Wizard of the Four Winds

A Shaman's Story

Wizard of the
Four Winds

A Shaman's Story

Douglas Sharon

THE FREE PRESS
A Division of Macmillan Publishing Co., Inc.
NEW YORK

Collier Macmillan Publishers
LONDON

The Free Press
A Division of Macmillan Publishing Co., Inc.
866 Third Avenue, New York, N.Y. 10022

Collier Macmillan Canada, Ltd.

Library of Congress Catalog Card Number: 78-3204

Printed in the United States of America

printing number

1 2 3 4 5 6 7 8 9 10

Library of Congress Cataloging in Publication Data

Sharon, Douglas.
    Wizard of the four winds.

    Includes bibliographical references and index.
    1. Shamanism—Peru.   2. Tuno, 1930-   I. Title.
BL2370.S5S53   1978   299'.8   78-3204
ISBN 0-02-928580-1

To Kaye

Contents

Preface

This book is about a unique individual, Eduardo Calderón Palomino, a Peruvian folk healer *(curandero)*. I have two reasons for telling Eduardo's story. First, as an anthropologist I am attempting to document a modern shaman's view of the world, a topic that has received little attention in the anthropological literature. Second, as Eduardo's friend I am trying to understand his struggles as a man, and above all, his personal search for meaning. Thus my approach is not biographical in the strict sense of the word; that is, it is not simply a chronological portrayal of events, mainly in the past tense. Although such an account is presented early in the book, it is meant to serve as a frame of reference for the balance of the work, which seeks to probe below the surface into the psychological and cultural factors motivating Eduardo.

At first sight many aspects of Eduardo's odyssey will appear foreign, even exotic. However, there are similarities between Eduardo's quest and that of human beings everywhere. It is this common ground underlying the amazing variety of human cultures, events, and behaviors that is explored by Eduardo the shaman. His genius in manipulating symbols and in combining the old and the new to learn about himself and others makes him stand out as a very special human being.

✧ ✧ ✧

My principal method of data collection involved apprenticeship to Eduardo during four visits totaling seven months of field work over a four-year period (July 1970 to March 1974). I have visited Eduardo twice since then (January 1975 and February–September 1977). Data collected on those two occasions will not be presented in this book, since I spent the 1975 visit mainly as an ethnographic consultant for an archeological film and the data from the 1977 visit are still in rough form at this writing. However, some of the latter materials are incorporated into a film on Eduardo funded by a grant from the National Institute on Drug Abuse, Washington, D.C., and due for release in 1978.

It was possible for me to assume the role of apprentice because of a long friendship with the healer. This tie was further strengthened when I became the godparent of one of his sons in the summer of 1970; in Latin American society this initiates a ritual kinship relation between the godfather and the parents of the child. My residence as a boarder in Eduardo's home not only established my membership within the community but also gave me an opportunity to observe the constant flow of patients and others who sought Eduardo's advice.

My apprenticeship included participation in, as well as observation of, all-night curing sessions. I spent the first research period (July and August 1970) more as an observer than as a participant; however, during the second season (September and October 1971) I became one of Eduardo's two assistants and was expected to take a very active part in all ceremonial and curing rituals. In addition to learning through practice and observation, I also developed a series of open-ended questionnaires for Eduardo that grew out of the learning experience, as opposed to carrying a preconceived set of questions into the field.

My primary interest was in Eduardo's version of *curanderismo*. I felt that if my major concern was to test anthropological theory that had already been conceptualized I would miss vital aspects of his work. Therefore, an inductive, exploratory technique was applied in field work. Interviews frequently developed into dialogues in the classical Socratic sense, with one question leading spontaneously to a new one. In order to give the reader a clear picture of the interaction between Eduardo and myself, transcriptions of our conversations in the following pages often include the whole dialogue that grew out of each question. I feel that much useful material was uncovered by this technique.

My field methodology was influenced by a basic premise of anthropology. This is the idea of putting aside one's own value judgments and attempting to record the native's categories and meanings for the acts and artifacts of his world. For example, by following Eduardo's example and treating his curing ceremonies and ritual gear* as "symbolic domains," or vehicles for meaning, I was able to discover the principles of organization governing his therapeutic system. This approach provided great insight into the dynamics of therapy

*Both ceremonies and ritual objects are referred to collectively by the same term: *mesa*, literally, table. A *mesa* is an altarlike arrangement of power objects laid on the ground for use in curing, fertility, and divination rituals. In northern Peru the term also is applied to the rituals performed with the power objects.

and into Eduardo's world view—conscious and unconscious. The cosmological notions underlying Eduardo's system, when placed in a historical and comparative framework, demonstrate the great antiquity and continuity of his beliefs and practices.

⋄ ⋄ ⋄

I am aware that data elicited from a single informant raises the question of reliability: Does such information adequately reflect the overall social context? If one is attempting to determine social structure or measure group behavior, this may be a valid consideration. However, when dealing with something as subjective as *curanderismo,* involving certain unique individuals with whom it is often very difficult to establish rapport, the researcher is not going to get very far unless he or she focuses intensively on the specialist who knows the profession best. That single-informant methodology can provide valuable information has been attested by several works on Latin American shamanism, most notably Furst (1965, 1967, 1968a, 1968b, 1968–69, 1972, 1973), Furst and Myerhoff (1966), and Myerhoff (1968, 1970, 1974), working with a Huichol shaman; Castaneda (1968, 1971, 1972, 1974), working with a Yaqui shaman; and Wilbert (1972b), working with a Warao shaman. Reichel-Dolmatoff (1971) was most successful in interpreting Tukano religious symbolism by working with an acculturated member of this Colombian jungle tribe. In Africa, Griaule's (1965) work with a Dogon elder is a classic example of in-depth religious information obtained from a single individual. Eliade (1958: 5–6) makes a good case for the use of knowledgeable individuals in the study of the religions of other cultures, while Spiro (1951: 43), says: "Personality and culture . . . are not different or mutually exclusive titles; they are part and parcel of the same process of interaction. Both personality and culture reside in the individual . . . and there are as many cultures as there are personalities."

In observing and reporting Eduardo's beliefs and practices I have tried to remain as objective as possible. Those parts of Eduardo's art that seem to lend themselves to objective analysis are rendered in conventional ethnographic style. However, since the understanding of certain aspects of Eduardo's life and art required personal experience on my part, I have chosen to convey my own experiences in a subjective and narrative fashion. By taking this approach I hope to come to terms with two problems involved in the observation of human behavior. First, no observer can totally separate his personality from his field methodology. Second, the researcher always carries some assumed value judgments and theoretical predilections with him to the study. These judgments shape the perception, documentation, and interpretation of data. I doubt that these two problems can be eliminated completely from anthropological field work, but I feel that if the investigator is as explicit as possible about his role and assumptions in collecting and interpreting field data, he increases the validity of his conclusions. The narrative portions of this work should clarify my role in eliciting field data and my apprentice relationship to Eduardo. Here I shall state the assumptions regarding *curanderismo* that guided the formal aspects of my research.

The major underlying assumption was that Eduardo was not performing simple hocus-pocus. Rather, I suspected that he was manipulating a coherent system of symbolic communication. A linguistic analogy borrowed from anthropological theory can best illustrate this assumption. I felt that Eduardo's system existed on two levels. One level, like spoken and written speech, consisted of observable acts (curing rituals) as well as artifacts (power objects) that "amplified" these acts. The other level, like the unconscious semantic principles structuring speech, consisted of a nonverbal "code" patterning Eduardo's ritual behavior and artifact manipulation. In other words, influenced by Geertz (1965) and Goodenough (1957, 1961), I distinguished between patterns *for* behavior (the code) and patterns *of* behavior (acts, artifacts). I felt that observation of Eduardo's interaction with patients and manipulation of ceremonial artifacts, combined with internalization of his system through apprenticeship, would eventually make it possible to explain his behavior by deciphering its underlying code. Of course, this explanation was contingent upon Eduardo's practices actually constituting a system of communication. After the first field season, in the summer of 1970, it was quite evident that such was the case: Eduardo was the sender, the patient was the receiver, the rituals and artifacts were the medium, and "balance" (Eduardo's core concept) was the message. (For a detailed explanation of the use of the communication model in anthropological analysis, see Leach, 1976.)

This orientation has some of the features of the structural viewpoint: human behavior patterns as symbolic codes exhibiting linguistic characteristics, the search for reality at a different level, the limits of phenomena determined by man's innate structuring ability. However, I disagree with the structuralist position in its Platonic placement of reality in a dehumanized "beyond." I prefer a more humanistic approach, since I feel that reality, or "deep structure," is more congruent with empirical "surface structure" than the formalist is willing to concede. Often information overload makes it difficult to decode the message. Thus phenomena vary in their degree of decipherability. But I believe that the empirical level reflects reality more effectively than structuralism will allow.

A cultural-historical corollary of my major assumption is that *curanderismo* represents an abstract system of magico-religious knowledge firmly rooted in an indigenous ideological substratum and manifesting a remarkable capacity for adaptation. The very fact that it is still alive after four hundred years of intensive social and psychological pressures exerted by Spanish culture, as well as more recent socioeconomic pressures brought to bear by modernization, attests to this tenet. I also assume that *curanderismo* represents not so much a nativistic reaction to Spanish Catholicism as a true syncretism—that is, a functional synthesis between aboriginal and Catholic religious forms with a great deal of tenacity and stability. In short, folk healing appears to represent a blending of archetypes common to Christian and Indian religious experience—a truly *mestizo* religious form ideally suited to contemporary Peruvian culture.

A basic premise of this study follows a suggestion by Barth (1967) that to understand change (in this case, from an aboriginal to a syncretic pattern) it is necessary to specify the continuity within the system or between the situations in which change occurs. Complementary to this premise is the work by Graves and Woods (1973) that quantitatively establishes the concept—long held by anthropologists on more impressionistic grounds—that man's values, ideas, and beliefs resist change (or, perhaps more correctly, are readapted) long after alterations in material culture, technology, economics, and social structure have occurred. In northern Peru it seems that a traditional cultural complex or system *(curanderismo)* is adapting to the demands of the twentieth century, just as it adapted to the demands of the colonial and republican periods of Peruvian history.

[margin annotation: could not be objective]

The question of ethics has been a paramount consideration in this study. From the beginning Eduardo and I agreed that an honest, straightforward strategy would be best. During the first season he preferred that I use a pseudonym for him in my writings, but during the second season even that restriction was removed. At séances I was introduced to patients as an apprentice and anthropologist studying *curanderismo*. Permission to tape sessions was always solicited from patients, and private information has been held in the strictest confidence. In addition, Eduardo has been informed of the content of my publications. During the most recent field season recorded here, the format for this book was discussed in great detail, and I sought and obtained his permission for the use of specific interviews and biographical data.

[margin annotation: as if portrayed modern surgeon without making reference to patients that died from complications]

In what follows I attempt to stay as close as possible to Eduardo's version of his art in an effort to avoid the pitfalls of extreme formalism. Since Eduardo is very articulate, I quote him at length on key issues. And in my translations I try to retain the slightly archaic tone of his use of the vernacular. However, I would not be responsible or honest if I did not acknowledge that the final product represents my perception of Eduardo's life and art from my par-

[margin annotation: even if Eduardo's good, others could suck.]

ticular point in space and time.* This is especially true for the ethno-historical, ethnological, and psychological interpretations of events. But my perception is strongly influenced by Eduardo's opinions regarding folk healing, which provide the guidelines for this book:

> Everything related to *curanderismo* is discoverable simply through the study of natural forces applied to these so-called mysteries that are not mysteries. Rather, they are very, very susceptible to those persons who really feel the desire to learn.

> It is necessary to teach [sincere seekers] all so that they know what it is all about. One must never keep secrets—secrets that are not secrets. Rather, one must bring all out into the light.

---

*A recent monograph, *Tuno: El Curandero* (1977), by the Peruvian anthropologist José Gushiken reproduces Eduardo's explanations of his shamanism verbatim. Although the author takes a different approach to Eduardo's work than I do, his documentation confirms the veracity of my ethnographic reportage.

Acknowledgments

Some of the material in this book has appeared in a different form in professional publications. The author wishes to thank the following publishers for permission to incorporate parts of the works cited below into the chapters indicated:

The American Museum of Natural History, *Natural History* magazine, New York, "Eduardo the Healer," vol. 81, no. 9, copyright © November 1972, pp. 32-47 — Eduardo's life history and our first meeting in chapter 1; sessions two and three in chapter 2.

The Regents of the University of California, UCLA Latin American Center Publications, Los Angeles, "Becoming a *Curandero* in Peru," in *Enculturation in Latin America: An Anthology*, edited by Johannes Wilbert, copyright © 1976, pp. 359-75 — Eduardo's "call" and "pact" in chapter 2; the conclusions regarding applied anthropology in chapter 12.

Praeger Publishers, Division of Holt, Rinehart, and Winston, Inc., New York, "The San Pedro Cactus in Peruvian Folk Healing," in *Flesh of the Gods: The Ritual Use of Hallucinogens*, edited by Peter T. Furst, copyright © 1972, pp. 114-35 — Eduardo's herbal lore and use of the San Pedro cactus in chapter 4; Eduardo's descriptions of a sorcerer's kit and of his cat amulet in chapter 5.

The Archaeological Institute of America, *Archaeology* magazine, "The Magic Cactus: Ethnoarchaeological Continuity in Peru," with Christopher B. Donnan, vol. 30, no. 6, copyright © November 1977, pp. 374-81 — history of the use of the San Pedro cactus in chapter 4.

Mouton Publishers, Division of Walter de Gruyter, Berlin/New York, "A Peruvian *Curandero*'s Séance: Power and Balance," in *The Realm of the Extra-Human: Agents and Audiences*, edited by Agehananda Bharati, copyright © 1976, pp. 371-81 — Apocalypse symbolism in chapter 8.

The Regents of the University of California, UCLA Latin American Center Publications, Los Angeles, "Distribution of the *Mesa* in Latin

America," *Journal of Latin American Lore,* vol. 2, no. 1, copyright ©
summer 1976, pp. 71-95—appendix A.

The author also gratefully acknowledges permission from Professor
Clement W. Meighan, UCLA Department of Anthropology, to use his ideas
regarding the power concept among California Indians as discussed in
chapter 5.

Wizard of the
Four Winds

A Shaman's Story

Opening the "Account"

I met Eduardo ("Chino") Calderón in July 1965. At the time he was the artist in charge of frieze reconstruction at the archeological site of Chan-Chan, the ancient capital of the Kingdom of Chimor (ca. A.D. 700–1475), located near the modern city of Trujillo, Peru. I was working in Trujillo with an explorers' group that was collaborating with the Chan-Chan project.

During the time I spent at Chan-Chan, thirty-five year-old Eduardo was hard to miss. Broad and heavyset, he had a dynamic, agile bearing that almost kept one from noticing that he bulged at the beltline. His round, full face was as plastic as the moist clay he manipulated to restore the adobe friezes. Capable of producing a wide variety of animated expressions, Eduardo had a confident, friendly personality and a robust sense of humor. There was a great warmth to him that seemed to emanate from a deep reservoir of inner strength. I liked him immediately.

As I became better acquainted with Eduardo I discovered that he was a wonderful storyteller. During work breaks and at lunchtime I found myself listening in amazement to his accounts of the long years he had spent as a fisherman and stevedore before joining the Chan-Chan project. He had fished from one-man reed boats of the type used by the ancient inhabitants of the Trujillo Valley and from modern tuna clippers working out of Chimbote, Peru's fishing capital to the south of Trujillo. The sea had taught him respect for the force and power of nature. But his encounters with fishermen, sailors, adventurers, and drifters had also taught him much about man. He had seen human pettiness and greed in the frontier-like atmosphere of Peru's newest and fastest-growing industry. At the same time he had known courage and camaraderie in the company of hearty mates as they faced the perils of the sea together. Eduardo's tales revealed a wealth of knowledge about human nature.

Eduardo's stories made it clear that the sea had cast a spell over him. He was raised in Trujillo, which was a few miles inland, but in his early twenties he had taken up residence in a nearby fishing village. Although he did not now expect to earn his living from the sea again as he often had in his youth, Eduardo vowed that he would never leave his hamlet by the ocean. The nights he spent in Trujillo were always sleepless, he said; to be at peace with himself, he needed the sound of the sea nearby. Listening to Eduardo, it was easy to understand why the ancient inhabitants of Chan-Chan had worshipped the sea. It seemed appropriate that this artist-fisherman should be bringing their art forms back to life.

As our conversations progressed, it became still more apparent how appropriate it was that Eduardo had become involved in the revival of Chimu culture. One day he talked about an American student who had lived near him the year before. They had become good friends, and Eduardo noted with pleasure how well the young man had learned Spanish and adapted to the life-style and customs of the community. In particular Eduardo noted the young man's fondness for *chicha*, the fermented corn beer of the region, and the drinking sessions they had enjoyed together. Somewhere in the conversation I missed a shift to another traditional practice that the young American had found interesting. I thought Eduardo was still talking about their drinking bouts, especially when he told me about seeing people and events at a distance. My first thought was, "That *chicha* must really have been fermented!" But as his description continued, it dawned on me that Eduardo was talking about night healing sessions conducted by himself and attended by the American student. He was telling me that he was a *curandero*.

⟡ ⟡ ⟡

Curanderos are the contemporary counterparts of the pre-Columbian magico-religious healers who were highly skilled in performing cures with herbs and simples. In the Kingdom of Chimor these specialists, called *oquetlupuc*, were treated with great respect and were well rewarded for their services. However, if a patient died under treatment the healer was killed by flogging. His body was then tied to the corpse of the patient, which was duly buried, while the doctor's body was left aboveground for the birds of prey to devour (Calancha, 1638: 556). Let us say no more regarding professional responsibility!

The modern *curandero* also has a vast knowledge of herbs, including the use of several hallucinogens, especially the San Pedro cactus *(Trichocereus pachanoi)* and floripondium *(Datura arborea)*, which serve as catalytic agents for his psychic powers. Reputedly capable of curing more than physical illness, he is said to be able to locate lost or stolen property, divine certain events and circumstances, assure success in personal projects and business, cure alcoholism and insanity, and undo love magic and witchcraft. Unfortunately, it is often difficult to distinguish between a *curandero* and a *brujo*, or sorcerer. The *brujo*, by making a secret pact with the devil, can usually perform the same feats as a *curandero*, and in addition can practice witchcraft and adverse love magic that cause misfortune, bad health, and even death. This is one of the reasons that both *curanderos* and *brujos* have been persecuted by the Catholic Church and the law since the Spanish Conquest. Despite the fact that such persecution forced ancient practices underground, they have persisted to the present through an oral tradition passed on from *curandero* to apprentice through the centuries. Folk healing has bowed to clerical pressures by adopting many of the trappings of Christianity, but it has preserved much of the ancient shamanistic content of Chimu culture.

⬧ ⬧ ⬧

Once I realized that Eduardo was referring to night healing sessions, it occurred to me that exposure to twentieth-century technology and life-styles might have very little influence on one's conception of the supernatural and the practices such a conception could induce. Listening to Eduardo reinforced this slowly dawning realization, for here before me was a rational, cosmopolitan individual.

I learned that Eduardo had been educated at Trujillo's Catholic seminary and at one time had considered entering the priesthood. Although his restless, creative spirit had eventually rebelled against the idea of becoming a priest, he had nevertheless been at the seminary long enough — and during his formative years — to be carefully indoctrinated against the "errors" and "superstitions" of his forefathers. Then a year of art studies in Lima had exposed him to life in a big city. And he had spent most of his adult life in the modern fishing industry, where it was necessary to deal with heavy machinery and modern techniques. This exposure to the machine age was reinforced by years of stevedore work on the docks of Trujillo's port-town, Salaverry, where an untimely instance of mythopoetic contemplation could result in an unexpected release from the mayhem of the twentieth century in the wake of a plummeting packing crate. Finally, his present duties required him to deal with archeologists, tourists, and visiting intellectuals from many parts of the world. In the time I spent at Chan-Chan I had an opportunity to see how well he handled himself in such an environment.

Before meeting Eduardo I had had only one other encounter with a *curandero*. In 1964, during an archeological exploration of the highland jungle area near Cuzco, the first phase of the rainy season was upon us, and we knew that we would have difficulty getting badly needed porters and machetemen to go with us into the tropical rain forest. The expedition leader decided to hire a *curandero* to conduct rituals that would assure the success and safety of the expedition. Regardless of whether the rituals worked, he argued, they would help overcome the fears of the people we wanted to hire and thus guarantee us enough manpower. A *curandero* was found, and although the weather could not have been worse we were able to hire everybody we needed.

Our men had not at first appeared to be impressed with the *curandero* hired for the expedition. Nevertheless, whenever he divined with coca leaves or invoked the spirits of the mountains and forest, it was quite obvious that he had a profound effect on them. After that expedition I was willing to admit that there was a community of traditional belief—at least in the Cuzco area—that supported the activities of contemporary *curanderos*. But I had assumed that this was true only in areas where the influence of modern society had yet to penetrate.

My conversations with Eduardo at Chan-Chan suggested to me that *curanderos* were adapting to modernization and urban environments. For Eduardo was certainly far removed from the Quechua-speaking Indian practitioner I had met near Cuzco. Yet here he was at the Chan-Chan project, recounting his experiences as a *curandero* in a very matter-of-fact and earnest fashion.

Eduardo was proud of his abilities as a *curandero*. When he learned that I was interested in this phase of his life he was willing to discuss it in great detail. He gave me an open invitation to attend his nighttime curing sessions. His honesty, seriousness, and confidence in his own curing powers were quite impressive. Yet he was never pompous, and he exhibited a marvelous capacity to laugh at himself. Whenever we met, after our first conversations about his *curandero* role, he would look at me in mock seriousness and say in his scanty English, in a deep voice, "I am a wizard." Then he would roll his eyes back in his head and pucker his mouth in feigned awe. This would be followed by a broad smile and a hearty chuckle.

In my conversations with Eduardo I discovered details about his life that shed light on his character. He was born in 1930 in Trujillo, where his parents had settled after migrating from the Andean highlands near Cajabamba. At an early age Eduardo began to make his own contribution to the family's income. From the time he was eight to age fifteen he worked with his father making shoes, sold chocolates in front of local theaters, loaded cargo in the market, and even butchered animals at the slaughterhouse.

The necessity of working caused Eduardo to fall behind in his studies; at age ten he still had not completed the first year of primary school. But he readily admits that part of the fault was his, for he was an adventuresome, undisciplined child who often played hookey in order to roam by the sea or through the countryside exploring the mountains, dry riverbeds, and sandy wastes of the desert beyond the Trujillo Valley. Often these excursions took him to one of the many archeological ruins around Trujillo, where he would wander in search of pot shards and artifacts from the Indian past. Although he is frequently called "Chino" in recognition of his unusually Mongoloid features, his adventures also earned him another nickname—"Tuno" (truant, cunning rogue), which has stayed with him over the years.

At about the age of ten, however, Eduardo suddenly took an interest in his studies. Once his natural curiosity was aroused, he was quick to learn. This new interest in human knowledge was paralleled by a desire for self-expression, which began to find an outlet in artistic production. Eduardo's father was an artisan and handyman, a jack-of-all-trades who could do anything requiring manual dexterity. Exposure to his father's skills instilled in Eduardo an interest in ceramics and sculpture in wood and stone. Thus art and scholarship began to emerge as twin motivating forces in Eduardo's life.

When he was ready for high school in 1947 his thirst for knowledge led him to enroll in Trujillo's Catholic seminary, where he could obtain a better education than that provided by the public high school. In addition this provided an opportunity to test his interest in becoming a priest. At the seminary, although his favorite subjects were psychology and drama, his eclectic curiosity was stimulated by the classical curriculum. Even today Eduardo reads extensively in theology and philosophy as well as in psychology, archeology, art, medicine, and the occult (indeed, he corresponds with the Rosicrucians in the United States).

During his high-school years Eduardo covered some of his expenses by working after school in a Chinese dry-goods store. He also began migrating to Chimbote during vacations in order to earn extra money in the fishing industry. Port life for Eduardo was another kind of schooling. He still bears the scars from a brawl in which, unarmed, he took on a waterfront troublemaker who had a switchblade.

In his late teens Eduardo experienced a disillusionment with the priesthood. Then, for a brief period, he considered the navy as a career. Medicine was another profession that attracted him, but this proved economically unfeasible. Nevertheless, some of his early interest in that profession found expression in his later practice of *curanderismo*. Finally, he realized that art provided the best medium of expression for his developing personality.

Despite his aspirations, it was more often his strong back than his skilled hands that earned a livelihood for him. Years of carrying cargo in the market and fishing in Chimbote had toughened his stout, muscular physique. In addition, in his early teens he had taken up weightlifting. Toward the end of his fourth year of seminary studies in late 1950, Eduardo went to Lima as captain of the weightlifting team from the Club Gimnasta de Trujillo to participate in the national championships. Once there, he decided to seek his fortune in the big city.

In Lima he earned his living working as a bricklayer with his uncle while studying at night at the School of Fine Arts. But even art, approached as a formal academic discipline, bridled Eduardo's freedom-loving spirit. He left art school before completing his first year of studies, and years later, in an interview with the Lima magazine *Caretas* (Lama, 1965: 27), had the following to say about his final encounter with academe:

> I didn't like what they wanted to do with me. The study of art was too pretentious and rigid. No one can be taught to be an artist. One is, or one is not, and nothing else. . . . Of course, they can help to temper character, but they don't make artists. I preferred to return to my home. If it is true that I am an artist, I am in a manner different than they. And here among the people of Moche are the things I love. . . .

The trauma associated with Eduardo's experiences in Lima was personal as well as professional. While in school he married one of his classmates. But the girl's parents looked down on this impoverished would-be artist from the provinces. They succeeded in breaking up the marriage and sent their daughter to live with relatives. After a frantic and fruitless search for his wife, Eduardo returned to Trujillo to nurse the wounds of his encounter with the big city.

Eduardo turned to fishing, using the traditional methods of the coastal village near Trujillo, where he eventually took up residence. These methods included the use of nets strung from the shore and hauled by donkeys as well as the casting of nets from one-man reed boats. In 1952, at twenty-two years of age, Eduardo began courting María, a sweetheart from his teens. She was a fisherman's daughter and also a fine ceramist. Although his divorce was not finalized until the early 1970s, Eduardo and María have been together ever since his return from Lima. As of 1974, they had ten children.

Fishing with traditional methods was not enough to support Eduardo's growing family. In the 1950s they had to migrate to Chimbote every year during the fishing season; in the off-season he worked as a stevedore at Salaverry. The first few years of seasonal fishing were harsh. Eduardo and María would set up a temporary reed-mat house on the sands outside Chimbote along with other migrants. Working conditions were primitive and dangerous, and salaries were low. Nevertheless, through hard work and frugality Eduardo became a crew foreman and eventually saved enough money to build a house near Trujillo. Although he pursued his artistic bent, holding occasional exhibitions of wood sculpture and pottery in Trujillo and working part-time as an artist in the archeological museum of the University of Trujillo, the sea provided his major source of livelihood into the early 1960s.

In 1962 the American hospital ship *Hope* docked at Salaverry for a year. The staff enthusiastically discovered Eduardo's works in clay and wood, and their support gave him a chance to pursue his art almost full-time. When the ship left, Eduardo was offered a contract in the United States to commercialize his talents on a large scale. At that time, however, his mother was seriously ill, and since his father had abandoned the family, Eduardo, as the oldest son, felt obliged to stay and look after his younger brothers and sisters. So once again he took up his stevedore's hook and his fishing net.

By 1964 Eduardo had accumulated enough capital to buy his own boat and net. Thus he became an innovator, introducing modern fishing methods for the first time to the local fishermen. But in 1965 the Peruvian fishing industry suffered a bad year because the warming of the coastal waters eliminated the cold-water diatoms upon which the fish chiefly fed. Small fishermen like Eduardo were forced out of business.

Through his exhibitions and work for the *Hope* staff Eduardo had become known locally for his artistic talents. This reputation, plus his earlier experience at the archeological museum, allowed him to get a job restoring murals with the Chan-Chan project. Now Eduardo had the opportunity to make a living exclusively from his artistic talents. In the 1965 interview, *Caretas* characterized Eduardo's work at Chan-Chan as "a re-encounter with his land. With his people and with the clay of his people." It quoted him as saying: "Clay is plastic and vital; it attracts me . . . I feel that it is linked to the original forms with which my ancestors constructed their palaces of molded earth. Therefore, when I was commissioned to work on the friezes of Chan-Chan, I felt a mixture of anxiety and respect."

It was during his first months of work at Chan-Chan that I met Eduardo. In the years that followed he truly breathed new life into the "clay of his people," for in addition to helping restore the ruins of the past he taught for two years at the regional School of Fine Arts in Trujillo and produced some two thousand copies of pre-Columbian ceramics for sale to tourists.

My time at Chan-Chan in 1965 came abruptly to an end when our group organized an expedition to the highland jungles east of Trujillo. The expedition and subsequent trips and research prevented me from seeing Eduardo again for over a year. On this occasion I took a graduate student in anthropology, Christopher Donnan, out to Chan-Chan to meet Eduardo. Chris was interested in ancient coastal ceramic technology, and I told him that Eduardo knew and used all the old techniques.

Eduardo was just leaving the site for home and invited us to come with him. Once there, after helping Chris, he brought out an ancient sorcerer's kit, consisting of a set of stones of various shapes and sizes, which had been found at a nearby ruin. Eduardo laid them all out on a table and explained their functions and significance. He said that they corresponded to many of the personal artifacts laid out on his *mesa*. I knew that throughout pre-Columbian Peru stone was venerated as an embodiment of the first ancestors. On the coast, sacred stones regarded as sons of the sun were referred to as *alecpong*, or deities in stone (Calancha, 1638: 553). It is also known that Indian households kept collections of stones of various shapes, colors, and sizes, known in the highlands as *conopas* and on the coast as *morpis* (household gods), much like the Roman *lares* and *penates* passed on from father to son (Arriaga, 1968: 28-29, 68). My interest in Eduardo's magical beliefs and practices was kindled anew, but another expedition in Peru and my subsequent departure for the United States in 1967 kept me from investigating further. This was an inquiry that eventually commanded my attention, however; the man's personal quest was contagious.

As fate would have it, in 1970, after obtaining a fellowship from the University of California (Los Angeles) to study *curanderismo*, I returned to Trujillo hoping to work with Eduardo. I found Eduardo at his home in the midst of his happy family—bent over a clay pot. We had barely exchanged greetings when I impetuously blurted out the purpose of my visit and asked him point-blank if he would be willing to accept me as an apprentice *curandero*. For a moment my enthusiastic onslaught caught Eduardo by surprise. But after brief reflection he told me he was always willing to teach anyone who was sincere and sought knowledge. On that simple note was launched a remarkable adventure into an unexplored realm of the human psyche, rivaling anything I had experienced in my years of exploration in the Peruvian hinterland.

In the previous year, the restoration work at Chan-Chan had been discontinued, and Eduardo had turned to full-time work at home producing copies of pre-Columbian ceramics for tourist shops. Because of the fluctuating demand for the ceramics, it was often very difficult for him to make ends meet. At the same time, his situation was a boon for me, for I was able to spend most of the day talking with him in the privacy of his home while he worked on his pots. It also made it much easier for patients to find and consult with him. Divination of the course of a recent undertaking or business venture; love and marital problems; sickness; simple advice; and the possibility of witchcraft—all were routine concerns for Eduardo. Arrangements could be made to assure good luck in a business venture or to bring back a spouse who had abandoned a household.

For consultations involving business or love, Eduardo would go off into a separate room and perform cartomancy with a deck of Spanish divining cards. For sickness or the suspicion of witchcraft, which often went together, he would rub the patient with a live guinea pig, vivisect it, and perform entrail divination, since the sensitive guinea pig was believed to take on the body "humors" and ailments of the patient. If the patient had an organic disorder, the corresponding organ of the guinea pig was believed to become spotted or to turn black. In a case involving witchcraft the spine of the animal broke, indicating that a night curing session would be necessary to remove the hex. If the guinea pig revealed a serious organic disorder, Eduardo would indicate the organ affected, prescribe certain herbs combined with a special diet, and then urge the patient to seek medical attention. His diagnosis of organic ailments was facilitated by the medical knowledge he was acquiring from a correspondence course in nursing completed later that year with a school in Miami that provides lessons in Spanish.

But not everyone who visited the Calderón residence was a patient. During the days I spent at Eduardo's house there was a steady stream of friends, relatives, and *compadres* (godparents of his children). There were old fishing companions, stevedores, mechanics, teachers, university professors, shopkeepers, accountants, students, athletes, artists, businessmen, farmers, truck drivers, old people, youngsters, and drifters, among others. I had all I could do to keep up with the flow of names and faces. Eduardo loved the company of his fellow human beings. And conversation was an art—even a way of life—at which he excelled. Busy though he was, he had time for everyone, and if the visitors stayed long enough usually someone was sent out for a gallon of *chicha* and a snack was served. It appeared as if the outside world had beaten a path to Eduardo's door. As I watched his daily interaction I realized that Eduardo's greatest masterpiece was his own life. He molded it with the same deliberation and dexterity that shaped his ceramics.

As Eduardo slowly revealed his *curandero* lore, I began to realize that it was the expression of a profound system of abstract thought. In addition to embodying traditional beliefs and practices elaborated over centuries, it was grounded in personal experience. This was not the idyllic pastoral prattle of that European delusion, the "noble savage." Rather, there was a lusty, earthy quality to Eduardo's system that reflected a direct contact with nature and a realistic perception of the joys and sorrows of the human situation. There was nothing of the lotus-eater in this worldly man of action. At all times he emphasized to me the need for perseverance and constant practice in learning to become a *curandero*. He said that I could learn only by doing. The *mesa* he set up at night and the rituals he conducted during sessions were direct manifestations and applications of his philosophy. To understand them I would have to watch them used, assist in their use, and eventually use them myself.

Once back in the United States after the 1970 season, I did not know when I would return to Trujillo. But in the fall of 1971, after a summer of field training in Guatemala, once more I found myself on Eduardo's doorstep. This time I had a grant from the National Geographic Society and was accompanied by David Brill, a photographer assigned by the Society.

My training as Eduardo's apprentice advanced considerably during my second "official" visit. In the summer of 1970 I had simply observed nighttime curing séances. This time I worked as one of Eduardo's two assistants while participating in curing rituals. Eduardo was still working at home, but he was developing plans to build his own ceramic workshop on an empty lot adjoining his house. In addition, his spiritual leadership had been given formal recognition by his election as the first secretary general of his community of about two thousand people.

My last visits with Eduardo relating to this book occurred in the fall and winter of 1973–74. By then he had managed to build his ceramic workshop. Also, he had secured another teaching position—this time at the Centro Artesanal Mixto de Trujillo. New educational reforms in Peru indicated that this would be a permanent position. Government promotion of Peruvian arts and crafts for exportation seemed to offer hope that the creative talents of Eduardo Calderón would finally receive the recognition they deserved.

This, then, is the story of my mentor. Apart from his ceramic art, his work at Chan-Chan, and the ancestry of his family in the *sierra*, there is nothing very Indian about Eduardo's way of life. On the contrary, he is a typical *mestizo*—Spanish-speaking, literate, worldly, Catholic, apparently with only the most tenuous ties to native Indian culture. As can be seen from the foregoing, the main current running through this part of his life was adaptation to the day-to-day demands of his society. But through hardship and crisis, Eduardo also learned to make "reality" adapt to him. It is to this aspect of his life that we now turn.

2

Germination: The Spiritual Beginnings of Eduardo the Shaman

RETURN FROM DEATH: THE "CALL" AND THE "PACT"

Throughout his long career in a variety of jobs, Eduardo the artist and family man was evolving as Eduardo the *curandero*. For, in addition to adapting to the demands of his sociocultural milieu, his life was forged by a restless search for meaning that gradually led him to a rediscovery of his own cultural heritage.

The wanderings of Eduardo's childhood were more than expressions of a mischievous nature. When he was very young, Eduardo experienced disturbing dreams and visions. Here is how he described them:

During my youth from more or less the age of seven or eight years I had some rare dreams. I still remember them. I remember dreams in which I flew, that my ego departed from the state in which it was, and I went to strange places in the form of a spiral. Or I flew in a vertiginous manner: sssssssssssss, I departed. I tried to retain myself and I could not. Strange dreams, strange. I had these until the age of more or less twelve or thirteen. . . .

I have seen things as if someone opens a door and the door is closed. I have had nightmares, but not ordinary ones. I have seen myself introduced through a hole in the air, and I went through an immense, immense void. I have felt numbness in all my body as if my hands were huge but I could not grasp; I could not hold up my hand.

Eduardo did not know where to turn in coping with his unusual experiences. He was afraid that people would think he was crazy if he confided in them. So he learned to keep his inner world to himself, handling these frightening events to the best of his ability, alone and unsupported.

During his adolescence Eduardo discovered that his growing interest in his studies brought some relief from the tensions in his psyche. He found the realm of ideas a fascinating place peopled by thinkers who had struggled — as he was doing — to understand the world around them and the people in it. It was this newfound motivation to learn that led Eduardo to enroll in the Trujillo seminary instead of the public high school. He felt a deep yearning to help alleviate human suffering, a "calling to serve humanity," and for a while seriously considered studying for the priesthood. But it was not long before he realized that the discipline and obedience required by orthodox religion were stifling his personal growth. In the end what had begun as a step to self-discovery became a crippling frustration.

Medicine seemed to be the next best avenue of expression for Eduardo's idealism, but it was not economically feasible. His frustration, however, was temporarily mitigated by his growth as an artist. Toward the end of his studies at the seminary it became clear that art provided his best medium of expression. However, his experience in Lima at the School of Fine Arts only brought further disappointment. Just before his return to Trujillo in late 1951, at the age of twenty-one, he fell ill with a mysterious ailment that appeared incurable by modern medical treatment. He described this event as follows:

> In Lima I was studying fine arts and suddenly I began drinking and spending everything on drink. And I came down with a rare sickness. It happened that on one occasion I saw a cat on my left shoulder. It was enough that with that impression of a cat everything that I did was overturned. In other words, I couldn't find work, I drank, I didn't want to do things the way they should be done. Then I took off, wandering without a goal. Finally I decided to return to my home. I had just enough energy left to travel. I arrived home and came down with a sickness in which eruptions like volcanoes that did not emit pus broke out all over my body. They only emitted yellowish water and a kind of black worm stuck out its head and then hid. My whole body from my head to my feet [was affected], and I lost the power to hold things in my hand and to stand up. I completely lost all my strength. I could not hold myself up in a standing position and walked like a sleepwalker, according to what they tell me.

Both of his grandfathers had been *curanderos* in the highlands, so his family decided to see if a folk healer might help where doctors had failed. Eduardo underwent treatment and was cured. Here is his description:

> Frankly, I didn't believe in these things. But when my condition got worse, my mother and my uncle called in a friend who understood these things . . . a woman who understood witchcraft, and especially curing. She is a great herb specialist. Thus one night—I could not attend [the session] because I could not get on my feet—they brought me a brew prepared by her. I spent exactly $3 on this. It made me throw up black beer, as if I had recently drunk it. And I recovered from one day to the next. . . .

Although triggered by events in his personal life, Eduardo's experience is obviously akin to the "sickness vocation" discussed at length by Eliade (1964:

33-36). It is common for a future shaman to feel himself "called" through a serious illness that fails to respond to normal treatment and requires supernatural intervention. "Hereditary transmission" of shamanic aptitudes from grandparents is also quite frequent (Eliade, 1964: 20-23). In any case, Eduardo recovered from his disease. This personal experience enabled him eventually to cure similar maladies suffered by those who shared his cultural milieu.

At the time, Eduardo did not understand what had happened, but he felt an urge to learn *curanderismo*. He had already attended a few sessions when a friend, who felt he was suffering from a love spell, decided to go in search of a specialist capable of undoing the *enredo*, or entanglement. Eduardo offered to accompany him. At the town of Mocupe they tried the "clinic" of a famous *curandera*. However, she had become a drunkard and no longer possessed her power. So Eduardo and his friend went on to Chiclayo in search of a healer.

There they encountered a *brujo*, reputed to be a good *enguayanchero* (maker of love spells), who used a guitar with his *mesa*. But he also removed spells—if the price was right. Eduardo's friend was in desperation and willing to try anything. So the two friends arranged for a séance.

The *enguayanchero's* therapy was successful. During the séance it became apparent that Eduardo had good "vision," psychic insight, which aided in the cure. The *enguayanchero* asked Eduardo to become his assistant, but Eduardo declined. Although inexperienced in *curanderismo,* he knew instinctively that his nature was not inclined toward the path of darkness and intrigue.

Back in Trujillo once again, Eduardo began to experience a disturbing restlessness and a desire to return to Chiclayo, much like the feeling he had experienced prior to his return from Lima, though this time unaccompanied by illness. Enough was enough! María had an uncle who was noted for healing with hallucinogens and a *mesa*. A séance was arranged and the spell was broken.

Eduardo decided it was time to learn to be a curer in self-defense. He began his apprenticeship under his relative. In the years that followed, while earning a living as a stevedore at Salaverry, exhibiting his art in Trujillo, and fishing seasonally at Chimbote, he also gained sufficient experience as a *curandero's* assistant to serve as *rastreador* (literally "tracker," one who helps the *curandero* "see" during the healing session). Eventually he developed his powers to the point where, during one momentous session, he suddenly felt that the "Christ of the *mesa*" had chosen him to effect a part of the curing ritual:

> One time the *mesa* called me in the "account."* It called me. Christ called me; He said to me, "Come here." And He had me take the rattle and the dagger in my hands and sit at the place of the *maestro* [master, or

---

*See chapter 5 for a full explanation of this term.

curandero]. And the *curandero's* assistants realized that the account pulled me. In other words, this was the initiation—the supreme instance in which the Divine Judge pulled me.

After that session Eduardo decided that he had outgrown his teacher. But he did not yet feel ready to establish his own *mesa*. Instead he went north to work with famous *curanderos* in Chiclayo, Mocupe, and Ferreñafe. His discussion of his training in these towns reveals the highly individualistic nature of the initiatory experience in northern Peru, a reflection of *mestizo* culture. As can be seen from the following, this contrasts markedly with indigenous training and initiation, in which a relatively undisturbed cosmological and mythological system provides a clear-cut charter for the teacher to pass on to the initiate:

But where I was really initiated was with a *maestro*, a northerner also, a man from Ferreñafe. . . . He initiated me. I had a few artifacts already, and I liked *curanderismo* since I was pulled by the *mesa*. . . . But I went on creating my own accounts because he was the one who initiated me and he gave me very good advice. He said: "He who wants to enter the life of a *curandero*, who likes the art, must be frank and, more than anything, create his own things. Nothing that is of another [should be his] because when a *maestro* teaches another it is like following the same line without creating. With his bad account, they [the forces directed by a sorcerer that he opposes] dominate him, and the others [his students] also go. However, you, knowing that your account is your own, nobody knows you, nobody can reach you, never will they cross you on your path because you have something that is your own, not picked up from someone else."

(Question: How long did you remain there with this man from Ferreñafe?)

I worked with him in the highlands, I worked in Trujillo, I worked in Moche, I worked in several places. I was with him about six months, it wasn't very much time. He initiated me in the initiative sense, which is when one has artifacts and he "adjusts" them by means of his account within the field of the *curandero*. He adjusted my rattle, he adjusted my two staffs and my dagger, and with these I began to work. . . .

He made the sign of the cross over me; in other words, he initiated me in this by blessing me. He blessed me in front of his *mesa*, in front of his artifacts together with my artifacts as an initiate. Then I followed my own initiative and from then on began to work alone, creating my own, and studying books, et cetera. My dreams revealed certain things to me about obtaining my artifacts, making my staffs, and in this fashion little by little I grew in the art.

One's spirit has to bond itself with all of the artifacts that are there, that harmonize with the esoteric, the cosmic, and the earth. The *maestro* is the one who handles the levers of that motor, that mechanism, and I am part of the mechanism. I, as an initiate, am part of the mechanism. In other words, I separate myself from the mechanism, but I am part of the very force of that mechanism which is [the unity of] the *maestro* and his artifacts. Then I create my own world and live as an initiate blessed by him, but with my own ideas. As he said to me: "Make your own [account] and nobody will be able to cross you or bewitch you. Follow this advice and you will see."

When Eduardo returned from the north, at age twenty-eight, he was hesitant to practice on his own even though he had had four years of training. Then one of his cousins fell seriously ill. This is how Eduardo described his first cure:

> I came as a result of the sickness of one of my cousins . . . a girl who was in the last stage of an ailment which was going to drive her crazy into the streets. And my uncle was in a bad economic situation. Then I had to intervene because he begged me; for I didn't want to interfere. And I began to perform the first cure of my life. . . . I don't remember all of the details of the sickness of the girl, but it occurred in Chicama, in a town where there are sorcerers in quantity. The sorcerers there abound like the sand. It is the school of sorcerers. I arrived there to cure her. This girl couldn't look at mirrors because she saw the Devil there, she saw animals, she saw monsters, and a series of things. It seems as if they had worked on her hair, a common thing in witchcraft. Then in Chicama I placed two *mesas* for my cousin and cured her. That is where I began and was initiated with a handful of artifacts.

Thus Eduardo's career as a *curandero* working with his own *mesa* was launched. In gratitude to God, he made a vow never to abuse his powers and to work only for good in the service of humanity. This is what he had to say about his subsequent growth:

> Then I began with force in my life in this branch of these rites, which increased more and more as I went drinking these brews and entering into the problem of the famous "charms" — as they are called in *curanderismo* and witchcraft — until it seems that they spoke to me at night, in dreams. I went along acquiring knowledge each time that I manipulated these artifacts at night, acquiring much more superior knowledge each time — more and more, until today, as you see me relating these things. I know so many things that the artifacts have taught me. A mysterious thing, right? But it exists. Now with the passage of the years . . . I have arrived at a conclusion: Knowledge is acquired by means of practice. A logical, simple thing, right? Nobody can understand this. However, one arrives at one single thing, so simple, which is that by practicing, practicing one reaches understanding. That is what happened to me.

Today, after about twenty years as a full-fledged *curandero,* Eduardo is still learning and growing. His knowledge and power increase with practice and experience. He attributes this to the fact that he has never abandoned his "pact." He knows that he is dealing with dangerous forces, but his faith keeps him alert and strong. In addition, his active mind is constantly probing and seeking new challenges, as evidenced by his extensive reading and by his nursing course.

But his erudition only supplements the insight into human nature gained from his wide experience in the workaday world. He is open, direct, and candid in his dealings with his fellows. He does not believe in keeping his knowledge a secret and gladly shares his ideas with any sincere person who inquires about *curanderismo.* For Eduardo, *curanderismo* is simply a matter of "vision" gained by those who have a sincere desire to learn and who practice on a regular basis. But, although *curanderismo* requires hard work and constant practice, it is my suspicion that *curanderos* are born, not made; they are the unusually gifted and perceptive members of their communities. Whatever the case, Eduardo himself is not an ordinary person. He sums up his philosophy very simply:

> I work under a faith more than anything, a promise that I made when I was initiated as a *curandero* — for one must make a promise, of course — a promise to serve man without thought of gain, whoever the man may be, whatever his circumstances.

NINE NIGHTS OF MAGIC

During the research periods covered in this book (summer 1970, fall 1971, fall 1973, and winter 1974), I participated in nine evening sessions conducted by Eduardo. The following brief summary of these sessions is offered to help the reader conceptualize Eduardo's *curandero* practices.

I attended three sessions with Eduardo during the summer of 1970. The first seemed rather uneventful. It was conducted in the yard of an auto-repair shop among tools, tires, and dismantled trucks. The owner of the shop was suffering from a backache, which he felt was caused by a curse placed on him by a disgruntled client. (I remember wishing that we had such recourse against bungling mechanics in the United States!) He was accompanied by a friend who came along for moral support. During the divinatory segment of the session Eduardo, unprompted, offered a description of the culprit which matched that of the man suspected by the patient. Eduardo remarked that there was a great deal of bad feeling involved but insisted that this was not a case of witchcraft; it was the mental anguish caused by the incident that was affecting the mechanic's health. Eduardo gave the patient some advice and performed a purification rite for the garage.

When my turn before the *mesa* came, Eduardo divined a series of events in my life. First he saw my wife appear on my right, holding a baby boy in her arms. He said she wanted a son. Then he saw my brother, noting that he was concerned about the shipment of a Peruvian reed boat and was bothered by a sore throat. Regarding my work, he said that my study would be very successful and that this would not be my last trip to Peru—adding that I should tape everything possible. He also saw me receiving a sum of money in the future and studying ways to invest it. I asked about a former employer, who had announced his retirement from archeological exploration, and Eduardo saw him planning a new expedition.

In the months that followed, every one of these divinations was confirmed. At the time of the session my wife had been visiting friends who had a newborn son and she had held the baby in her arms. A son was born to us four years later. When I visited my brother I learned that he had in fact been thinking a great deal about a reed boat he had arranged to deliver to a Canadian museum, and he had experienced a throat infection at the time of the séance. (Since Eduardo had made the boat, his knowledge of my brother's concern could have been good guesswork, but the divination of the sore throat was a little out of the ordinary.) In reference to my work, that first summer with Eduardo led to several publications, a dissertation, the present work, and three more visits to Peru. Three months after my return from that first trip I did indeed receive an unexpected sum of money in the form of a bond, which I promptly put away for safekeeping. Four months later I found myself cashing the bond and investing the money, after considering several ways of doing so. (Unfortunately, I did not ask Eduardo for any tips; eventually I took a substantial loss!) Regarding my old employer, weeks after that first session with Eduardo a letter from a friend reported a new expedition, which was confirmed by newspaper reports shortly thereafter. And so it went with the aftermath of that "rather uneventful" first session.

The second session I attended (first described in Sharon, 1972b: 43–44) was held for the treatment of an entire family. The father was a practical-minded businessman who had been quite successful in the past. Now his business was declining, and he was bedridden, unable to walk. Medical attention had not explained or alleviated his state. At the same time, his children, who were normally responsible, had been dropping out of school or quitting their jobs and simply loafing. This was the man's second session with Eduardo, and although he was beginning to walk again he was still very skeptical about the *curandero*'s ability to help him. He didn't believe in witchcraft and had decided to consult with Eduardo only after much urging by a business associate who had previously been helped.

In the course of this second séance, the therapeutic manipulation of artifacts and rituals became quite clear. At first the atmosphere was charged with tension. As the individual members of the family took their turns before the *mesa* and Eduardo made divinations about them and events from their lives, their increasing amazement was obvious. After divination, a patient must "raise the staff"—that is, inhale a perfume or a liquid mixture of boiled San Pedro cactus and tobacco while holding one of Eduardo's magical staffs over his head. Eduardo defines the operation of "raising" (which is performed by the curer, his two assistants, and the patients several times during the session) as a "libation, offering, or tribute to the cosmos intended to clear the mind."

During this particular séance each person had a difficult time raising the staff after the divination—a certain sign that witchcraft was involved and that the forces responsible for this witchcraft were resisting the therapy. At one point a screech-owl flew overhead and let out an eerie cry. With that our nervousness increased, since the owl is considered to be an extremely bad omen associated with black magicians and evil sorcery. Then the hood of a truck in the yard where the session was being held suddenly buckled, as if someone had put pressure on the metal and then let it go. There was probably a natural explanation for this sound, but we all jumped. By now we had a feeling of dark foreboding.

At this point a daughter of the family took her turn before the *mesa*. When divining, Eduardo warned her about certain envious friends who wished her ill. Events proceeded normally until she tried to raise the staff. After several attempts and much coughing and sputtering she began to regurgitate the brew. Tension mounted. It did not seem that she would ever succeed in getting the San Pedro and tobacco mixture down her nostrils. She began to lean crazily backward. Panic set in, and someone exclaimed that a monster was pulling the girl's hair from behind to carry her away. Suddenly, without warning, Eduardo raised the brew on the girl's behalf, snatched one of the swords at the head of the *mesa*, and charged into the open area behind her. Before we realized it, he was conducting a furious sword battle, slicing and slashing like a buccaneer. Then, with incredible agility and grace, he executed seven successive rapid-fire somersaults, holding the sword over his head with the blade outward at the beginning of each turn. The direction of his movements over the ground formed a cross. The entire spectacle was over almost before we were fully aware of what was happening, and Eduardo returned to his seat at the *mesa* breathing heavily.

Catching his breath, Eduardo resumed the curing routine, proceeding to the next ritual as if nothing had happened. The tension melted away, and from then until the end of the session everything progressed smoothly.

Afterward, the girl asked Eduardo to explain what had happened. The essence of matter-of-fact paternalism and self-confidence, he chuckled and told her simply that she had confronted forces with which she was unfamiliar, but that like everything else in life, they could be dealt with once one understood their function. Later I asked him for a fuller explanation, and he told me that the sorcerer responsible for the family's misfortunes had attacked the session, making emergency action necessary. The sword battle and somersaults (called *siete mortales*), in addition to breaking the sorcerer's spell, were also intended to shock him.

There was one more session with this family (first described in Sharon, 1972b: 43–44) before I returned to the United States. It went along very smoothly with no problems. There was no tension, and no one had trouble raising the staff. When I left Peru the father was better, and his family and business were beginning to return to normal. But it was difficult to determine if Eduardo had overcome the father's original skepticism.

One year later I attended my fourth session. It was the second session for the evening's principal patient, Eduardo's uncle. He had been bewitched by a jilted ex-lover. The other major patient was Eduardo's mother. This was also her second session, her first having been held a year earlier. She was suffering from witchcraft caused by bundles planted near the doors and external passageways of her house by a man with whom she had had legal difficulties. Also present was a friend of the family, a municipal employee who wanted to make sure that his mistress was still loyal to him. A young man was there to try to improve his luck, since he had just lost a good job with a fish-canning company. Eduardo's brother—in addition to working as one of his two assistants *(alzadores)*—wanted to consult about the health of his wife, who was convalescing from a recent operation, as well as to check on a business matter. Eduardo's wife, María, acted as the other *alzador*. About all I could determine regarding the outcome of this session was that everyone appeared to be satisfied. It was obvious that during divination Eduardo had alluded to many personal matters understood only by the patients.

In the weeks that followed, Eduardo and I probed the depths of his system between visits from friends, relatives, and patients. One day we had an unexpected visitor: the skeptical businessman whose sessions I had witnessed the year before. This time he was accompanied by a relative who had traveled all the way from Cajamarca for guinea-pig divination. After vivisection, the animal's spine was perceived to be broken. The patient had to return to Cajamarca but intended to have a session the next time she was in Trujillo.

I asked if the businessman could give me a lift to Trujillo in his car. This gave me an opportunity to talk with him without his having to worry about pleasing Eduardo. I learned that his luck had changed; he was back on his feet, literally and figuratively. He attributed the outcome to Eduardo's therapy, although he was completely baffled by just how Eduardo had done it. He invited me to lunch the following Sunday, when I had a chance to observe that the family was back to normal and living quite affluently.

Three weeks later, while setting up the *mesa* for another séance (my fifth), Eduardo realized that his brother was not going to show up to act as one of his assistants. When a patient asked who was going to replace him, Eduardo, after muttering something about his brother probably being drunk someplace, nodded in my direction. So that evening I reluctantly stepped out of the comfortable role of participating anthropologist and began to take an active part in the all-night ceremony.

My first experience as a shaman's assistant turned out to be a real initiation. On this occasion it was necessary to exorcise a malevolent spirit that was haunting the patient's house—part of the black magic directed against him by a disgruntled laborer who had fought with the victim over agricultural wages. This meant that in addition to Eduardo's therapy (sucking a pathogen out of the man's back), the two assistants had to raise the hallucinogenic brew at every door in the house. It was only a one-story adobe structure, but it had eight doors! By the end of the session I felt that I could handle any assistant's duties.

Within the next week there were three more sessions, which gave me the opportunity to apply my newly acquired expertise. The first in the series was held in the pre-Columbian adobe ruins of Chan-Chan. This sixth session was held to divine the past of a certain group of buildings in the ruins being studied by an archeology student. The distant roar of the ocean and the eerie shadows on the crumbling adobe walls added to the mysteriousness of the atmosphere as Eduardo began his prayers, chants, and whistlings to the rhythmic beat of his gourd rattle. It was easy to imagine the ghosts of Chan-Chan whispering their secrets to this confident, commanding manipulator of the sacred realm as he handled his sacramental paraphernalia, invoked Catholic saints and guardian spirits, and served the hallucinogenic brew.

After the divination for the archeology student was over, two more clients took their turns before the *mesa*. The first was a farmer who was advised regarding the crops he was sowing and the deals he was making for the sale of his harvest. The second man was encouraged about the outcome of a lawsuit.

Two nights later Eduardo held a "diagnostic" séance (my seventh session) in one of the shantytowns on the desert fringe surrounding Trujillo. He did this as a favor to the healer who had cured him of witchcraft many years before. She now maintained a herb stand in the local market as well as a "clinic" in the shantytown, where patients suffering from a variety of ailments could stay for a few days to be cured through diets and the use of herbs.

There were ten patients waiting for the séance when we arrived, none of whom Eduardo had ever seen before. The *mesa* was set up in the patio, and Eduardo proceeded to divine efficiently the causes of each patient's ailment. Most were fairly routine and involved only a prescription of diet and herbs. But one case turned out to be a classical example of witchcraft. While peering through the darkness, Eduardo asked about the patient's affairs and about certain people he saw. He concluded that there was a great deal of envy being directed toward the patient and that her malady was not simply organic. The patient had to be back in Lima the next day, but she intended to return to Trujillo for a curing session with Eduardo. The other patients were cases that Eduardo's colleague could attend to at the clinic.

The last session I attended with Eduardo in 1971 (my eighth) involved a mild case of love magic. The young man being treated had been neglecting his job and other responsibilities as a result of unrequited love. Eduardo's discourse was a combination of divination and astute psychotherapy, in which he chided the patient for his unmanly melancholy. Eduardo also divined the whereabouts of lost objects for a lady who thought they might have been stolen for use in a curse against her. She was greatly relieved to learn that they had simply been misplaced.

During my last season with Eduardo, in early 1974, he held only one night session. (Eduardo was kept so busy teaching in Trujillo and setting up his ceramic workshop that he did not have the time for more.) However, that single session proved to be quite important in that it provided cross-cultural information on the phenomenon of witchcraft. The clients were two Americans on their first visit to Peru, who could not speak a word of Spanish.

The divination for the first client, which I translated, was quite routine. Eduardo discerned people and activities related to the client's work. The divination for the second client seemed to be developing in a similar fashion until events took a dramatic and unexpected turn. After inquiring whether there was anything in the American's background that might be keeping him from achieving his aspirations, Eduardo suddenly confided to me that the patient had been transformed into a hideous fanged monster, illuminated by what appeared to be the headlights of a car. I was admonished not to tell the American about this, while Eduardo continued probing into his life. Toward the end of the divination the Virgin of Carmen, governess of Purgatory and celestial fire, appeared — and Eduardo saw a flaming arrow in the client's side. After the usual ritual of raising the staff, the client resumed his seat on the reed mat to my left, and his turn before the *mesa* appeared to be over.

But, once seated, the American asked me if it was too late to ask questions. He had not queried Eduardo throughout the divination, even though he knew that it was one of his prerogatives to do so. I told him to go ahead, by all means. The American offered a lengthy explanation for what he thought might have caused the arrow in his side. He said that a palmist in the United States had told him that when he was a child a sorcerer had cut off locks of his hair and placed them in a coffin, and this was the source of the Devil in him which throughout his life had caused numerous setbacks. He would never be free of this negative influence, the palmist had added, until something was done to remove it. Eduardo nodded, confirming that the curse lay behind the monster face he had seen, and that the Virgin of Carmen was in charge of removing witchcraft. The patient asked me to tell Eduardo that a close friend, observing him from an angle, had also seen the fanged monster face.

Eduardo affirmed that it was time to do something about the curse. The American was sent out in front of the *mesa* once again. This time he was instructed to jump back and forth over a small bonfire in the form of a cross, while holding the sword of Saint Paul as if going into battle. Then, while the other assistant and I imbibed red *cananga* perfume, the patient was instructed to stamp out the fire. As he was performing this act, both he and Eduardo reported that they smelled burning hair.

Here ends the summary of my experiences as Eduardo's apprentice through nine séances—during the last five of which I participated actively as one of his assistants. Over the years I have observed the evolution of this man of magic who believes that constant innovation and growth are essential to his curing practices. Recurrent germination seems to be the essence of his shamanism. My observations have convinced me that anthropologists need to reevaluate seriously their concepts regarding traditional therapists and their role in twentieth-century societies.

3

Seeds of Discontent: The Social Context of Peruvian Witchcraft

INSTITUTIONALIZED ENVY

We know that black magic (which included poisoning) was practiced in pre-Columbian times. Since we know also that Chimu herbalist-doctors in north coastal Peru were put to death if an attempted cure failed, and thieves and adulterers were likewise put to death, it seems highly unlikely that the fate of a proven sorcerer could have been any better. We know, too, that the Incas considered sorcery to be one of the most heinous of crimes, punishable by death for the sorcerer and all his family (Cobo, 1956:92: 116). Thus the question arises: How did witchcraft (*daño*) become so predominant in Peru? Part of the answer is provided by Kubler (1946: 398).

> The proliferation of the sorcerers practicing an infrasocial or antisocial magic was a colonial phenomenon. . . . The number of sorcerers had increased enormously, and Polo de Ondegardo [*corregidor* of Cuzco in the mid-sixteenth century] assigns the increase to the general spread of indigence in the colonial communities.

The natives of Peru were certainly impoverished after the Conquest (Steward and Faron, 1959: 148-153). In addition to suffering a generation of revolution and looting by the *conquistadores,* the Indians were ruthlessly exploited through a system of excessive tribute levies (*encomienda*) coupled with forced labor (*mita*) and the expansion of the native institution of personal servants (*yanaconas*). Although in theory the *encomienda* system did not permit direct land use or interference in native affairs by Spaniards, in practice excessive tribute demands, exacerbated by the complications of Spanish law, led to increasing loss of community lands and the eventual rise of individually owned Spanish estates (*haciendas*). As a consequence, a vast homeless population constantly on the verge of starvation was created. This rootless, floating proletariat included landless farmers but was composed mainly of *yanaconas*—servants and artisans—who were enticed away from their native communities by exemption from tribute and forced labor.

In the late sixteenth century the Spanish Crown made an effort to curtail the virtual slavery produced by the *encomienda* system, with its attendant alienation of Indian lands. This was done by instituting the *corregimiento*, whereby Crown officials (*corregidores*) took over most *encomienda* grants, thus removing Indian lands from the market. At the same time the number of *yanaconas* was strictly regulated. These measures placed large reserves of native labor in the hands of the government, which channeled them into forced labor for newly discovered mines. Overnight the agrarian emphasis of the economy was shifted to mining. The total effect of the changes in colonial administration was to lock the Indian into a community system that existed mainly to provide labor and food for the mining economy. Despite the growth of towns and small-scale manufacturing in the eighteenth century, this socioeconomic pattern persisted until the wars of independence in 1821, and the *corregimiento* remained the basic institution of Peruvian colonial government.*

As delineated by Wolf (1955: 456-61), the characteristics of the "closed corporate community" best describe the structure of the Indian communities that contained the majority of the population and supplied the labor and tribute for the colonial economy. Under this system, the community's members were made participants in its political and religious affairs and co-owners of a landholding corporation. The Crown adopted the system in order to keep the *conquistadores* from becoming too powerful and independent; also, it fitted well into the Spanish political and legal structure, and it facilitated the imposition of forced labor and tribute. The characteristics of the corporate peasant community were poverty, location on marginal lands, use of traditional technology, jurisdiction over land allocation, a political-religious system establishing traditional roles within the community, social sanctions to prevent nontraditional behavior, a need to search for supplementary income in an outside market (wage labor on the *haciendas* or inter-village exchange), and much physical labor within the family.

Wolf's discussion (1955: 460) of institutionalized psychological sanctions against nontraditional behavior as operative in a "closed corporate community" shows how this type of social organization fostered the growth of witchcraft in colonial Peruvian society:

> Paralleling the mechanisms of control which are primarily economic in origin are psychological mechanisms like institutionalized envy, which may find expression in various manifestations such as gossip, attacks of the evil eye, or in the fear and practice of witchcraft. . . . Witchcraft, as well as milder forms of institutionalized envy, has an integrative effect in restraining non-traditional behavior, as long as social relationships suffer no serious disruption. It minimizes disruptive phenomena such as economic mobility, abuse of ascribed power, or individual conspicuous show of wealth. On the individual plane, it thus acts to maintain the individual in equilibrium with his neighbors. On the social plane, it reduces the disruptive influences of outside society.

*See Rowe (1957) on the abuse and corruption of the *corregimiento*.

We know very little about the history of the north coast during the colonial period. According to Rowe (1948: 53-55), the soldier-historian Cieza de León travelled along the coast in 1548. He attributed the scanty population he encountered throughout his travels to the twenty years of civil war between the *conquistadores* that followed the Conquest. New diseases brought by the Spanish probably contributed to the depopulation. In 1578 heavy rains and floods, followed by locusts, destroyed homes and farms, leaving the Indians destitute and starving.

Rowe tells us that "a cultural blow as severe as the economic ones . . . was the great campaign against idolatry of the first half of the seventeenth century." The coastal campaign was the most intense, and Rowe contends that it was probably a major cause of the disappearance of Chimu culture, which, despite the Inca and Spanish conquests, was still strong in the early seventeenth century. Kubler (1946: 400) informs us that during this campaign "very stern repressive measures were taken against the professional practitioners of idolatry. . . . In 1617-18, systematic idol- and witch-hunts were conducted." In the latter campaign, 679 "sorcerers" were discovered in a single coastal *corregimiento*.

The Jesuit missionary Arriaga, who participated in this campaign (see Arriaga, 1968: 38-39), discovered a type of witchcraft that bore many similarities to the European belief in vampires. The practice was performed in the towns of the coast, where "in the various clans and factions there are teachers of witchcraft whom they now designate by our Spanish word for captain, and each of these has his disciples and soldiers." Here is Arriaga's account:

> That night the master goes to a house of his choice, accompanied by one or two disciples. While they stand outside at the door he goes in, scattering a powder made for the purpose from the bones of the dead. Then using I know not what words and signs that he has prepared, he puts the entire household to sleep, so that no one in the house will move or hear anything. Then he goes up to the person he wants to kill, and with his fingernail takes blood out of some part of the body and sucks as much of it as he can. This is why in their language witches are called bloodsuckers. Then what they have sucked out in this manner they put into the palm of their hand or into a gourd and take it to where the rest are gathered. They say the Devil multiplies this blood or converts it into meat (I am inclined to believe that they add other meat to it) and they cook it together and eat it. The result is that the person whose blood has been sucked will die within two or three days.

The following passage from the same report alludes obliquely to some of the social conditions underlying these practices:

> One of them remarked without shame or fear: "I have killed three boys," and another said, "I have eaten this many." When the visitor [the ecclesiastical in-

vestigator] confronted them with each other in order to find out I know not
what fact, one of them said: "You ate my son." "That is true," he answered, "I
have already said so to the visitor. I ate him because you took away my farm."

This episode occurred nearly a century after the Conquest. In the interim
the Spanish colonial policies, including abuse and mistreatment of the Indians, had time to take their full effect. We have already noted that as early
as the middle of the sixteenth century Indian poverty and social disruption
had caused an enormous increase in the number of sorcerers. Religious
persecution only exacerbated the social conditions that encouraged the practice of malevolent magic. Thus, by the seventeenth century the seeds of
discontent had been sown and were ripening; witchcraft had become a fact
of life in the coastal towns, especially the late medieval Christian variety,
which had itself been fostered by oppression, religious intolerance, ig-
norance, and poverty.

Throughout the colonial period, northern Peru remained on the periphery
of all of the major revolts and events that occurred in the central and
southern regions around the great mining centers. What historical data we
have from the late colonial period in the north gives us a clue to the roots of
northern quiescence. In addition to the fact that the mineral wealth of the
north was not as extensive as that of the southern and central regions, there
were hardly any native peoples left for either large-scale labor draft or revolt.
That the depopulation observed by Cieza de Leon in 1548 had not been overcome by the 1760s is verified by the writings of the *corregidor* of Trujillo,
Feyjoo y Sosa. Von Hagen (1964: 17, 19) summarizes his observations:

> Herein one reads that the province was almost void of people. There were only
> 2,513 Indians in the several valleys that formed the area, and these were en-
> gaged in agriculture, mostly sugar, and in the upper valleys they worked in
> clothing factories. The reader was informed of the large *haciendas* in the suc-
> ceeding valleys, with vast stretches of desert emptiness between them. . . .
> [T]he population of these northern desert valleys had shrunk, and land was held
> in vast *latifundias* by only a sprinkling of aristocracy, while the people, mostly
> Indian or Mestizo descendants of the Chimu and Mochica empires, were living
> on the bare edge of penury.

Von Hagen (1964: 18) further observes that "wars, disease, and inadequate
medical services had decimated the population . . . the natural resources
had been reduced to the point of disappearance." Thus indigence and social
marginality, the nutrients of witchcraft, were still rife in the coastal valleys of
northern Peru during the late colonial period.

DAÑO, THE BITTER HARVEST

Independence from Spain and the establishment of a republic in the 1820s
at first did little to change the colonial status of the vast majority of the peo-

ple of Peru. *Encomienda*-like tribute was collected until 1895. Mining declined during the eighteenth century and did not revive until late in the nineteenth century, but forced labor was still used for the *haciendas* and for public works. A phenomenon similar to the *encomienda* system of the sixteenth century was the rapid growth of huge estates (*latifundias*), made possible when landlords, now free from colonial trade restrictions imposed by Spain, began to produce specialized export crops for the world market. Many traditional corporate communities, enticed by monetary returns, also began to produce cash crops. This often led to individualization of land holdings, which, in addition to eroding community cohesiveness through competition, caused land loss because the small farmer could not compete with the large estates.

As in the colonial period, the north figured negligibly in the politics of the *caudillos* (military leaders) who dominated the early republican period. However, in the 1880s several foreign-owned corporations began to purchase land and improve the irrigation systems of the northern coastal valleys in order to plant and process sugar cane for export. This accelerated the socioeconomic changes and modernization initiated by *latifundismo*. As a result of increasing involvement in the world market, the "closed-corporate" nature of the social structure gave way to an "open" type of peasant community, which paved the way for the predominance of the middle class in the twentieth century.

Because of increasing technological innovation, improved transportation and communication facilities, greater involvement in a modern market economy, and public education, the middle class today is the dominant segment of the population of the northern coastal region. Thus the majority of the people now live and work in urban environments or are involved in an interdependent economic network regulating the flow of goods and services. Capital investment is concentrated largely in the sugar, cotton, and fishing industries. Most of the smaller sugar *haciendas* have been consolidated into several large ones, which were owned by American, British, and German interests until nationalization in 1969. In addition to the urban middle class, there is now a rural proletariat working and living on the *haciendas*, as well as a small peasant population living in a few marginal "indigenous communities" that have been preserved in order to maintain some food production for the local markets.

Another subculture that has begun to increase is composed of migrating peasants from "corporate" highland communities who live in fast-growing shantytowns on the nonproductive fringes of the valley oases of the north. These people come to the coast in the hope of finding better work opportunities, but lack of sufficient industrial diversification and educational facilities is preventing the creation of new jobs and job training programs. Sugar and cotton (and, to a lesser degree, fishing) have so monopolized the economy that there is room for diversification only in service employment. In addition, there has been little upward mobility in the sugar and cotton industries. As a result, the cities of the north, like many Latin American cities, suffer from an excess of services built on a limited industrial base—which causes much overlap and severe restriction on expansion of opportunities to meet increasing job demands from all strata of the society. Needless to say, there is a great deal of competition for those jobs that are available; salaries are low, and the cost of living is high in proportion to personal income.

The Peruvian social psychiatrist Mario Chiappe, in a study of north coastal *curanderismo* (1968), described the interplay between these socioeconomic factors and psychological mechanisms of adaptation. He found that patients and healers agreed that witchcraft was caused by the "envy" of enemies of the patient. Belief in envy as the motivation for witchcraft was so pervasive that community members exercised great care to avoid behavior that might arouse this sentiment in their neighbors—a situation similar to the one already described for the closed-corporate peasant community, and probably a reflection of the social effects of heavy rural-to-urban migration.

Analyzing northern social structure, Chiappe noted the overspecialization in the sugar and cotton industries that has monopolized regional resources, as mentioned above. He showed that this limited economic base produced rigid social stratification with little upward mobility, stiff competition for jobs, and a high level of insecurity. Endemic frustration and aggression were denied most forms of expression by the total dependence of the population on the dysfunctionally rigid social structure. However, expression was provided in the form of a projective mechanism: the widespread envy that Chiappe discovered throughout the north. This projective mechanism fed directly into the practice of witchcraft. Thus, if someone felt envious he could seek out a sorcerer to help him express his covert aggressions. If he suffered illness or personal tragedy he could blame it on the envy of an enemy and seek alleviation from a folk healer. Witchcraft, then, was depicted by Chiappe as an escape valve, permitting aggression resulting from frustration to express itself without attacking fundamental institutions upon which the population was so dependent.

Chiappe (1968: 34) noted increasing sophistication and adaption to modern medicine by *curanderos* near urban centers such as Trujillo. Dragunsky (1968), in another study of northern *curanderismo*, indicated that belief in witchcraft (and in the ability of healers to overcome it) was widespread throughout the north among all strata of the society. He attributed this to three factors: (1) underdevelopment and backwardness, (2) lack of political leadership capable of forging a nation-state, and (3) extensive unemployment among large segments of the population. These factors combined, he felt, to cause the transference of many traditional rural beliefs and values to the whole of contemporary society by means of a semi-proletarianized peasant class. In addition, Dragunsky felt that folk healing was adapting to culture change. As he put it, the role of the *curandero* tends to reshape itself; it isn't done and finished. Even more, the role tends to change. . . . The people of Lima and the large cities, sick of inhuman relations, discover millenial folk healing as an old "remedy" for new ills. . . . [Thus, folk healing] takes on new vitality, nourished by the peasantry and by the large city, in adapting itself for new problems, new forms, congruent with the medium and the age, but the same content: ancestral magic. (1968: 20-21)

The findings of Chiappe and Dragunsky parallel some of Redfield's (1941), uncovered during one of the earliest studies of witchcraft in Latin America. Studying four communities in Yucatán, ranging from folk to urban, Redfield found a belief in witchcraft in all of them. However, the frequency of witchcraft activity increased with the size of the community. The explanation offered by Redfield (1941: 334-35) was that

black magic . . . is an expression of the insecurity of the individual in the unstable social milieu of the city. Life has greater uncertainties in the city than in the village. The forces of economic competition affect people in different ways and therefore tend to isolate the individual from his family and his local group. The lack of an integrated culture and the breakdown of the familial and religious controls . . . make it difficult to predict the behavior of others. The social world in which an individual moves is large and complex, and the roles of individuals within it are often unclear and are unstable. . . . None of those cases of black magic which were encountered in the villages involved its practice by one resident of a village against another of the same village. The solidarity of the local and the familial group is great. But in the city one's neighbor may be one's enemy, and not rarely is.

Thus the social seeds sown by the technically advanced Europeans of the Conquest are today being reaped in an impersonal, dehumanized environment that is also the product of Western technology. However, in all fairness to contemporary Peruvians it must be acknowledged that in recent years much has been done to overcome the effects of those aspects of their heritage which have meant oppression and injustice for so many.

EDUARDO'S VIEW OF HIS SOCIAL ROLE

As we have seen from his biography, Eduardo is intellectually inclined. This side of his personality was reinforced by his work with archeologists as well as by his teaching experience. In addition, he is well informed and politically aware. Thus, unlike many *curanderos,* he is most articulate about his art and its place in his society. It seems fitting, therefore, to quote what Eduardo had to say about the relationship of the socioeconomic base to envy and witchcraft:

In general the socioeconomic base plays a principal role within

witchcraft and folk healing owing to the phase of acculturation among the
people of Peru. The cultural variety that exists among the people is one of
the principal factors. Within the society three factors—customs rooted in
ancestral culture, lack of economic means, and lack of work—coincide to
cause envy. For example, here in Moche there are those who work, who
dedicate themselves exclusively to their work. And there are those who do
not work, who depend upon that man who has his four cents, his small fortune. Then the latter tend to focus on the worker a principle of envy, of
resentment. On the basis of this hidden, guarded resentment, whenever a
dispute occurs the envy comes into operation in a general and damaging
fashion, producing witchcraft. They look for a motivation, something with
which they can justify themselves in bewitching him in order to see him
"unbalanced" so that he does not surge ahead, so that he regresses or lives
on a cultural and socioeconomic level with them.

(Question: Why do some bewitch others? What is the reason for witchcraft?)

For the purpose of seeing the victim suffer, and more than anything, to
set him back in his desire for progress. Knowing that he is bewitched, he
gets sick, physically and spiritually. Then the individual, instead of pro-
gressing, becomes debilitated economically and physically. When the vic-
timizers see that the victim is approaching calamity they feel satisfied.
Then they confront him: "Where is your money? See! So you think what
you tell yourself is going to help you!" And so on.

(Question: Do you think it is possible that witchcraft exists as a sort of
"escape valve" for society—for example, for the expression of hostilities
that society itself does not permit to be expressed?)

It is possible. Given that one cannot assault in a direct fashion such as
taking a revolver and putting a bullet in a person, many do it in an in-
direct fashion, taking advantage of the mystical field, of the esoteric, of
the field of mystery that includes witchcraft, of secrecy by which the blame
can be laid upon a sorcerer who knows to whom the witchcraft has been
done. . . . And since there is no evidence that this is effective—as in reality it is—and in view of the fact that modern society denies that these at-
titudes are effective, a man can die or end up in bankruptcy.

(Question: For one who gets sick, do you think that belief in witchcraft
helps him as an "explanatory" function? . . . For example, if it is a
psychosomatic sickness that the doctor cannot cure, but the patient says "I
am sure that I am suffering from witchcraft," do you think that this helps
the patient?)

Up to a certain point, yes, because if he assumes the burden of
witchcraft or thinks that he is really bewitched, this is going to help him in
"unraveling" his sickness. Because it is a psychosomatic case, right? Then
automatically he is auto-curing himself in a real fashion by thinking that it
is witchcraft. Then the *curandero* joins mentally in a telepathic manner

and knows what is the reality, and by means of his drink of San Pedro he "visualizes" the thing much more precisely. Then he knows where to go, what is the reason.

When questioned further about envy, Eduardo described it as one of the principles, one of the preambles of evil. Envy is ingrained in man, always to envy the things belonging to one's fellows: if he has and I don't have, and why does he have. This is one of the preambles, as I said, for the occurrence of evil, witchcraft, reprisal. In all of the towns that I have seen and all the cases, they have been performed out of envy. Always envy enters into this field, since through envy the individual channels his feeling into witchcraft. And, being on this plane of envy, of aversion, of hate caused by the things that he cannot possess, he is already practicing his influence over the person.

(Question: In other words, it is a kind of hate that aids bewitchment of other persons?)

Yes. By the very fact that one is feeling this problem one is already doing harm to another. It begins there. Therefore, certain sorcerers in Australia, for example, have their rites when they want to harm a person. . . .They take a spine and begin to thrust it in from far away. And it turns out that the other person is dying. . . .

(Question: In other words, you think that envy plays a key role in witchcraft, it is the basic principle?)

Yes, the basic principle by which witchcraft or sorcery comes about.

(Question: What is the mechanism that works here? How does envy function to cause witchcraft or sorcery?)

By the intention, the will of man, and thinking, always thinking, evil, always trying to opaque that personality [of the victim]. It is necessary. If there isn't this, there is no witchcraft. . . .

(Question: In other words, evil thought works against a man when one is thinking in this fashion?)

Of course, it's logical.

(Question: Does the sorcerer concentrate the envy or the hate of the one who asks for his services in order to perform the evil?)

Certainly, in that both are of the same stock. If the one hates for a reason, the sorcerer is the individual in which is concentrated all evil. Then the client pours out his afflictions, his sorrows, his intentions, and the sorcerer increases them, duplicates them, triplicates them, raising them to major potency with his knowledge, with his power. Then the witchcraft is stronger, more instantaneous, more potent.

(Question: In other words, there exists a kind of covenant between the client and the sorcerer?)

Logically there has to be, because if there is no affinity between the two there can be no witchcraft. Or if the client thinks of doing harm and sud-

denly becomes discouraged, then the sorcerer loses his will in that moment. Those two forces have to be allied there in order to go directly and
coincide in the place.

When asked how he perceived the social role of the *curandero* in Peruvian
society, this was his answer:

> It is possible that the *curandero* who tends toward frankness is a nexus
> between the traditional and the modern. . . . It would be a very strong,
> very abrupt change for the individual confronting a growing society to sud-
> denly abandon his forms, his ancestral principles, traditions leagued to the
> old society of his grandparents, of his ancestors. Thus the *curandero*
> diminishes the force of the blow, but, more important, he provides a
> beginning, an entrance, an opening in a smooth fashion toward the society
> to which one is going to adapt. He is a shock-absorber between both social
> fields, between that which is being left and that which is being
> entered. . . . Thus the *curandero* comes to be the link of amalgamation,
> of connection between what is behind and what is ahead. He is the bridge
> in the social field.

> (Question: It seems to me that the adaptation that many *curanderos* are
> making toward modern medicine helps in this work as a bridge.)

> Yes, that is true. Things that cannot be cured with natural herbs — ad-
> vanced things — require the application of the wisdom and the techniques
> of modern science. . . .

> (Question: In your work do you encounter many middle-class patients
> having ample knowledge of modern medicine who have come to you for
> consultations anyway, even though they have been to the doctor also?)

> Yes. . . . Even here I am still a shock-absorber. The average middle-
> class citizen still has this tendency to believe in the remedies, the herbs.
> And in effect they find relief, they get better. What are they going to do?
> They aren't going to go to the doctor and ask him for herbs for a stomach
> ache. They come to the *curandero*. Then the *curandero*, such as I am,
> gives them an herb to alleviate their ailment. Then, in my case, I speak to
> them about the question of medicines and I prescribe a medicine,
> something, and I send them to the doctor. . . .

> (Question: Do you find that many people of the middle class believe in
> witchcraft and come here to be cured of witchcraft?)

> The majority, yes. The majority believe. However, in the north there are
> many deceivers, many tricksters, as they are commonly called. This has
> resulted in the emergence of a group of individuals who cheat, which in
> turn has caused certain members of the middle class to hate and repudiate
> the sorcerer because they have fallen into his clutches, in his noose of
> trickery and shamelessness. I always try to oppose these sorcerers.

From the foregoing we get an impression of Eduardo's milieu and the way
in which it influences his *curandero* role and associated ideology. Envy and

witchcraft, these are the results of tensions created by the ongoing collision of cultures: Indian, *mestizo,* and Western. But the socioeconomic picture presents only one level of reality. Other, older seeds have been planted and nurtured in the rich cultural soil of Latin America. Their roots run deep and still provide nourishment for their people. It is to this deeper stratum of *curanderismo* that we now turn our attention.

4

Magical Flora: *Curandero* Plant Lore

ENCHANTED HERBS AND FALCON TOBACCO

Owing to its location near the equator and its great ecological variety—including, for example, coastal desert, Andean highlands, *montaña* (high tropical rain forest), and *selva* (lowland jungle and river country)—Peru supports a wide range of exotic flora, much of which has medicinal properties. Some of the medicinal plants have been properly classified by botanists or analyzed by pharmacologists in modern times, but many have not. However, through millennia of trial and error, *curanderismo* has developed an empirical tradition in the use of these plants that is carefully passed on from generation to generation. *Curanderos* are well versed in the medicinal properties of the Peruvian flora, which they conceive of not in purely physical or mechanical terms but also in terms of the supernatural context in which the plant is administered. But it is not necessary to be a folk healer to be well acquainted with this tradition. In Peru today, every marketplace has its herb stands, owned by merchants who have a very extensive knowledge of plants and their uses. These stands receive shipments from all the ecological zones of the country.

San Pedro is only one—though the principal one—of a great number of "magical" plants used by *curanderos*. These plants (some of which are medicinal as well as magical) are carefully distinguished from the purely medicinal plants known to the *curandero*. The great majority of the magical plants are herbs collected at sacred lagoons on hillsides in the Andes at altitudes of twelve to thirteen thousand feet, or lower down on "powerful" mountains in the north coastal region. There are several areas in the northern highlands where such lagoons and mountains are found. The most important lagoons, called collectively Las Huaringas, are located above the town of Huancabamba, near the Peru-Ecuador border. Many *curanderos* have been initiated at Las Huaringas and make periodic pilgrimages to the area to collect herbs.

Initiation and curing rituals at Las Huaringas involve a midday bath in a lagoon, during which one "sows" one's shadow, or soul, in its waters. Regarding this ritual, Eduardo says:

When one works with or bathes in the lagoon, the herbs themselves "call" one. If he is for good, the good herbs are attracted to him and come near; and the bad herbs come to him who is for evil. All this is according to the affinity of the herbs, according to their function and their application.

Of particular importance in northern ethnobotany is "mountain lore." In pre-Columbian times mountains were the sacred dwelling places of the ancestors and the chthonic deities of fertility and the underworld. Among the Quechua- and Aymara-speaking Indians of the southern highlands this pre-Columbian belief system is still very much alive. Such beliefs have less overt influence among the Spanish-speaking *mestizo* peoples of the north coast, where Christianity has exercised a greater influence than in the highlands. Nevertheless, mountains play a vital role in contemporary northern folk healing. They are "power spots" invoked by *curanderos* in their nighttime curing sessions. The two most important mountains along the coast, Chaparrí and Yanahuanga, are also sites of initiation where magical plants can be collected.

According to Eduardo:

Chaparrí and Yanahuanga are two of the great powers, or "charms." They are mountains. According to *curandero* legends, they were two kingdoms: the high Yanahuanga and the wide Chaparrí. . . . They are in the Lambayeque region inland around the town of Ferreñafe. These two mountains are completely bare. The legend says that the two ancient kingdoms hated each other. One represented good, the other evil. They fought with each other. Thus it happened that Divine Providence converted them into mountains because the Devil had come between them. But they vindicated themselves in order to do good to others. On one side are found the good herbs and on the other the bad herbs. The white herbs are on one side on Yanahuanga, and the black herbs are on the other side on Chaparrí.

Almost all of the *curanderos* make pilgrimages to Chaparrí and Yanahuanga to look for the magical herbs. There are no mountains as bare as these two. Thus the *curanderos* have to wait for the moment when the mountains induce a dreamy state causing them to fall asleep. Suddenly the *curanderos* wake up and their steps go directly to the site where the herbs are to be found. They pick only the herbs that they need—those their temperament, their idea, their "account" has "called" in their dreams, showing where the herbs can be found. And they come down from the mountains in a tranquil state. And they return with the plants to cure others.

They have to have made a "pact" as *curanderos* in order to be able to make this pilgrimage. Otherwise it is not possible, because if they go the mountains begin to rumble and loosen boulders . . . causing one to run away. According to the *curanderos* who make the pilgrimage to collect the herbs, it is dangerous. One must have a special gift for bringing the herbs from there. This is developed in a pact that the *curanderos* make.

From the foregoing it can be seen that north Peruvian plant lore represents a syncretic blend of Christian moralism and the pre-Columbian belief that all nature is animated by spirit, with certain objects and places having greater concentrations of spirit than others. Chaparrí and Yanahuanga and the plants that grow there give concrete expression to a dualistic ideology that underlies all northern folk healing and its use of magical herbs. The good/evil dichotomy is Christian, but, as we shall see in chapter 7, pre-Columbian religion was also dualistic. However, native dualism tended to be less moralistic, and the opposites—left/right, male/female—were perceived as complementary, not dissociated. When we analyze Eduardo's *mesa* in chapter 6, we shall see that even the opposition of good/evil is mediated and rendered complementary.

Magical herbs, once collected at a power spot, are placed in the healer's *seguro*, a special glass jar, along with several perfumes to preserve them. During the curing part of a session, the *curandero* pays much attention to the *seguro*, which he considers to be his "second person," or alter ego. According to Eduardo, when he is concentrating on the *seguro* the magical plants contained therein, previously activated by the ceremonial part of the session and by the drinking of San Pedro, "talk" to him. During diagnosis, some plants indicate to the curer symbols of his art that are appropriate to the case, as well as the causes of the patient's ailment; others, which have both symbolic and medicinal value, indicate what herb or herbs should be used in treatment.

The action of the magical plants, and their relation to San Pedro and to Eduardo, are of vital importance in his work. He elaborates their role as follows:

> According to my evaluation as *curandero,* the herbs have their spirits, because they speak and direct the activities in the realm of *curanderismo* during the nocturnal session. . . . Their spirits are susceptible to the *curandero* who manipulates them. They can advise or warn him. . . . They indicate to him how the cure is to be effected by means of the San Pedro infusion, which is the principal base of *curanderismo.* They enumerate the dangers to watch out for, and what is to be done about the sickness. If one does not drink San Pedro, there is nothing. . . . The herbs . . . have power to manifest themselves. It seems that possibly they have a spirit that is matched with the power of San Pedro and the intellectual power of the *curandero.*

When asked about the power of the magical plants, Eduardo explained:

> The *curandero* or *brujo,* upon invoking the power of the plants within

his curative power, also influences them. He imposes his personal spiritual force over the plants . . . activating that magic power that plants contain as a result of having been rooted in the earth and partaken of its magnetic force. And since man is an element of the earth, with the power of his intelligence . . . he emits this potentiality over the plants. The plants receive this influence and return it toward man, toward the individual in the moment when he invokes it. In other words, all of the spirit of the plants is . . . fortified by the influences—intellectual, spiritual, and human—of man. He is the one who forms the magic potentiality of the plants. Because of the fact that they are in an isolated place, a place untouched by strange hands, by foreign elements, the plants together with water produce the magic power by virtue of their duality.

It appears that once the curer's inner power is activated by San Pedro, the magical plants provide a medium for renewing his contact with the earth in a reciprocal flow of energy.

My introduction to esoteric plant lore under Eduardo's tutorship should help to illustrate the reciprocity between man and plant inherent in *curandero* ethnobotany. During my first week of apprenticeship, while showing me his artifacts, Eduardo came across a small bag of dried plants. He spread them out on a table and explained their respective names and symbolic meanings to me. Then he casually wrapped four or five of them in a small section of newspaper torn from a copy at hand and told me to take them home. That night the package fell out of my pocket while I was preparing for bed. I placed it on a nightstand, intending to put it somewhere in my gear the next morning. I had a restless night. In the early morning hours I was awakened by a dream in which I felt as if an electric current were passing through my body. I awoke so fast that at first I had no sense of my body. After getting over the jolt, I had difficulty going back to sleep.

The next day at Eduardo's, I was busy interrogating him about the *mesa* when he suddenly cocked his head in a quizzical fashion and asked me if anything unusual had happened during the night. I related my experience and asked him why he had asked. He told me that he had given me the plants the night before for a special reason; my early-morning experience had been caused by the "spirit of the plants" imparting "power" to me!

In addition to the magical plants, a liquid tobacco mixture (*tabaco*) acts as an auxiliary catalyst in support of the visionary function of San Pedro. It is imbibed through the nostrils by everyone present during the ceremonial acts of a night session prior to the drinking of the pure San Pedro infusion at midnight. It is individually prepared for each participant by Eduardo, who mixes the following ingredients in a bivalve shell: dried leaves of a black tobacco plant (the principal ingredient, from which the mixture gets its name), San Pedro juice, sugar, sweet-lime juice, Tabu cologne, a red perfume (*cananga*), a light-colored scented water (*agua florida*), and cane alcohol. San Pedro is included because of its power to arouse the spirit. Sugar, sweet lime, and cologne symbolize sweetness, the force that renders the patient's spirit susceptible to therapy once aroused. Red perfume represents the purifying fire of Purgatory used in exorcisms; light perfume, the magical herbs. Cane alcohol symbolizes the intoxicating force of the Devil and the powers of evil, which must be invoked to get at the causes of disharmony.

Eduardo described the purpose of the tobacco in the mixture as follows:

> Pure tobacco—*sayri* or *huaman tabaco,* the famous falcon, as the an-
> cients called it—gives power to "visualize" . . . and very rapid sight,
> mind, and imagination. It is for this reason that in ancient times they used
> *rapé* made from ground tobacco to "clear" the mind. It is in exactly the
> same fashion that we . . . the *curanderos* . . . utilize tobacco: to clear
> our minds and speed our thoughts toward the ends we seek.
>
> (Question: Why do you take it through the nostrils?)
>
> Because it is near certain motor nerves that transmit to the brain. There
> it touches these olfactory papillae* that go directly to the brain. Then its
> power is more rapid.

The power of the magical flora, then, seems to come from a projection of the *curandero*'s own inner psychic force catalyzed by the action of the prin-cipal magic plant, the hallucinogenic San Pedro cactus. The activity of San Pedro is reinforced by the auxiliary catalyst, tobacco.

La Barre (1972: 277) indicates the Amerindian ideology behind the use of such catalytic agents of psychic projection:

> Whether shaman alone, or shaman and communicants, or communicants alone
> imbibe or ingest *Ilex* drinks, *Datura* infusions, tobacco in whatever form, native
> beers and wines, peyote cactus, ololiuqui or morning-glory seeds, mushrooms,
> narcotic mint leaves or coca, the *ayahuasca* "vine of the dead spirits"
> (*Banisteriopsis caapi*), or any of the vast array of Amerindian psychotropic
> plants, the ethnographic principle is the same. *These plants contain spirit*
> *power.*

He adds that the Amerindians' "epistemological touchstone for reality was direct personal psychic experience of the forces in nature; their shamanism fits the individualism of hunters" (1972: 278). This matches the "warrior" and "hunter" philosophy taught to Castaneda (1971, 1972) by his Yaqui shaman-mentor, don Juan. But the Andean and Mesoamerican shamanic traditions, because of a relatively long history of agriculture, also include elements of the psychology of planters. In northern Peru this latter influence is indicated by the manner in which the magical herbs embody the dualism

---

*Some of Eduardo's recently acquired medical terminology (gained through a correspondence course in nursing) renders his meaning here quite clear.

of "good versus evil," and the way in which they "call" the *curandero* or *brujo* to his shamanic art. Agricultural ideology also finds appropriate symbolic expression through the characteristics of the primary magical plant, San Pedro, which is part of an ongoing cultural tradition of respectable antiquity.

THE HISTORY OF A MAGICAL PLANT

Because of the overlay of Christian symbolism and many Hispanic cultural traits, early researchers thought that northern folk healing, like the witchcraft it treats, was a product of colonial Peruvian society. As our knowledge of the hallucenogenic San Pedro plant grows, however, it becomes increasingly apparent that its use is firmly rooted in the pre-Columbian past. It is now possible to demonstrate that the ritual use of San Pedro has a long and uninterrupted history reaching back to the very beginnings of Peruvian civilization.

San Pedro is a smooth, relatively thin, night-blooming columnar cactus of the genus *Cereus*. When it has any spines at all they are small and few in number. It is possible that the spines, like the flowers, are seasonal. San Pedro was first described and classified in 1920 as *Trichocereus pachanoi* by botanists N. L. Britton and N. J. Rose, who noted its distribution area as Andean Ecuador. The German botanist Curt Backeberg (1959) agreed with this classification but expanded the area of distribution to include northern Peru and Bolivia. Britton and Rose reported San Pedro growing at altitudes of two to three thousand meters. However, I have also found the cactus growing at sea level in many places along the coast of northern Peru. Figure 4-1 (see photo insert) shows a large San Pedro plant in the coastal city of Trujillo.

Pharmacological analysis of San Pedro has shown that mescaline is its active alkaloid (Friedberg, 1959; Poisson, 1960; Gonzalez Huerta, 1960). The mescaline content is approximately 0.12 percent of the fresh plant, and 2 percent when it is dried. The Swedish pharmacologist Stig Agurell (1969a, 1969b) has recently discovered seven other alkaloids in San Pedro, but none of these are present in significant quantity.

According to *curandero* lore there are several types of San Pedro, distinguished by the number of longitudinal ribs. The kind most often used by *curanderos* has seven ribs. Four-ribbed cacti, like four-leafed clovers, are considered to be very rare and very lucky. They are believed to have special curative properties because they correspond to the "four winds" and the "four roads," supernatural powers associated with the cardinal points invoked during curing rituals. The varieties of San Pedro found in the Andean foothills are said to be most potent, whatever the number of ribs, because of the higher mineral content of the soil.

Preparing San Pedro for a folk-healing session is a very simple process. At noon on the day of the session, four cacti (the thinnest are believed to make the best brew), purchased from an herb stand in the local market, are sliced like a loaf of bread (see photo insert figure 4-2) and boiled in a five-gallon can of water for seven hours (see photo insert figure 4-3). The completed brew is set near the *curandero*'s other power objects on his *mesa* (see photo insert figure 4-4).

For most cases brought to the folk healer, nothing is added to the boiled San Pedro infusion. However, in cases of illness caused by a sorcerer's magic concoction of powdered bones, cemetery dust, dust from archeological ruins, or other substances, certain botanically unidentified plants—known as *hornamo blanco, hornamo amarillo, hornamo morado, hornamo cuti, hornamo caballo,* and *condor purga*—are boiled separately and later added to the portions of San Pedro served to the patient. A purgative brew made from another unidentified plant (*condorillo,* or *yerba de la justicia,* or *mejorana*) is prepared to be taken after San Pedro and the *hornamos* to induce vomiting. Finally, a portion of San Pedro infusion is set aside to be added to the ingredients mixed to produce *tabaco.*

Many *curanderos* in the Chiclayo area add *floripondio,* or floripondium (*Datura arborea;* see photo insert figure 4-5)—one of the numerous *mishas* or *Daturas*—to San Pedro, but Eduardo usually prefers not to do so. He was initiated by healers who used these potent plants and is aware of their toxic properties and adverse effects on many patients. He does not feel that such drastic shock therapy is always necessary to alleviate the ailments of those seeking his services. (See my experiences with *Datura* in chapter 10.)

Since the use of San Pedro is clearly a fundamental aspect of present-day folk-healing, one might assume that its hallucinogenic properties have been known to *curanderos* for a long time. Only recently, however, have scholars been able to show that this cactus has been used for more than three thousand years. We now can identify artistic representations of the plant in many of the ancient Peruvian art styles.

The earliest depiction of San Pedro is found in a block of stone recently excavated from a circular sunken plaza in the court of the Old Temple at Chavin de Huantar in the northern highlands. This representation (see photo insert figure 4-6) is incised in low relief, showing a side view of the principal Chavin deity: an anthropomorphized mythological being with serpentine hair, fangs, a two-headed serpent belt, and harpy eagle claws. In its outstretched right hand the figure holds a four-ribbed San Pedro cactus. The Chavin style flourished in the Andean area ca. 1400–400 B.C., and this incised stone dates from ca. 1300 B.C.

Chavin textiles recently discovered on the south coast of Peru suggest that San Pedro was being used in that area in the first millenium B.C. The cactus depicted on these textiles is spineless and is shown is association with a feline and what may be a hummingbird. Throughout South America the feline is believed to be the alter ego of the shaman (see Furst, 1968c). Moreover, present-day *curanderos* believe that the hummingbird symbolizes the shaman's capacity to suck magic pathogens out of victims of sorcery.

Chavin artists also created ceramic depictions of the San Pedro cactus. One of the earliest of these is from the north coast of Peru. Thought to date from ca. 1000–700 B.C., it shows the magical plant in association with a deer (see photo insert figure 4–7). Today the deer plays a vital role in the lore of modern shamans, and is an important part of their therapy. It is represented on Eduardo's *mesa* by its right front foot. Symbolizing swiftness and elusiveness, the deer is used by the shaman to detect attacking spirits and to exorcise spirits in cases of possession.

The San Pedro cactus is juxtaposed with the jaguar on five other Chavin vessels thought to date from ca. 700–500 B.C. (for example, see photo insert figure 4–8). Each of these depicts four-ribbed San Pedro cacti in association with a spotted jaguar and volute designs (stylized spirals). The volutes may symbolize the subjective experiences produced by San Pedro (described in chapter 9).

Another Chavin ceramic vessel, also thought to date from ca. 700–500 B.C., shows what may be three stylized four-ribbed cacti joined to a gourdlike circular figure by a ceramic tube (which also serves as a handle). Perhaps the idea portrayed here is the extraction of the plant's hallucinogenic content through the tube into the gourd, for it is the juice of the plant that is used in healing today.

Apparently San Pedro usage persisted on the south coast of Peru after the decline of Chavin influence. Such persistence is shown by large ceramic urns from the Nasca culture (ca. 100 B.C.–A.D. 500). Some of these urns appear to be in the form of mummy bundles with a stalk of San Pedro cactus on each shoulder (for example, see photo insert figure 4–9). Five such urns are known to date, all of which are in the Museo Nacional in Lima.

In Inca times the word for royal mummy—*mallqui*—also meant "seed." If such a conceptual analogy formed part of the Nasca cult of the dead, then perhaps the message conveyed by their San Pedro funerary urns was that the dead person was being buried like a seed for germination in the afterlife. Possibly the San Pedro stalks symbolize the capacity of the carefully buried seed-person to be reborn out of darkness—exactly as the night-blooming San Pedro is every spring.

Still another ceramic representation of San Pedro can be found in the Salinar style of the north coast of Peru (ca. 400–200 B.C.). One type of Salinar vessel that is clearly a stylized representation of the San Pedro cactus has a decorated chamber, with a spout and modeled protrusion joined by a strap handle. The modeled protrusion is in the form of a stalk of San Pedro. Whereas the Chavin representations of San Pedro sometimes showed four-ribbed stalks, in Salinar *all* of the representations show this number. These four-ribbed cacti, as was mentioned earlier, may represent the concept of the "four winds" or "four quarters," and the crossroads ("four roads") that lead to them—a cosmology shared by present-day *curanderos*. An invocation to the four winds and four roads opens and closes a night curing séance. (See appendix B, pp. 170–74. This rite consecrates the sacred space occupied by the *mesa*, thus confirming its supernatural power. Although to date we have no solid ethnohistorical evidence for the ritual orientation to the four cardinal directions in Peru, we do know that this practice was central to Indian cosmology and ritual throughout the New World. That the four quarters were important in pre-Columbian Peru is suggested by the Incas' name for their empire: *Tahuantinsuyo* (The Four Quarters of the World). They also built four roads running from their capital, Cuzco, to each of the four divisions of the empire.

In the art of the Moche period (north coast, ca. 100 B.C.–A.D. 700) San Pedro is often found with a shawl-clad female figure in a curing scenario. Often she has the features of an owl, the alter ego of modern female curers (see photo insert figure 4-10). Eduardo believes that this figure is a female herbalist and *curandera,* a wise old woman associated with the traditional wisdom and herbal lore of the pre-Columbian peoples. The *curandera* appears frequently and is normally shown holding something in her outstretched hand. In most instances this object is only sketchily depicted and cannot be identified. When it is clearly represented, however, as on one example in the Museo Larco Herrera in Lima, it has the form of a slice of San Pedro.

The *curandera* holding a San Pedro cactus was a subject for north-coast artists throughout the next millennium. Some of their representations, like many in the Moche style, depict the San Pedro in a sketchy fashion. Others (such as the bottle shown in figure 4-11, see photo insert) show the *curandera* holding a tall stalk of four-ribbed San Pedro, about the same size as the stalks used by healers today. This vessel is in the Chimu style, which flourished on the north coast of Peru ca. A.D. 700–1475. The *curandera* is here performing a *mocha* (blowing a kiss), a pre-Columbian gesture of reverence for holy objects and places that is still practiced by highland Indians.

Although the various pre-Columbian artistic representations clearly show San Pedro in use, actual remains of the plant itself have seldom been found in archeological excavations. Excavations at Las Haldas by the Peruvian archeologist Rosa Fung (1969: 43, 120, 195) yielded what appear to have been cigars made from cactus. These were found in Chavin refuse dating from approximately 800 B.C. Recent excavations by William Isbell and Rogger Ravines at Garagay, near Lima, uncovered mud bricks made with San Pedro spines.* These were associated with a temple structure. Considering the superb preservative environment characteristic of many parts of Peru, it is highly likely that more cactus remains will be found through archeological excavation.

The ethnohistorical records clearly show that the ritual use of San Pedro cactus was widespread in the Andean area at the time of European contact;

---

*The reader will note that although the San Pedro cacti normally do not have spines, the rare ones that did were highly valued and were perhaps sacred.

this use persisted throughout the colonial period. There are two clear references to it from about the middle of the seventeenth century—when the Catholic Church was mounting an intensive campaign to "extirpate idolatry" in Peru. San Pedro is also called *huachuma* in modern Peru. In 1631 Father Oliva (1895: 115–24) described the ritual use of *huachuma* (then called *achuma*) by Indian leaders to divine the intentions of an outsider:

> The principal *caciques* and *curacas* [leaders] of this nation . . . in order to know the good or bad will of some to others drink a beverage they call *Achuma* which is a water they make from the sap of some thick and smooth cacti that they raise in the hot valleys. They drink it with great ceremonies and songs, and as it is very strong, after they drink it they remain without judgment and deprived of their senses, and they see visions that the Devil represents to them and consistent with them they judge their suspicions and the intentions of others.

In 1653 Father Cobo (1956: 91: 205) wrote a brief account of San Pedro usage in which the Christian bias against native customs is apparent:

> This is the plant with which the devil deceived the Indians of Peru in their paganism, using it for their lies and superstitions. Having drunk the juice of it, those who drink lose consciousness and remain as if dead; and it has even been seen that some have died because of the great frigidity to the brain. Transported by this drink, the Indians dreamed a thousand absurdities and believed them as if they were true. . . . One can use its juices against fevers and kidney burn.

The brew mentioned by Cobo more than likely also contained some other hallucinogenic plant, probably *misha* or *floripondio*—that is, floripondium (*Datura arborea*); active ingredient, scopolamine—which many healers mix with San Pedro today. San Pedro alone does not have such violent effects. Apparently the chroniclers overlooked the use of *Datura* as an additive to San Pedro, not realizing how powerful it is. But Cobo came close by noting that the white, bell-shaped flowers of this plant were placed on church altars inside the holders for votive candles. He relates that the perfume from a single flower placed in a room was so powerful that it caused anger and a headache for anyone who smelled it for too long (1956: 91: 218).

The bishop of Cajamarca (in the northern highlands) recently published the documentation of a legal case conducted against a native curer in 1782. The shaman was accused of curing with a brew made from *gigantón*—another alternative designation for San Pedro. Although the curer escaped from the authorities, amulets and talismans used to set up a *mesa* were found among his confiscated possessions. His power objects were similar to those used today. Witnesses for the prosecution described curing séances of which the details were remarkably similar to modern practices (Dammert, 1974).

Despite the Catholic persecution of traditional folk healing, the practice lives on today as a combination of pre-Columbian and European cultural traits. It is interesting that the tradition of the *curandera* survives as well. She is represented on Eduardo's *mesa* by a wooden staff, carved in the form of a woman with a shawl over her shoulders in the Spanish style (see photo insert figure 4-12). She is still thought to govern magical flora, especially the San Pedro cactus, as well as the sacred highland lagoons.

The documentation of San Pedro use over a span of more than three thousand years suggests an amazing continuity of magico-religious tradition in the Andean area. It represents the physical manifestation of an ideology, many aspects of which have also survived through the centuries. To learn more about this ideology we now turn to Eduardo's explanations of his use of San Pedro.

VISIONARY SAN PEDRO

Unfortunately, the ancient Peruvians left no written documents describing their religious beliefs and customs. For such information we must rely on archeology and the Spanish chronicles. But even this material, scanty though it is, shows the persistence of San Pedro usage. Given this continuity, Eduardo's comments on San Pedro seem particularly important, for, while informing us about a contemporary *curandero*'s perception of his therapy, they can also shed light on the past.

We start with the basics, Eduardo's description of San Pedro:

> San Pedro, *huando hermoso, cardo, huachuma* [are] various names applied to this cactus. . . . It is medicinal. It is diuretic. It is utilized in general for cases of healing and witchcraft. . . . It is used . . . for both [types of] magic—white and black. . . . It is always recommended that after taking San Pedro one must follow a diet: not to eat any food that contains hot peppers, salt, animal fat, or grease, or anything that "entangles"; for example, foods that grow on climbing vines, such as beans, peas, lentils, et cetera. . . .
>
> San Pedro has a special symbolism in *curanderismo* for a reason: San Pedro is always represented, "accounted" with the saints, with the power of animals, of strong personages or beings, or serious beings, of beings that have supernatural power. . . . The symbolism of San Pedro is to locate in all the regions of the territory the elemental thought and potentiality of man.

Another interesting power claimed for San Pedro is the protection of houses:

It cares for the house . . . as if it were a dog. It is "accounted," it is in tune [with the *curandero*'s own powers and with his other magical artifacts and herbs], and it is "raised" with *tabaco* in the proper manner. Then it cares for the house. It serves as guardian. In the night it appears to strangers who want to enter as a man in white, wearing a hat. Or else it whistles. It whistles with a peculiar sound so that anyone who enters who is not of the household . . . comes out at top speed, like a bullet.

During conversations with Eduardo and participation in his curing sessions, it was made clear to me that the hallucinogenic San Pedro cactus is experienced as the catalyst that enables the *curandero* to transcend the limitations placed on ordinary mortals: to activate all his senses; to project his spirit, or soul; to ascend and descend into the supernatural realms; to identify and do battle with the sources of illness, witchcraft, and misfortune; to confront and vanquish ferocious animals and demons of disease and sorcerers who direct them; to "jump over" barriers of time, space, and matter; to divine the past, present, and future—in short, to attain "vision," to "see." And "seeing," in this special sense, is very different from "looking at."*

The physical effects of San Pedro, according to Eduardo,

are first a slight dizziness that one hardly notices. And then a great "vision," a clearing of all the faculties of the individual. It produces a light numbness in the body and afterward a tranquility. And then comes a detachment, a type of visual force in the individual inclusive of all the senses: seeing, hearing, smelling, touching, et cetera.—all the senses, including the sixth sense, the telepathic sense of transmitting oneself across time and matter. . . . It develops the power of perception . . . in the sense that when one wants to see something far away . . . he can distinguish powers or problems or disturbances at great distance, so as to deal with them. . . . It [also] produces . . . a general cleansing, which includes the kidneys, the liver . . . the stomach, and the blood.

When asked how San Pedro affects patients, Eduardo replied:

San Pedro tends to manifest itself in the form of vomiting, perspiration . . . sometimes in dancing. At times during diagnosis a patient automatically starts to dance alone, or to throw himself writhing on the ground. And there "unfolds" the power [that is, the ailment, or evil power] placed into the person.

It seems that . . . not all of us are resistant. Some are very susceptible, very unstable, and San Pedro tends to reach the subconscious . . . and the conscious, in such cases. It penetrates the blood . . . rises to, let us say, the intellectual nervous system. Then it "visualizes" and opens up a sixth sense. . . . Then the individual, sometimes by himself, can visualize his past or . . . the present, or an immediate future.

*Cf. Castaneda (1971) for a complete discourse on "seeing."

What does the concept of the subconscious mean to Eduardo? Here is his answer:

The subconscious is a superior part [of man] . . . a kind of bag where the individual has stored all his memories, all his valuations. . . . One must try . . . to make the individual "jump out" of his conscious mind. That is the principal task of *curanderismo*. By means of the magical plants and the chants and the search for the roots of the problem, the subconscious of the individual is opened up like a flower, and it releases these blockages. All by itself it tells things. A very practical manner . . . which was known to the ancients.

Again and again Eduardo returned to the *curandero*'s attainment of vision as the major focus of the curing session. Vision not only involves seeing problems "at a great distance" but also refers to experiences on ecstatic journeys in trances induced by San Pedro:

I called certain saints, mountains, ancient shrines; and I disappeared. There was an unfolding of my personality. . . . I was no longer at the *mesa*. . . . That is to say, my personality had departed to other places. The human mind has great power, a supernatural power. And one must exercise it, of course, in order to conduct a session. During my sessions at times I have been looking for a certain force — for example, an ancient shrine or a mountain — and suddenly, [while] I was whistling and singing, the account was activated and I felt myself enter the mountain, which opened all its passages, all its labyrinths. And suddenly I returned again. I had "seen" and I had "visualized" with my spirit.

Some of the major destinations of the soul during ecstatic magical flight in northern Peru are the sacred highland lagoons (especially Las Huaringas), to which the spirit of the *curandero* literally ascends from the low coastal desert. Here is what Eduardo says about such soul journeys:

The flight is spiritual. . . . One invokes, and his spirit soars to those haunts. One asks for the lagoon, invokes, and then the spirit makes the trip. The journey of the spirit also causes one to visualize the lagoon in . . . an almost objective manner. . . . Spiritually one is there and one sees it up close.
(Question: Does your being actually arrive there?)
My material being, no. My spiritual being arrives, yes; and I perceive in an objective fashion, as if I were in the place.

When an illness has been produced by the concoction of a sorcerer, Eduardo's flight-induced vision helps him to see that the spirit of the concoction

comes to look for what it is lacking. A light in the form of a firefly blinks on and off and comes looking for its "bone," which the sorcerer has introduced into the patient's stomach, killing him, consuming him. And until the patient throws up that element, the firefly is there circling.

In certain serious cases, the illness-causing forces are believed to be powerful enough to attack the patient during the actual curing session, in an effort to thwart the *curandero*'s therapeutic measures. This situation is extremely critical and requires vigorous emergency action. The *curandero* conducts a ferocious battle with the attacking forces (which only he can see, in his San Pedro trance vision). Then he performs seven somersaults (*siete mortales*) while grasping the sword horizontally in both hands with the sharp edge held away from his body; the direction of his movements over the ground forms a cross. This is intended to drive off the attacking spirits and shock the sorcerer who is directing them.

If the hostile forces are sufficiently strong, they may even attack the *curandero* himself. In that case he must rely on the aid and protection of higher beings:

> In certain trances, on paths closed to most men, rare beasts have confronted me with harmful intentions. And the presence of the Lord and his powerful light have helped me out of these places unharmed. And I always get out unharmed because there are beings in the other "mansion" [realm] such as great *curanderos*. . . . [By] calling these spirits via the prayers that I know, they come and assist in any trance.

Such trance experiences as just described—visits to sacred lakes or water holes, entering the earth or hills, spirit projection, physical combat against disease demons and ferocious animals doing the bidding of sorcerers, the magical introduction of foreign objects into the body to cause illness, and assistance from dead shamans and benevolent supernatural beings—are all typically shamanistic (see Furst, 1973-74). Somersaulting also is a not-uncommon shamanistic phenomenon, utilized especially for purposes of transformation. In neighboring Bolivia, for example, shamans of the Tacana perform somersaults in one direction to turn themselves into jaguars (their alter egos) and in the opposite direction to reassume human form (see Hissink and Hahn, 1961).

The hallucinogenic San Pedro infusion, then, is the magical substance that activates the curer's inner powers, as well as those inherent in the objects of his *mesa*. For the patient it opens his subconscious "like a flower" and renders the forces that made him sick visible and susceptible to the curer's therapeutic powers. By means of San Pedro the curer awakens all his senses, including a vital sixth sense, and by their interaction attains vision—the true object of the curing session and the healer's supreme achievement. For aid, guidance, and protection during these arduous and dangerous sessions, the *curandero* places his faith in higher spiritual beings, including those of the Christian faith as well as the aboriginal Indian pantheon.

Perhaps the single most important aspect of *curandero* therapy is the symbolic element in San Pedro usage. San Pedro produces beautiful aromatic white flowers that bloom at night, approximately at midnight. The object of a nighttime curing séance is to make the *mesa*, its artifacts — and by extension the *curandero*, his assistants, his patients, and his friends — bloom (*florecer*). The climactic moment when this occurs is at midnight. From then until the end of the session the power accumulated by such symbolic action is applied in magical therapy. Thus, in essence, what a *curandero* does during a séance is to replicate symbolically the growth cycle of the San Pedro, which provides the prototype for traditional *curanderismo*. (We shall have more to say about this aspect in chapter 8.) As a result, the symbolic context of San Pedro usage — perpetuated by a cultural tradition over three thousand years old and manipulated by charismatic *curanderos* — is every bit as vital to successful therapy as is the hallucinogenic factor. For, as the Peruvian scholar Tamayo Herrera (1970: 253) has noted, Andean man sees himself as "one plant more in the countryside, fixed in the earth and dependent upon her." In this respect, Castaneda (1972: 7-8) acknowledges as "erroneous" his earlier assumption that the hallucinogenic aspects of his shaman-mentor's teachings represented "the only avenue to communicating the learning that don Juan was attempting to teach me." Finally, to place the plant metaphor right on our doorstep, it is extremely interesting to note that "night-blooming cereus" occurred in the visions of an American patient after successful culmination of Jungian psychotherapy (see Jung, 1972: 64, n. 172).

Rising Sap: Power and Essence in the Shamanic Universe

POWER CONCEPTS: "MAGNETISM" AND "ACCOUNT"

Probably the central concept of shamanism, wherever in the world it is found, is the idea of power. Simply stated, this is the notion that underlying all the visible forms in the world, animate and inanimate, there exists a vital essence from which they emerge and by which they are nurtured. Ultimately everything returns to this ineffable, mysterious, impersonal unknown. The varied religious expressions of humanity are attempts to develop a meaningful and/or practical relationship with this power. The ancient Chinese called it life force or vital energy; the ancient Hindus referred to it as *prana;* among the Polynesians it is known as *mana*. Its manifestation in the universe is described by modern physical science through such concepts as the mass/energy equation and the space/time continuum. Modern psychoanalysis refers to its manifestation in the human psyche as libido. But only the shaman and the mystic actually identify with power through direct personal experience. Apparently all humanity has the potential for such identification, but few realize this potential, perhaps because most are unaware of it or do not know how to develop it.

Perhaps the best definition of shamanic power is that given to Carlos Casteneda (1968: 213) by his Yaqui shaman-mentor don Juan. Describing the "ally," the main tenet of his teachings, don Juan defines it as "a power capable of transporting a man beyond the boundaries of himself." This accords very well with the definition of shamanism supplied by Mircea Eliade (1964: 4). On the basis of a cross-cultural analysis of the literature on shamanism, Eliade defines shamanism as a "technique of ecstasy." Webster's dictionary defines ecstasy as a "state of being beside oneself," which parallels don Juan's definition. Although ecstasy and power are closely related, we will postpone further discussion of the former until chapter 9.

The elusive concept of power remains the pivot of shamanism. Although there is no substitute for personal experience in dealing with this topic, there seem to be certain observable characteristics by which it can be described.

The ideas for the following description are derived from what is known about the power concept in California Indian shamanism.* They correspond to what I have observed in Eduardo's shamanism and to Castaneda's (1974) descriptions of the concept. According to this formulation (which I have slightly expanded), aspects of power include:

1. *Knowledge,* especially ritual knowledge, and a correct perception of reality, omens, and symbols. Knowledge is wisdom about the true nature of things, the capacity to "see"—discussed at great length by Castaneda (1971).

2. *Fate.* Power can be sought, but seeking it does not guarantee that one will attain it. Ways of seeking include drugs, fasting, mortification of the flesh, dreams, prayers or supplication, and meditation or concentration. But fate, or one's inner nature, determines whether or not one actually receives power. More often one receives a "call" or suffers "sickness-vocation" (as in Eduardo's case). True power seeks out the shaman.

3. *Individuality,* which comes only to individuals, and only to those who are worthy or ready. It does not manifest itself to groups, and it cannot be given by one shaman to another (although shamans can partially transmit it through exchange of power objects). To try to do so is dangerous to both the giver and the receiver. Those who have attained it know; it shows in their charismatic personalities.

4. *Variability.* Everyone has some power, but its amount and intensity vary from person to person. It can increase or decrease through life. Shamans have more than the average individual, and there are different degrees among shamans. No one is born with shamanic power. It must be acquired through strenuous effort, though fate will determine its reception. The oldest shamans are considered to have the most power, since they have had the most opportunity to receive it.

5. *Success.* Without power a person is helpless. With it, one is successful, especially in curing or in practicing magic against enemies. The shaman can guarantee good fortune (including wealth, if this is a value held by his society).

6. *Focus.* Although power permeates everything, it is focused in certain individuals (shamans), power objects (especially crystals, rattles, and wands or staffs), plants (especially hallucinogens), and natural locations (especially mountains and water holes).

7. *Ambivalence.* Power can be used for good or evil—however these may be defined by the shaman's society—depending upon the innate disposition of the user. Most shamans are excellent performers, quite capable of playing the role of the trickster when the occasion demands. Thus

*This material is drawn from a lecture by Professor Clement W. Meighan at UCLA on 26 January 1973, in a course entitled *Native Peoples of California, Ethnography.*

there can be "black" shamans (sorcerers), "white" shamans, and "in-between" shamans. Observation by peers over a period of time usually reveals a shaman's proclivity for largely positive or negative behavior in accord with his inner nature.

At the time of the conquest of Peru, the Spanish chroniclers recorded the shamanic underpinnings of Peruvian religion by the concept of *huaca*, a belief that is still very much alive today, especially in the more isolated communities of the Andes. Brundage (1963: 47) provides one of the best summaries of this concept, culled from the Spanish sources:

> A *huaca* was both a localization of power and the power itself resident in an object, a mountain, a grave, an ancestral mummy, a ceremonial city, a shrine, a sacred tree, cave, spring, or lake of origination, a river or standing stone, the statue of a deity, a revered square or a bit of ground where festivals were held or where a great man lived. The power which enabled skilled artisans to produce curious pieces of goldwork or fine tapestry or rich dyes or the like was also *huaca*. Coca, the narcotic leaf from the *montaña*, was *huaca*.

Although Eduardo—like most people in northern Peru—uses the term *huaca* to refer only to archeological ruins, the importance of power to his healing practices is made particularly clear by two terms he uses frequently: *magnetismo* ("magnetism") and *cuenta* (literally, "account"; more precisely, "history" or "power relationship"). Most often *magnetismo* is used in reference to persons, although it is conceived of as a force in nature that is channeled through both living beings and inanimate objects. *Cuenta* is used specifically in relation to power objects from a *mesa* and denotes their special magical relationship to the shaman's powers.

Eduardo explains magnetism as "essential and important."

Magnetic force is one of the innate essences in the individual, in man. For the person who does not put it to work in his body, the essence manifests [itself] almost automatically without one being aware. But he who applies this essence with principles, with wisdom, with knowledge, is a person whose acts lead to an essential, profound triumph. The majority of the *curanderos*—since they know these natural principles of the magnetic force of man and of the elements—apply them in an empirical fashion without [scientific] knowledge. But they know that this is good, that doing this act is good. If they knew how to apply these principles in a scientific or semiscientific manner, it would be much better.

Magnetism operates in everything concerning the natural elements: man, the place where he walks, the very earth. The earth is crisscrossed by networks of water which are good conductors of the terrestrial magnetic current which governs the individual. The individual has two legs and two hands. The . . . magnetic current rises up the left leg and down the right. . . . It is the same with the hands. . . . Therefore there are cases in *curandero* work which require the laying on of the hands. The magnetic force of the individual is very strong. Thus the laying on of a hand—depending upon which hand is placed—on a place where there is pain causes the release or relief of that pain by the force of magnetic intuition. . . . The mind corresponds to the [magnetic or] electromagnetic field and acts as the general battery. The encephalic cavity is at the same time the accumulator and the generator of currents which govern these things. . . . The hands, the ends of the fingers are the antennae from which the magnetic current emanates or sparks.

Eduardo frequently mentions a sixth sense that plays a key role in *curandero* therapy. Here is how it relates to magnetism:

Magnetism is the activating electrical force of the individual to unite with others. All have a magnetic point, a magnetic force linked with the earth, since all are elements of the earth. Thus by forming a magnetic chain, the attraction of the individuals, the telepathic force, the intellectual effort, unites all beings along this nexus in a magnetic fashion. That is, magnetism is the thread and the telepathic force is the transmission of the elemental force along the thread.

The power objects of the *mesa* are not just a random collection of things assembled when the *curandero* begins his work. Rather, they are gradually accumulated over the years of his practice. The healer begins with the bare essentials—utensils and a few key artifacts. Through the years he enlarges the collection. Each item is carefully selected or acquired under special circumstances—for example, as a gift from a fellow *curandero* or a grateful patient, or as a discovery in a dry riverbed, on a mountain, or at an archeological site. Each has unique significance to the healer, along with its own *cuenta,* which is activated by the catalytic action of the hallucinogenic San Pedro infusion. Many artifacts are made by the *curandero* from materials carefully selected in accord with inspiration received in dreams. Within the standard symbolic framework passed on from *curandero* to initiate, there is room for personal elaboration once mastery has been gained over the curing art. The same is true of the *curandero's tarjos,* or ritual chants. He learns the traditional rhythms, but as with the various power objects—positive *and* negative—he elaborates on the basic complex with his own particular talents and according to the inspiration he receives from a variety of extrapersonal and supernatural sources.

To understand how the artifacts function it is important to remember that to the *curandero* they are not lifeless objects. Cosmologically, each represents a particular force in nature. Psychologically, each is a projection of the healer's own inner spiritual power, which becomes activated whenever the *mesa* and its accounts are manipulated in conjunction with the drinking of the San Pedro infusion.*

*There is the implication here of oneness with the cosmos, which is dramatized in the séance, as we shall see in chapters 6 and 8.

According to Eduardo, the account of an artifact is

its relationship with the world, the magical world [and] the actual
. . . world in which one lives. Let us take, for example, the account of St.
Cyprian [a statue that is one of the objects on Eduardo's *mesa* and is considered to be the "governor" of an important symbolic zone related to his
curing powers]. St. Cyprian makes one remember, by means of the account, how he acted within the field of magical "charms." He is dead, but
his spirit persists, it lives. Thus, by means of the account one makes a kind
of "call" to the spiritual field. When one activates the account of Saint
Cyprian, his spirit begins inside oneself.

(Question: In other words, each artifact has an account that one must
invoke when the *mesa* is working?)

Yes. For example, the account of an artifact, of an object that we have
on the *mesa*, is related to the site from which it was brought. In reality, the
account is everything concerning history, geographic points, and, more
than anything, the power that it contains. If one "accounts" an artifact for
a certain magical end, one's spirit has to impregnate itself little by little
into the artifact, into the material of the artifact, within the instrument.
For example, we have a staff, a *chonta* [made from the tropical hardwood
of that name], which is a special wood that becomes impregnated—by
means of one's spirit, one's potency—with the spiritual form of the
curandero, the magician, so that this artifact has all of the inherent
characteristics of the spirit of him who prepares it. Then, once and for all,
the account becomes all the essential memory of him who formed that
prayer, that history, that reference. And by means of this, through all the
time that it is manipulated, it contains a major quantity of potency—that
is, magic—within the field of its application; for example, for a sickness,
for something that one is looking for, regarding a robbery, regarding a
love charm, and so on. The artifact casts its account for whatever it has
been destined. If there is no account, there is nothing. The artifacts move,
they have their dynamic, as does the *maestro* who makes them move with
his magnetic force. All this influences.

(Question: Does an artifact have to have a kind of account, or personal
history, for the *curandero*?)

Yes. Each *curandero* has his own account. There are also acquired accounts—that is, discovered accounts or accounts given as gifts. For example, an artifact given to me by Mr. X; this artifact has been accounted by
another. Then it is added to the other artifacts, but it is accounted in a
personal manner with the old account and the new account of its new
owner. One has to dominate it. One has to try to "call" the artifact with
one's own account. In other words, one must give it the profound force of
the person who is going to possess it.

(Question: Does the *curandero* begin with a few artifacts and increase
his supply of artifacts during his life?)

Yes. In my opinion this is most essential. But there are *curanderos* who have acquired the art from their fathers, from their family, who have received it as a legacy. And since they are accustomed to the account of the clan, of the group of *curanderos,* then it is more likely that they already know and belong to the family. . . . If one finds an artifact with an unknown account one has to submit it to a "tracking" or a "tracing" [activation of the artifact on the *mesa* with the other artifacts]. And, by means of this tracking, one discovers what it's for, where it's from, and why; all is revealed in the tracking.

Eduardo's description of what happened when he found an ancient sorcerer's kit (a pre-Columbian ceramic containing stones in the shapes of animals, human beings, body parts, and so forth) at an archeological site and took it home in the hope of "dominating its accounts" for use in his own work demonstrates the importance to the curer of tracking new power objects to make sure their accounts harmonize with his own power:

I took it in order to track [it] to see what type it was. As a result these artifacts rebelled. Rare animals and monstrous beasts issued forth with hunger and the desire to seize people. Then, when I placed the kit on my *mesa,* everything was distorted and turned black. The artifacts began bleeding. Several personages with huge fangs gushing blood came forth and demanded my wife and children. Then I tried to throw them out. I purified the kit with holy water and burned it because the day that I brought it home there had also begun a noise on my roof like the galloping of wild beasts. And they didn't leave me alone until I made cabalistic thrusts with my swords to countercheck these influences. . . .

For me [the kit] was of no use. It was a black artifact, an artifact of witchcraft. That is, this was used in witchcraft . . . in remote ancestral times by the Mochica or Chimu peoples . . . to destroy farms, crops, [human] organs, etc. And all the evil has been preserved for centuries for one reason, which is that this [the kit] is designed, or accounted, under the influence of a person of this character. . . . When accounted, the object absorbs the potentiality, let us say, the intellectual potentiality of the man who manipulates it and it remains impregnated forever.*

One of Eduardo's most important power objects, activated by the hallucinogenic San Pedro infusion and utilized in certain especially virulent cases of witchcraft or sorcery, is "the cat." His description of how he obtained it and how it is used is of particular interest, not only because of the role of "cats" in European witchcraft lore, but also because of the intimate relationship of felines to traditional South American shamanism and the considerable feline symbolism to be found in the ancient ritual art of Peru.†

*This incident was first described in Sharon (1972a: 127).
†For the role of the feline in South American shamanism see Furst (1968c) and Reichel-Dolmatoff (1975). For feline symbolism in pre-Columbian Peruvian art see Tello (1923).

Eduardo's description also demonstrates how some of the hunting ideology of archaic shamanism persists today:

> I have some talismans that I prepared by means of my own ideas and illuminations that I have had in my dreams. The cat plays a principal role in witchcraft and its glance has great power. When a cat dies . . . the eyes remain open. Then there is reflected all concerning the tragedy that has happened in the hour of its death. And it carries in its pupils the moment of [its] abduction toward the tomb. . . .
>
> Therefore, I purposely prepared this talisman. I grabbed a cat and killed it and drank the blood three times and then I took out the eyes. After I took out the eyes I cut off its right paw, the right claw. I gathered all this together and placed it in a receptacle with *agua cananga* [red perfume] during one complete cycle of the moon. . . . After that I added *agua florida* [scented water]. And after the *agua florida* I added cane alcohol at the end in order to give this feline bravery and power to intoxicate with his glance. I sewed the eyes together with green and red silk thread and tied them to a flint arrowhead that I found in an ancient archeological tomb.
>
> I carry this talisman with me, and I use it at night, when I want to countercheck the power of a cat, of a feline, of some exterior spirit attack of a sorcerer who wants to attack or perturb me. All I do is launch my savage cat by means of a few sparks made with the flint arrowhead. And it has its power. The cat goes out to the hills screaming and screeching. . . .
>
> I use it on a block of crystal. This block of crystal is like a mirror, and the cat sees what moves in this mirror. For whatever [disturbance] it is there, looking. The eyes light up as if they were light bulbs. This is one of the talismans purposely prepared by us in accordance with the idea that one has, or the inspiration of a dream, or the intuition.*

Eduardo's examples provide a vivid picture of the significance of individual power objects located on his *mesa*. In addition, he says, the objects on the *mesa*, taken as a whole, constitute a microcosmos

> in which is represented all of the powers and mysteries of nature situated in that small space with its staffs, with all those things. The staffs are like antennae that pull and emit and transmit radiations. And the stones are like representations of the places of the universe — that is, the world, the earth. . . .
>
> (Question: In other words, we have land and also space or sky?)
>
> Of course, land (or matter), earth, space, and in general the aggregate — all with the spirit of the individual, of the *curandero*, with the physical potentialities, etc., inherent there. They harmonize with or . . . compose the cosmos. It is a small cosmos, a microcosmos.

*This description was first published in Sharon (1972a: 126–27).

(Question: I suppose that the *curandero* emits an influence over this microcosmos in order to be able to influence the macrocosmos.)

Yes, of course. He is like a small receiver and transmitter which catches and emits. Therefore I say that when an individual is in a dream state or asleep, the subconscious opens for him, it opens itself. . . . Then it begins to emit its waves. . . . Then the making or procreation of the principle of "transistoriality" occurs. I don't know if there is any work in psychology or parapsychology that has treated transistoriality. In other words, the individual upon going to sleep, upon entering a dream state, emits waves. And he also receives. This is the moment in which the shamans realize their opening also, and their spiritual transmission through the cosmos to other beings—for example, like me—who are attuned to this work.

(Question: In other words, working with the "remedy" and the accounts and the artifacts of the *mesa* is like having a conscious power over the subconscious and all the forces of the universe?)

Yes, exactly. With the remedy, the spirit—or, more correctly, the physical faculties—are turned outward or are made more attuned, more susceptible, more apt to receive, together with the spirit which reinforces this orientation, this stimulus, principally when the power of man is exercised. Thus he gives himself greater priority, greater stability, force, and power in all of the aspects of the esoteric, in the whole field of the esoteric.

Such is the essence of Eduardo's modern version of the ancient shamanic concept of power: its description as magnetism, a medium of telepathy and curing force; its concentration in the account of individual power objects, which in aggregate constitute a microcosmic *mesa*. Psychologically, power objects are also a projection of Eduardo's personal power; the *mesa* is an extension of the shaman as receiver/transmitter. Before turning to this matter in chapter 6, let us look at an example of transmission of power.

OLD MAN MAXIMÓN

We have noted that occasionally *curanderos* exchange power objects. The following incident is a good example of the transmission of power between shamans in the form of seemingly innocuous artifacts.

In fall 1971, when I began my second period of apprenticeship with Eduardo, I came to Peru from Guatemala, where I had been doing field work in the town of Santiago Atitlán. In Atitlán, a famous if somewhat ambiguous character is Maximón, a life-sized wooden mannequin carved from the sacred *pito* tree *(Erythrina);* he wears a mask carved from the same wood as his body and is dressed in Indian garb. His devotees keep him supplied with draughts of *aguardiente* (fermented sugar-cane alcohol) and cigars, for which he has a great affinity. The people of Atitlán believe him to be an avid traveler, and many claim to have seen him taking an evening constitutional along the tortuous, narrow streets of Atitlán. He has many names, such as Pedro Alvarado, Judas, Simón, and Mam.

According to local folklore, Maximón was introduced into the Mayan/ folk-Catholic ritual and agricultural cycle of the town about ninety years ago by an *ajkún* (the Guatemalan Indian version of the Peruvian *curandero*) named Francisco Sojuel Pablo, who was considered to be a prophet. Maximón became the patron of the *ajkúns*, since he was believed to be able to heal sickness, including that caused by witchcraft; to bring success in farming and commercial activities; and to help in matters of the heart. Consultations with the folk-saint Maximón require the intercession of an *ajkún*, who burns candles and incense in front of him while performing special prayers for the petitioner. Maximón is housed by *cofradía* Santa Cruz, one of the hierarchical religious brotherhoods of Atitlán responsible for the care of Catholic saints and their public festivals. Here his cult has managed to survive despite a vigorous effort in the early 1950s to purge such "paganism" from the Catholicism of Atitlán.

Prior to my visit to Atitlán, Maximón, living up to his reputation for multiple personalities, had suddenly appeared in the form of a new mannequin at another *cofradía*, the one dedicated to Saint John. This was a singular event because it is believed that the sacred *pito* tree from which Maximón is made can be carved only by a powerful *ajkún*. Anyone else who tries it is supposed to go insane. I eventually located the man who had created the new Maximón and told him about my apprenticeship with Eduardo and my interest in *curanderos*. Before the summer was over we had become good friends. His assistance was invaluable to me in my work. When I left for Peru, he gave me some very special gifts: a cigar that had been in the mouth of Maximón, a candle blessed before the same image, two newly carved Maximón masks, and eight red "beans" from the *pito* tree used for divining by Guatemalan *ajkúns*. One mask was for me, the other for Eduardo, and we were to divide the beans between us. The cigar and candle were to be used to consecrate Eduardo's mask. I was assured that the masks would help both of us in our undertakings.

Back in Peru, I went out to Eduardo's house, where I recounted my adventures in Atitlán and delivered the mask and beans, along with a taped message from their donor. I thought that the gift, once accounted, or prepared in a night session, would make a good power object for Eduardo's *mesa*. I had no idea how good!

For the next few days I was busy in Trujillo. A session was planned at the home of one of Eduardo's relatives a few evenings later, so I decided to meet Eduardo there. On the night of the session I arrived early so that I would have a chance to find out how the Maximón mask had been received.

The first night Eduardo had the mask in his house he had apparently had difficulty sleeping, and his wife, María, had been suffering from stomach cramps. While she was asleep a person who identified himself as Maximón asked her about her problem. When she told him what was wrong he placed his hands on her stomach and said that she would be all right the next day. She woke up feeling fine. The following night Eduardo left his *mesa* artifacts—including the mask—with his relatives in preparation for the forthcoming session. Several people had difficulty sleeping and blamed it on the mask, which they said was restless.

When Eduardo set up his *mesa* the mask was placed in the Middle Field, the focus of his supernatural "vision" and the embodiment of his personal philosophy of "balance" (to be explained in chapter 6), since he felt that Maximón had to be a peer of Saint Cyprian, governor of this segment of the *mesa*. During the first, ceremonial part of the session, Eduardo paused at an appropriate stage in the ritual and asked me to help him account the mask in accord with the donor's elaborate instructions. The mask—and Maximón—were now ready to help Eduardo in his work. And apparently they did. Part of the way through the curing division of the session, between patients, Eduardo turned to me with an expression of unmitigated joy on his face. He informed me that the mask was working better than any other artifact he had ever had. He said that its lips actually moved and told him things about the cases before him.

Eduardo wanted to know more about Maximón, so the next week I gave him a Spanish copy of an excellent study conducted in Atitlán in 1952-53 by the anthropologist E. Michael Mendelson (1965). Eduardo was fascinated by Maximón's story. He understood the *cofradía* system, for in his youth a similar system had existed in the nearby community of Moche. He decided to set up his own personal *cofradía* in the house. The Maximón mask was carefully balanced on a manual sewing machine. A candle holder was placed in front of the mask, and a flower arrangement set on either side. Eduardo said that he was going to hold all future consultations with patients in front of the mask, requesting that they burn candles there and invite Maximón to have a cigar, as is done in Atitlán when an *ajkún* intercedes for a patient before Maximón.

From that day forward, everyone who came to Eduardo with a problem was escorted to the new altar. Eduardo began to use divining cards less often than before, for he said that the mask talked to him and presented matters clearly and directly. As the word got around to some of Eduardo's regular clients, people began showing up with flowers to replace those that had wilted, and a supply of cigars began to build up on the altar.

During the first week of the *cofradía* Eduardo's sister-in-law came for a visit. She was recuperating from surgery to remove a tumor and was still in a great deal of pain. Later in the week she returned with flowers for the altar, which she had brought in gratitude for Maximón's help. The evening after her previous visit she had been scheduled to see her doctor, but half an hour before the appointment the pain subsided. However, that night she had difficulty sleeping. When she finally fell asleep, she dreamed that Maximón came to her with some advice. For several days she had been thinking about changing doctors. Maximón told her not to do so and said that her present doctor would cure her. Maximón also identified himself as Simon Cireneyo, the person who helped Christ to carry His cross on the way to Calvary. When he left, the pain ceased and the woman felt much better.

The way Eduardo and his patients adapted the Maximón mask to their own situations seems to illustrate how Christian religious forms and symbols have been reshaped to meet the needs of the Indian and *mestizo* peoples of Peru. It certainly illustrates the concept of power held by contemporary Latin American shamans, as well as Eduardo's eclectic capacity to restructure his symbolic framework to accommodate new forms. This adaptability seems to explain the persistence of folk healing from the time of the Spanish Conquest to the present. In any case, Maximón's restless spirit has found a new home. He has now been accounted, like the other power objects on Eduardo's microcosmic *mesa*.

SACRED STONES

Many of the power objects on Eduardo's *mesa* are stones. Belief in the magical properties of stone has a long history in Peru; in fact, the cult of stones was the most prevalent religious practice of the ancient Peruvians. The peoples of pre-Columbian Peru venerated stones as a manifestation of their first ancestors and of the Earth Mother, *Pachamama*. At the lowest level were the *conopas*, usually quartz crystals or unusual pebbles, in which the family ancestors were said to reside. *Conopas* shaped like corn, potatoes, and llamas were handed down from father to son and used to promote the fertility of crops and livestock. On a higher level were the large stones *(huancas)* placed in the center of a community or on a nearby peak and recognized as the mentor of the tribe to which the community belonged. Often these tribal guardians were grouped in divine families that differed according to locality; a local pantheon, for example, could consist of a male ancestral stone, his consort, and his offspring. An *apacheta,* or pile of stones, always marked the top of a mountain pass or other critical points on a road where travelers stopped to pray for strength and to make offerings.

The campaign to "extirpate idolatry" in the early seventeenth century eliminated most of the stones that served as public, tribal *huancas*. However, *apachetas* and *conopas* have survived to the present in many parts of the Andes. The latter, known today in the Cuzco region as *incaychus,* are small stones shaped like alpacas, llamas, or sheep and used by Andean herders to assure the fertility of their flocks. Recent research by Flores (1976) and Gow (1976) has greatly increased our knowledge of the esoteric lore associated with *incaychus.* Gow informs us that on August 1, the day on which the "earth lives," Quechua peasants go into the foothills in search of these stones, which are considered to be a memento from the indigenous gods, or *apus*. One's star or destiny determines the kind of stone one will find; those born to raise alpacas will find alpaca stones, llama herders will find stone llamas, and those destined to raise sheep will find stones shaped like these animals. Occasionally such stones may be found in the entrails of animals slaughtered on August 1, in which case they are considered to be a gift from *Pachamama*. Once blessed in the mass and sprinkled with holy water, these *incaychus* are used to cure animal sicknesses and the supernatural ailments caused by evil winds. They also ward off evil spirits, are taken along on journeys, and play an important role in animal fertility rituals.

The importance of the *incaychus* in contemporary highland communities becomes apparent during Carnival. The day before this *fiesta*, *mesa* rituals are performed for the livestock, the earth, the ancestors, and the *apus*. The *incaychus* are removed from sacred bundles in which they have been stored with coca leaves. After being sprinkled with carnations and *chicha* they are placed on the *mesa*, which is often a large flat stone. As one informant expressed it:

> Because the *incaychus* represent the animals they are respected. When the *incaychu* is on the table the *apu* himself repeats the same words they say. That's why the animals are all right. They don't sicken or die if their owner has *incaychus*. But those who don't have *incaychus* need medicines and the services of a veterinarian. (Gow, 1976: 197)

Gow (1976: 198) adds:

> The importance of this *incaychu* ceremony to individual peasant families is shown by the fact that it is the most secret of their rituals and almost impossible for outsiders to witness. The *incaychu* is said to contain the *animo* or life-force of the livestock.

Gow translates and quotes Flores (1976: 121), who defines the concept of *enqa* (or *inca*) of which the *incaychus* are the graphic manifestation:

> *Enqa* is the vital generating principle. It is the fount and origin of happiness, well-being, and abundance. . . . It has an immediate primary role in the procreation of the livestock, but its role is not limited to this aspect, since it is the permanent element capable of providing well-being and happiness by means of abundance. Besides, *enqa* is a special gift which permits good fortune to accompany the family, preserving the herds which support it.

In view of the persisting importance of stone in Peruvian magico-religious beliefs and practices, a discussion of its symbolism by the Jungian psychologist von Franz (1964: 221–27) offers some provocative insights. He suggests that the "just-so-ness" of stones makes them apt symbols of the self, noting that many people cannot seem to resist collecting unusually shaped or colored stones even though they cannot explain why. Since time immemorial people have collected stones, apparently assuming that certain types contained the mysterious life-force. For example, the ancient Germans maintained that the spirits of the deceased resided in their tombstones. Perhaps the custom of marking graves with stones relates to the belief that something eternal—the soul or psyche or self—remains after death. Although man is very different from stone, his inner being seems connected with it in a mysterious fashion.

Von Franz thinks that the practice in nearly all civilizations of erecting stone monuments to commemorate great men and events likewise stems from the significance of stones as symbols of the self. Other notable uses of this symbolism that he discusses include the stone that Jacob placed on the spot where he experienced his famous dream of the ladder to heaven; the placing of stones on the tombs of heroes and saints by simple folk; the references in the New Testament to Peter as a rock upon which the Church was to be built; the *Ka'aba*, or Black Stone of Mecca, to which all pious Muslims make their pilgrimages; the Blarney Stone of Ireland; and the Philosopher's Stone *(lapis)* sought by the medieval alchemists in their quest for the secret of matter. Some of them perceived this stone as the symbol of a quality that could only be found in the human psyche. Finally, von Franz mentions the unknown relationship between the human psyche and matter. He feels that "it is precisely toward such a relation that the symbol of the stone seems to point." (1964: 227)

Regarding the mysterious nature of stone, which induces man to make it sacrosanct, Mircea Eliade (1958: 216) contends that stone shows man

> something that transcends the precariousness of his humanity; an absolute mode of being. Its strength, its motionlessness, its size and its strange outlines are none of them human; they indicate the presence of something that fascinates, terrifies, attracts and threatens, all at once. In its grandeur, its hardness, its shape and its color, man is faced with a reality and a force that belong to some world other than the profane world of which he himself is a part.

We have seen that the natives of pre-Columbian Peru believed that stone, in some mysterious fashion, was an adequate symbol for the sacred power animating the universe. This was a belief shared by many ancient peoples of the world. By maintaining the tradition of sacred stones many contemporary Peruvians and their shamans preserve a link with a time when early man, aided by stone, began the ascent to civilization.

6

Sacred Space: Duality and
the Four Winds

The work of numerous scholars* has independently verified the fact that the major symbolic prop used in all northern Peruvian night healing séances to cure witchcraft is a *mesa,* similar to that used by Eduardo, which consists of power objects acquired under special circumstances during the *curandero's* years of practice. Many of Eduardo's artifacts are from specific "power spots" in northern Peru. Each object has a personal significance to him and embodies a special "account," or story representing a projection of his own inner psychic "power" or "magnetism." Each account becomes activated, together with the accounts of the other power objects on the *mesa,* whenever the objects are manipulated at night under the catalytic influence of the hallucinogenic San Pedro cactus, imbibed in liquid form (both mixed with black tobacco juice and alone) by the *curandero,* his two assistants, his patients, and accompanying friends or relatives. Taken as a whole, the *mesa* symbolizes the duality of the worlds of man and nature—a veritable microcosmos duplicating the forces at work in the universe.

Figure 6-1 (see photo insert) shows Eduardo's *mesa.* Appendix A gives Eduardo's detailed description of its power objects.

The spatial arrangement of Eduardo's *mesa* is the manifestation of a profound underlying philosophy. It has to be understood as representing two levels of abstraction existing at the same time and in the same space. One level can be labeled "balanced dualism" and is manifest in three unequal divisions of the *mesa.* The other level can be labeled "the four winds and the four roads" and is manifest in four triangles converging on the center, the crucifix (see figure 6-1, in photo insert).

On the first level of abstraction, Eduardo's *mesa* is divided vertically into two major zones called *campos* (fields), which are separated by a mediating *campo.* The smaller side of the rectangular *mesa,* called the *Campo Ganadero* (Field of the Sly Dealer, Satan), contains artifacts associated with the forces of evil, the underworld, and black magic—mainly

*Gillin (1947: 117-29), Mac-Lain y Estenós (1939; 1942: 409-14), Cruz Sánchez (1948, 1951), Friedberg (1959, 1960, 1963), Chiappe (1967, 1968, 1969a, 1969b), Dobkin de Rios (1968, 1968-69, 1969a, 1969b), Sharon (1972a, 1972b), and Rodríguez Suy Suy (1973).

fragments of ancient ceramics (nos. 6, 14, 16, 23, 27) and stones (nos. 2, 5, 9, 10, 11, 12, 13, 15, 17, 18, 19, 22, 24, 25, 26, 28, 29) from archeological ruins and power spots, along with cane alcohol (4), a deer foot (3), and a triton shell (1). This zone is governed by Satan, whose negative powers are concentrated in three "staffs" placed upright in the ground behind the artifacts of the *Campo Ganadero*. These are called, from left to right, Satan's Bayonet (I), Owl Staff (II), and Staff of the Single Woman (III). A sorcerer would use this negative zone for witchcraft or in curing for financial gain; a benevolent curer needs it for consultation in cases of witchcraft, adverse love magic, or bad luck, since this is the realm responsible for such evils and consequently is also capable of revealing their sources. The unlucky number 13 (symbolizing Christ's eleven faithful disciples plus Paul and the traitor Judas) is ritually associated with this zone.

The right and larger side of the *mesa*, called the *Campo Justiciero* (Field of the Divine Judge, or Divine Justice), contains artifacts related to the forces of good or white magic, including images of saints (nos. 41, 48, 55, 61), crystals (nos. 63, 64, 72, 73), shells (nos. 46, 53, 56, 65, 67), a dagger (47), a rattle (59), three perfumes (74, 75, 76), holy water (69), black tobacco (79), sugar (66), sweet lime (77), and a five-gallon can of the San Pedro infusion (XIII). This zone is governed by Christ, who is considered the "center," or "axis," of the *mesa* and Lord of all three fields. The positive powers of this zone are concentrated in the crucifix (51) at the center of the *mesa*, as well as in seven staffs, called, from left to right, Swordfish Beak Staff (V), Eagle Staff (VI), Grayhound Staff (VII), Hummingbird Staff (VIII), Staff of the Virgin of Mercy (IX), Sword of St. Paul (X), and Saber of St. Michael the Archangel (XI). (In 1970 the Sword of St. James the Elder, XII, was included in Eduardo's *mesa* as an eighth staff, but it was only on loan from a patient who wanted it "charged.") These staffs are placed upright in the ground behind the artifacts of the *Campo Justiciero*. The sacred number 12 (for the twelve apostles—the eleven faithful plus Saint Paul, who replaces Judas—and the signs of the zodiac) is magically associated with this field. The crucifix is the ritual storage place for this number, which symbolizes the twelve thousand accounts of the *Campo Justiciero*. The sacred number 7, the "perfect" number of Christianity—symbolizing the seven "justices," or miracles, of Christ—is also stored in the crucifix.

The *Campo Medio* (Middle Field) contains mediating artifacts in which the forces of good and evil are evenly balanced. This zone is governed by Saint Cyprian (in Christian folklore, a powerful practitioner of black magic who was converted to Christianity), whose "balanced" powers are focused in the Serpent Staff of Moses and Solomon (IV). The mediating objects are a bronze sunburst (31), a bronze disk symbolic of the "complete" sun (32), a stone symbolizing the sea and the winds (33), a glass jar *(seguro)* containing magic herbs that Eduardo considers to be his spiritual alter ego, a stone (35) from Las Huaringas (Shimbe Lagoon), a statue of Saint Cyprian seated on a deck of Spanish divining cards with divinatory runes at his feet (36), a "fortune stone" (37), and a crystal "mirror" with the cat amulet (described in chapter 5) on top of it (38). The sacred number 25—that is, 12 *(Justiciero)* plus 13 *(Ganadero)*—is magically associated with this Middle Field. The artifacts of the Middle Field are symbolic of forces in nature and the world of man that can be used for good or evil depending on the intention of the individual. For Eduardo, who is a "white" shaman, the emphasis is on good in accord with the pact he made when he was initiated. This commitment is further emphasized by the fact that the *Campo Justiciero* is the largest field of the *mesa*.

Eduardo explains the concept of balance governing the *Campo Medio* as follows:

> The *Campo Medio* is like a judge in this case, or like the needle in a balance, the controlling needle between those two powers, between good and evil. The *Campo Medio* is where the chiefs, the guardians, those who command, those who govern present themselves, since it is the neutral field—that is, the dividing field between two frontiers where a war can occur over a dispute. That is the place where one has to put all, all, all his perseverance so that everything remains well controlled.

The Middle Field represents the core of Eduardo's conscious philosophy, for the opposing forces of the universe—as manifest in this microcosmos known as a *mesa*—are not conceived of as irreconcilable. Rather, they are seen as complementary, for it is their interaction that creates and sustains all life. The Middle Field, in addition to symbolizing the concept of balance, or the complementarity of opposites, also provides guidance for practical action, since it is the zone that helps the *curandero* to concentrate his supernatural vision, or sixth sense (which is activated by the San Pedro infusion). It is this vision that distinguishes the *curandero* from other men and permits him to divine and cure. The Middle Field, as a balanced mediating area, helps to focus the *curandero*'s supernatural faculties on the problem at hand, thus making his therapy possible. Eduardo is fully aware of this first level of abstraction represented by the *mesa*. It reflects a rational, verbalized explanation of the forces activated and put to work through the medium of his power objects.

The three-part structure that expresses the dualistic philosophy of the first level of abstraction (shown representatively in figure 6-2) contrasts markedly with the structure of the second level of abstraction (see stylized figure 6-3)—that is, "the four winds and the four roads," a label derived from an invocation made by the *curandero* at the beginning and end of each night séance. Despite the contrast, this second level is an extension and refinement of the dualism of the first level. It is not so clearly verbalized by Eduardo as the first level but is implicit in his descriptions and in the strategic grouping of power objects.

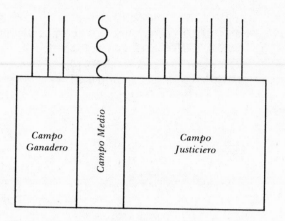

Figure 6-2. The three "fields" of Eduardo's *mesa*.

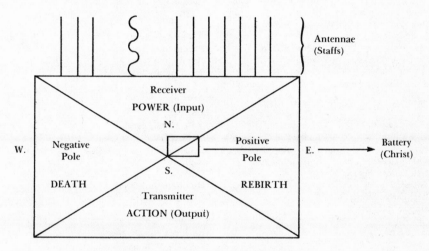

Figure 6-3. The transmitter/receiver.

Eduardo says that the four winds correspond to the four cardinal points of the compass, and the four roads are the diagonals that run from the central crucifix (51) of the *mesa*. Further inquiry reveals that he considers the east to be a "positive" or "safe" direction because the sun rises in the east, giving birth to light and a new day. The west is interpreted as a "negative" or "dangerous" direction because it is the region where the sun is swallowed up by the sea. The north is the direction of strong "magnetism" and "power" because of the location of the equator and the North Pole. The south contrasts with the power of the north because prevailing winds and winter come from the south. It is interesting to note that Eduardo always sets up his *mesa* with the sea at his back, since, as a fisherman, he considers it to be a protective force and a stimulus for action—much like his pre-Columbian ancestors,

Table 6–1.
ARTIFACTS GROUPED BY THE FOUR TRIANGLES:
FOUR WINDS AND FOUR ROADS

WEST (Death)	EAST (Rebirth)	NORTH (Power)	SOUTH (Action)
Mediators		*Antennae*	*Tools*
Shimbe Lagoon Stone, 35		Staffs, I–XI (XII)	*Receptacles*
			Pearl Shells, 46, 53
St. Cyprian, 36			Bowl, 52
Fortune Stone, 37		*Catalyst*	Cup, 71
Virgin's Breast Stone, 45		San Pedro, XIII	
Death (Witchcraft)	*Rebirth (Ascension)*	*Single Women*	*Defense/Offense*
Human	Christ Enthroned	Single Woman Stone,	Crystal Mirror and
Eye Stone, 9	Statue, 70	22	Cat Amulet, 38
Heart Stone, 10	St. John (Baptist)	Single Woman	Dagger, 47
Kidney Stone, 11	Shell, 56	Ceramic, 23	Rattle, 59
Phallus Stone, 12	Birth of Jesus Stone,	(Single Woman Staff,	Rope, 60
Double-Eyed Stone, 18	58	III)	(Cigars), 21
Knee Stone, 19	Moses & Red Sea		
Woman's Heel Stone,	Stone, 57	*Natural Elements*	
24	Jacob's Crystal, 63	Bronze Sunburst, 31	
Man's Foot Ceramic,	Noah's Ark Crystal, 72	Bronze Sun Disk, 32	
27	Chalpón Cave Stone,	Sea & Winds Stone, 33	
Bound Humans Stone,	62		
29		*Alter Ego, Mediator*	
		Herb Jar, 34	
Animal		*Animals (Staffs)*	
Snake Stone, 2	Snake Eye Crystal, 64	Serpent, IV	
Deer Foot, 3	White Ray Crystals, 73	Swordfish, V	
Monkey Ceramic, 6	*(Defense* also)	Eagle, VI	
Black Guinea Pig		Grayhound, VII	
Stone, 7		Hummingbird, VIII	
Black Parrot Stone, 8		Owl, II (& Stone, 13)	
Vampire Bat Ceramic,			
14			
Fox Ceramic, 16		*Christian Personages*	
		Virgin Mary	
Crops		Virgin of Carmen	
Wheat Stone, 26	Curer's Shell, 65	Statue, 43	
Bound Corn Stone, 28		Virgin, Immaculate	
		Conception Statue,	
Sorcerer's Spell		49	
Lagoon Stone, 15		Virgin Fountain Shell,	
Mountain Stone, 25		50	
Fire Stone, 17		(Virgin of Mercy Staff,	
Whistle, 20		IX)	
Cigars, 21			
		Mary Magdalene, 44	
Impurity	*Purification*	Child Jesus Statue, 42	
Cane Alcohol, 4	Purification Bowl, 68	St. Francis Statue, 41	
	Holy Water, 69	St. Anthony Statue, 48	
	Red Perfume, 74	St. Martin Statue, 55	
	Scented Water, 75	St. Paul Statue, 61	
	Tabu, 76	Soldier Stone, 54	
	White Sugar, 66	(Staffs: St. Paul, X,	

WEST (Death)	EAST (Rebirth)	NORTH (Power)	SOUTH (Action)
	Sweet Lime, 77	St. Michael, XI	
	Black Tobacco, 79	St. James, XII)	
Sex	*Sex*		*Sex*
Triton Shell (Vulva), 1	Shell (Phallus), 67		Shell (Vulva), 30
Defense	*Defense*	*"Charging"*	
Flints, 5	(White Ray Crystals, 73)	Patient's Herb Jar, 40	

who deified the sea. Since the Peruvian coast near Trujillo juts out to the northwest, by positioning himself with the sea at his back Eduardo usually faces the north.

One would expect the grouping of the artifacts related to the four cardinal points to reflect their respective interpretations. When one looks at the artifacts within the triangles formed by the four roads, a definite pattern emerges. The four cardinal points and the artifacts that are placed in their respective triangles are shown in table 6-1, which is keyed to figure 6-1 and to appendix A.

Careful scrutiny reveals that the power objects in each triangle all share certain generic qualities which elaborate and refine the dualism of the first level of abstraction—for example, east = rebirth, west = death, north = power, south = action. For example, the artifacts in the eastern triangle are all positive objects from the *Campo Justiciero* associated with rebirth and purification, whereas all but four objects grouped in the western triangle are negative artifacts from the *Campo Ganadero*, associated with death (by witchcraft) and impurity. The exceptions are three artifacts from the *Campo Medio:* Shimbe Lagoon Stone (35, symbolizing the powerful *curandero* of the lagoon, don Florentino García), Saint Cyprian (36), and the Fortune Stone (37, symbolizing the ambiguous forces of fate)—which balance the negative powers of the west through the mercy of the milk of the Virgin, symbolized by a fourth positive artifact, the Virgin's Breast Stone (45, from the *Campo Justiciero)*. This contrast is reinforced by the fact that the personages symbolized in the eastern triangle are spiritual men—Christ (70), Saint John the Baptist (56), Moses (57), Jacob (63), and Noah (72)—whereas most of the objects in the western triangle symbolize mortals or mortal parts that are often targets for witchcraft: for example, Eye Stone (9), Heart Stone (10), Kidney Stone (11), Phallus Stone (12), Double-Eyed (Whirlpool) Stone (18), Knee Stone (19), Woman's Heel Stone (24), Man's Right Foot Ceramic (27), and Tied Humans Stones (29); or animals associated with witchcraft, for example, Snake Stone (2), Deer Foot (3), Monkey Ceramic (6), Black Guinea Pig Stone (7), Black Parrot Stone (8), Vampire Bat Ceramic (14), and Fox Ceramic (16).

In addition, crop death by infertility is represented in the western triangle by the Wheat Stone (26) and the Bound Corn Stone (28). The forces of death are further accentuated in this segment of the *mesa* by stone representations of a lagoon (15, associated with an ancient ruin) and a mountain (25, invoked by sorcerers when casting a spell), as well as by a whistle (20) from an excavated tomb, used to invoke the spirits of the dead, and a Fire-Stone (17) and some cigars (21), symbolizing the fire and smoke used in certain spells. The impurity associated with death and witchcraft finds expression in a bottle of cane alcohol (4), which Eduardo believes symbolizes the intoxicating powers of the Devil. This contrasts sharply with the many substances of the eastern triangle associated with purification rites performed during a night séance: for example, a purification bowl (68), holy water (69), red perfume (74), scented water (75), Tabu perfume (76), white sugar (66), and sweet lime (77).

The greatest contrast to the symbols of death in the western triangle is provided by the many artifacts in the eastern triangle that symbolize rebirth and ascension: a small limestone carving of Christ Enthroned (70), depicting Jesus as Divine Judge after his ascension; Saint John the Baptist's Shell (56), symbolic of rebirth by a holy sacrament; the Birth of Jesus Stone (58), which symbolizes spiritual birth; Moses and the Red Sea Stone (57), symbolizing miraculous passage from one shore or plane to another (that is, rebirth); and Jacob's Crystal (63), described by Eduardo as a ladder with seven rungs, which is a symbol of ascent through seven heavens or planes. Other artifacts reinforce the theme of rebirth, such as Noah's Ark Crystal (72), symbolizing a new beginning for human and animal life after victorious emergence from the primordial waters, and the Cave of Chalpón Stone (62), representing initiatory death and rebirth.* The Snake-Eye Crystal (64) represents the clear capacity to "see" that comes with spiritual regeneration—an emphasis on the positive, skin-shedding ability of the snake, as opposed to the negative, deadly aspect of the Snake Stone (2) of the western triangle and the neutral, mediating qualities of the Serpent Staff (IV) of the Middle Field and the northern triangle. The three White Ray Crystals (73)—a bullet, a car, and one die—symbolize for Eduardo the speed and control over destiny made possible by the ascension of the soul, a "magical flight" produced by the ecstatic trance that Eduardo achieves through the San Pedro infusion (XIII). Finally, two spirally formed shells—one each in the upper corners of the eastern and western triangles—complete the contrast of opposites between east and west. The shell in the western triangle (1) has the shape of the vulva, while the shell in the eastern triangle (67) tapers down to a point, giving it a phallic shape.

Turning to the artifacts in the northern triangle, we see that all of them are power objects par excellence, like a conglomeration of magnets. This is obvious in the case of the eleven staffs (Eduardo refers to them as "antennae"), which are the foci of the forces at work in the manipulation of

---

*This cave, a modern Peruvian pilgrimage site, was inhabited during the nineteenth century by a Christian ascetic, Father Guatemala, who is believed to have ascended to Heaven.

the *mesa*. San Pedro (XIII), of course, is the catalyst that activates all of these forces. Most of the artifacts in this upper triangle belong to the *Campo Justiciero* and therefore have a positive connotation. Only a few artifacts of the *Campo Ganadero* are included: Satan's Bayonet (I), Owl Staff (II), Staff of the Single Woman (III), Stone of the Single Woman (22), Ancient Single Woman Ceramic (23), and Owl Stone (13). But these artifacts, despite the negative *Campo Ganadero* association, are especially potent objects that focus the forces of the left side of the *mesa* and make them available for therapy. This transformation is brought about by the proximity of the most important artifacts of the Middle Field: Serpent Staff (IV, mediator of duality), the bronze sunburst (31, locus of the element fire), bronze sun disk (32, symbol of the "complete" sun), Sea and Winds Stone (33, locus of the remaining elements of nature: water, air, earth), and the herb jar (34, Eduardo's alter ego). The remaining artifacts have as their referents personages from the Christian tradition considered by Eduardo to be particularly important: for example, the Virgin Mary (43, 49, 50, IX, symbolizing the beatitude and mercy of this Christian Great Mother), Mary Magdalene (44, conceivably an alter ego of the Virgin), Child Jesus (42, playing with the world in his hand as if it were a toy), Saint Francis (41, friend of birds and animals, but also a scourge against evil spirits), Saint Anthony (48, finder of lost objects), Saint Martin of Porres (55, a mulatto saint famous as a "doctor" and "cleanser of souls"), Saint Paul (61, the great lawyer of Christianity), and Soldier Stone (54, manifestation of the Church Militant). The last two artifacts work in close conjunction with the Sword of Saint Paul (X) and the Saber of Saint Michael (XI), in the line of staffs at the head of the *mesa*. Other staffs (Swordfish, V; Eagle, VI; Grayhound, VII; Hummingbird, VIII) represent Eduardo's helpful guardian spirits.

The northern triangle, like the Middle Field, expresses Eduardo's core concept: balance. This balanced zone is used to "charge" patients' amulets such as the second herb jar (see the chapter appendix, number 40, for an explanation).

The southern triangle is the emptiest. All of the objects placed here are veritable "tools of the trade" having a marked association with action and hence a utilitarian function. They are: two "Pearl" Shells (46, 53), for serving the San Pedro infusion and tobacco juice to assistants and patients during the curing séance (the personal shell used by the *curandero*, 65, is purposely placed in the eastern triangle of purification and rebirth); a bowl (52) for preparing the San Pedro and tobacco mixture; and a cup (71) for serving pure San Pedro infusion at midnight. (In figure 6-1 the cup has been moved up and to the right in order to make room for the three perfumes, 74, 75, and 76, which are normally placed upright more to the right, with the sugar, 66, occupying their present position.) However, some objects (crystal "mirror" and cat, 38; dagger, 47; rattle, 59; rope, 60) also have offensive/defensive functions. The dagger is held in the left hand of the *curandero* throughout the entire night session to guard against attacks by evil spirits (along with the rope, which is worn around his neck). In support of the dagger's function, the mirror with the cat amulet on top helps the *curandero* to "visualize" such attacks; he can counterattack by bringing to bear the energies of the feline aided by the rope, which he swings over his head to drive off the evil spirits. In addition, the mirror is also seen as a pyramid, in which are stored the twenty-five accounts that control the powers of the *Campo Ganadero* by balancing it with the powers of the *Campo Justiciero*. The rattle is held in the *curandero*'s right hand, in most instances, in order to activate healing accounts through songs and occasionally to defend against spirit attacks. Its curative action is supported by two borderline artifacts: the shell (30) and cigars (21). The shell is used to divine the character of female patients; while cigars are used to counter sorcerers' spells effected through tobacco smoke. Defensive functions are also supplemented by the flints (5) of the *Campo Ganadero,* located in the western triangle, and the bright White Ray Crystals (73) of the *Campo Justiciero,* located in the eastern triangle. It seems that the southern triangle is kept well guarded and relatively empty to facilitate defensive and offensive action by the *curandero* throughout the session.

In view of the fact that much of the defensive and offensive action initiated within the southern triangle involves a staff (when diagnosing and curing a patient) or a sword (when exorcising evil spirits), it is necessary to clarify their relationship to the four triangles of the *mesa.* As we noted earlier, as power objects par excellence these eleven staffs or swords belong to the northern triangle. However, when one of them is used in conjunction with San Pedro for diagnosing, curing, or exorcising, it is converted into one of the utilitarian tools of the trade and therefore temporarily belongs to the southern triangle. By the same token, we have seen that a staff or sword can manifest negative or positive attributes in accord with its association with one of the three "fields" of the *mesa.* At such times it manifests an affinity for either the eastern or western triangle. The fact that Eduardo refers to these artifacts at the head of his *mesa* as antennae suggests their multiple functions.

Finally, this analysis of the strategic arrangement of *mesa* artifacts would not be complete without a consideration of the axis around which the objects are placed: the "center" occupied by the crucifix (51) at the junction of the four roads that lead to the four winds. The crucifix is located slightly to the right of the exact center of the *mesa.* Nevertheless, the *curandero* emphasizes that it is the "actual" center, without which there could be no *mesa.* In shamanism throughout the world, ecstatic flights such as those achieved by Eduardo with the aid of San Pedro are achieved along the *Axis Mundi* (World Axis) joining three planes (Underworld, earth, sky). This World Axis, found at the center where earth and sky meet, can be conceptualized as a World Tree or Cosmic Mountain (Eliade, 1964: 259–74). The early Christians considered Golgotha (where Christ was crucified) to be the "center of the world" because it was at the summit of the Cosmic Mountain (268-69). Since we have already observed that throughout Andean South America (including the coastal areas) mountains and stone were, and in many places still are, considered sacred, the blending of Indian and Christian archetypes is most apparent on the *mesa;* the crucifix—elevated as it is above the other artifacts—is the Cosmic Mountain, which Eduardo ascends in ecstatic flight (symbolized by the Eagle Staff, VI) during the curing ceremony. But he can also descend to the Underworld along the Axis to retrieve lost souls and accompany the dead on their last journey when the situation demands. The Virgin of Carmen (43), overseer of Purgatory, stationed to the left of the crucifix, symbolizes this capacity, realized in search of drowned souls (an important service in the fishing village where Eduardo resides) with the aid of the Swordfish Beak (V), and mediated by her neighbor to the left, Saint Cyprian (36), who is in a position to strike a bargain with Satan (I). Here is what Eduardo has to say about journeys to the marine Underworld:

When it is a matter of a person who has died under unknown circumstances or when one wants to know what place he is in [whether Heaven, Purgatory, or Hell], then the Swordfish Beak together with the Virgin of Carmen are invoked in asking about the person and what place he is in, in what situation, in what "mansion" of the sea or the earth. Then if they say that he has drowned, I ask where the soul of that person is to be found. Then the artifacts take note and speak and "call" from the tomb to Purgatory and to Heaven. This is a special task, it is a special account and chant with which one looks in rarely encountered cases. But one does exactly . . . what the ancient Greek heroes did in making journeys to the center of the earth, to Hades to look for the dead. Also as the Egyptians in the accounts of Osiris and Isis. For example, when the sun dies Osiris travels through the mansion of the dead. Thus it is the same. It is a symbolism, but one which has a reality in these cases when one is trying to uncover a sign, a consequence. . . . According to his offenses, one has to go to the place that corresponds to him: Purgatory, or it can be Hell, or it can be Heaven also. If it seems to be Hell, one invokes the *Campo Ganadero,* or the *Campo Ganadero* reveals to the *curandero* that the soul is in that place. Then, in such cases, there is nothing that one can do.

Thus we see that each triangle corresponding to one of the cardinal points (four winds) contains artifacts that can be classified according to a common trait: east = positive energy, west = negative energy, north = input, south = output (see figure 6-3, this chapter, p. 65). The crucifix at the junction of the four roads unifies these four triangles, while the antennae perform input and output functions involving both negative and positive energies. Eduardo often calls the *mesa* a "receiver and transmitter," and the four triangles reveal this to be a good analogy. The balanced, quaternary structure of the four winds complements and completes the imbalanced, ternary structure of the three fields of the *mesa*. This reconciliation of opposites is achieved through ritual.

In an all-night curing séance Eduardo performs a ritual power build-up until midnight. First, opening prayers and invocations lead to the ritual activation of the center, or axis, associated with the number 7—the crucifix. Next, the right side of the *mesa*, the *Campo Justiciero*, associated with the forces of good and the number 12, is magically activated. Then the mediating Middle Field, associated with the number 25, is ritually activated; during this process the left side of the *mesa*, the *Campo Ganadero*, associated with the forces of evil and the number 13, is also brought to life. Finally, after ritual activation of the energizing San Pedro brew, the personal powers of the *curandero* are awakened by drinking the infusion. Once this is achieved, the ternary structure of the three fields is transcended by the manifestation of the *curandero*'s powers and the quaternary structure of the four triangles. Thus an imbalanced polar antagonism is transformed into a balanced, harmonious flow of forces that then can be put to work in solving patients' problems for the remainder of the séance.

Eduardo's manipulation of the quaternary format of his *mesa* may be considered to be marginally subliminal insofar as he has not verbalized it as clearly as he has described the ternary interaction of the *campos*. Once activated by ritual, however, the *mesa* becomes the sacred space in which the psychological (personal projections) and cosmological (cardinal points) meet and become one. In this sense the *mesa* truly is a transmitter of sacred power capable of achieving the magical meeting of man and cosmos.

7

The Cosmic Terrain:
Aboriginal Roots of the *Mesa*

The *mesa* plays a central role in north coastal *curanderismo*. Like the use of the San Pedro cactus, the ritual application of magico-religious paraphernalia is a remnant of an aboriginal pattern. A review of the ethnographic and ethnohistorical literature on Peru and other parts of Latin America reveals that the *mesa* is quite widespread today. It is used in order to cure, divine, locate lost property, punish thieves, harm enemies, retrieve runaway spouses, perform love magic, assure a safe journey, consecrate a new house, overcome bad luck, guarantee good fortune, influence the weather, avoid or overcome punishment by the ancestors and native deities, pay tribute to the spirits inhabiting the supernatural realm, and promote the health and fertility of crops, herds, and the community in general. In addition, the *mesa* appears to reflect an Indian *imago mundi* that is very old. Anthropologists are just beginning to discern the dim outlines of this ancient world view and its varied manifestations. A summary of findings from the literature appears in appendix C: "Aboriginal *Mesas*" and appendix D: "Aboriginal Cosmologies." The present discussion will be limited to the materials from Peru and Bolivia, since they will prove useful in interpreting Eduardo's *mesa*.

MOCHE

In the course of his ethnographic study of the Peruvian north coastal community of Moche, Gillin (1947: 117-29) provided one of the most detailed reports of folk healing recorded to date. To obtain his data Gillin participated in two nighttime curing séances, the second of which was performed exclusively for him and involved careful explanations. The material was checked by a daytime set-up and demonstration of *mesa* artifacts.

Gillin's informant was about sixty-years old and had been trained in his youth by one of the great *maestros* of Salas, the so-called capital of north-coast *curanderismo*. His introduction to this ancient art came when he was cured of a "case of worms in the leg." Since he could not pay the curer's fee, he was obliged to work with him as an *alzador* for six months. During this time he became interested in becoming a practitioner. The *maestro* tested him for another year of work as an assistant. Gillin (1947: 118) informs us that "one must have an innate ability to learn the techniques, and to see visions, but above all, the candidate must be absolutely sincere in believing in the power of the herbs."

According to Gillin curing sessions start at 9:00 P.M. and often continue until daybreak. Their purpose is to discover who has done magical harm (*daño*) to the patient and how it has been performed. After invoking the Christian Trinity, the curer lays out his *mesa* artifacts on a white cloth. Then, by the light of a candle, the two assistants are instructed to "raise the table" (*levantar la mesa*)—that is, snuff through the nostrils a mixture of cane alcohol, scented water, and jasmine perfume. These substances are presented in two flat seashells called *perlas,* reserved for use by the *alzadores.* The procedure is believed by the curer to purify the *mesa* and protect if from evil influences.

Once the *mesa* is raised, the candle is blown out and the curer raises the same substances as his assistants, using his personal shell. Then he orally sprays the *mesa*—twice with jasmine perfume to keep evildoers away, twice with scented water, and twice with white sugar to "sweeten the table."

Next the healer begins to call the spirits, believed to be represented by the *mesa* artifacts. First he chews a small piece of *misha negra*. The invocation consists of chanting and whistling a special sacred tune (composed by the healer) to the accompaniment of his rattle.

During the invocation, if counterspirits (*shapingos*) appear the curer throws an iron magnet at them. If this does not chase them off, he instructs an assistant to seize a long dagger at the head of the *mesa* and fight a shadow battle. If the assistant fails to drive off the invading spirits, the healer takes up the battle. It is considered to be very dangerous to the patient if the master is overcome in one of these spirit battles.

Once the *shapingos* are routed, all stand; the healer invokes the Trinity and continues to call the spirits of the herbs, replenishing his cud of *misha* from time to time and ingesting alcohol and perfume through his nostrils to drive off additional attacks of counterspirits. It is believed that at 11:00 P.M. the counterspirits begin coming in the greatest numbers, necessitating a raising of the patient. This is performed by the two assistants—one on each side of the patient. It consists of again sniffing alcohol and perfumes through the nose, this time lifting the shell containing the brew with both hands in three phases to demarcate the sections of the patient's body: (1) feet to waist (followed by imbibing), (2) waist to neck (followed by imbibing), and (3) neck to crown of the head (followed by imbibing). In addition to purifying and protecting the patient, the operation is said to "raise the soul."

After this procedure "an even more powerful method and one also prescribed for certain conditions of the patient, of which the master must be the judge," is to serve the San Pedro brew. In addition to boiled San Pedro cactus this brew contains powerful herbs (among them *misha negra*) from two *seguros*. Gillin notes that the mixture is reputed to cause "vomiting, diarrhea, and visual hallucinations" and that some healers administer "this brew or something similar to all persons present at the séance." (1947: 121-22)

As the session progresses, the tempo of the master's "singing, whistling, and monologic exclamations" increases and he begins to express greater certainty regarding the source of the patient's ailment. Eventually he again lights the candle and begins to concentrate "as if in a trance" on framed pictures of the saints at the head of his *mesa*. Finally he breaks the silence with an expression of conviction regarding the matter at hand. Then he calls others present to come and look at the pictures while concentrating on the patient's problem. After receiving some expressions of agreement regarding what can be discerned in the background of the pictures, the healer interrogates the patient about particulars of his or her case. If he still is not completely certain about the case, he blows out the candle and continues to call the spirits.

Once he has decided on the diagnosis and necessary treatment, the curer informs the patient that he will convey this information the next day. In the meantime, the patient's symptoms have to be relieved in another "raising" ritual. This time the assistants move their shells all over the patient's body, ingesting the entire contents of their shells whenever they discover a painful spot. At the same time they press their heads against the troubled area. Then the shells are refilled and the search for sore areas continues. Meanwhile, the master speaks reassuringly to the patient and prepares an herb to be ingested immediately or at home. Gillin (1947: 122) states quite simply: "Patients usually feel better after this treatment." His data on curing séances parallel materials gathered by later researchers.*

Many of the fifty-four artifacts on Gillin's informant's *mesa* are similar to Eduardo's power objects and to the materia medica of other northern healers as recorded by subsequent research.† However, Gillin (1947: 124) points out that "each [curer] has specialties and peculiarities of his own," and "no two *mesas* are exactly alike."

Next Gillin (1947: 125-26) discusses the use of the guinea pig in diagnosis (*limpia con cuy*), another practice used by Eduardo and other northern healers. Then he translates a portion of the novel *El Daño* (1942) by Camino Calderón, who gathered the background material first-hand during a year and a half of residence at Salas, when he made the acquaintance of the leading healers. The material translated by Gillin (1947: 126-28) includes a reference to an important highland curing center near the town of Huancabamba. (We shall have more to say about this region in chapter 10.) It also provides a dramatic and insightful description of a healing séance.

Finally, Gillin's report (128-29) discusses evil witchcraft, including such

*See appendix B for these sources.
†See appendix A for these sources.

practices as sticking sharp objects into an effigy of the intended victim, transforming oneself into an animal or bird to harm crops, leaving powders on the victim's doorstep, placing potions in his food or drink, using toads in casting spells, and blowing *mal aire* (bad air) to harm victims.

QUECHUA

Shamanism and *Mesas*

The first major source for the shamanism of the Quechua Indians is Mishkin (1940, 1946), who studied the Andean village of Kauri, near Cuzco. He makes a point that is most relevant to our search for remnants of archaic shamanism in the Andean region: "The contemporary Indian is obviously still embedded in the cultural matrix which belongs to the earliest horizon known in the Andes. Survivals are apparent at a glance" (1940: 225).

According to Mishkin, Quechua shamans are able to perform both good magic and black magic and are also diviners and curers. There are three classes of spirits associated with the shaman's practice: the *ccoas*, or striped cats, whose phosphorescent eyes emit hail; the *aukis*, and *apus*, or mountain spirits; and the former *gentiles*, or ancient inhabitants of the area, who now reside in the lower portions of the earth (*Uku Pacha*) and cause a large number of the diseases that attack the Indians. The *ccoa* selects the shaman and gives him power by striking him with lightning; the *aukis* are invoked by the shaman to help him cure; and the evil spirits of the *gentiles* must be combatted to overcome illness.

The Quechua distinguish between a superior shaman, called *alto mesayoq* (or *altomesa*), who has been struck by lightning three times, and an inferior shaman, called *pampa mesayoq* (or *pampamesa*), who has been struck by lightning only once. Although both can practice black magic and divination as well as cure and combat black magic, the essential difference between them lies in their relationship to the spirits. The *alto mesayoq* can converse with the *aukis*, his principal means of divination, whereas the *pampa mesayoq* is guided only by the *ccoa*. It is interesting to note that we encounter the word *mesa* incorporated in the titles of supernatural specialists.

In August, when the earth is believed to be alive, several kinds of stones (the *incaychus* mentioned in chapter 5) are thrown up in the fields, and they are used as amulets. There are seven classes of stones—named after foodstuffs, two kinds of cattle, sheep, llamas, and two kinds of shamans—which are supposed to protect their namesakes or help the bearer to obtain or benefit from them. It is necessary to consult a diviner to discover if a stone has magical properties and to classify it properly.

In curing by invocation of the *aukis*, the shaman first enters the sickroom containing a table holding cane alcohol, coca, sugar, a whip, and some money. After placing a white piece of paper on the ground, the shaman darkens the room and calls forth his tutelary *auki.* The door is closed, the curer whistles three times, and the *auki* enters through the roof and settles on the paper. Then the shaman and his spirit guide converse until the *auki* reveals the cause of the illness and advises a remedy. Sometimes the familiar spirit strikes the healer and the patient with the whip. At the end of the session the *auki* leaves through the roof. The curer lights a candle, takes his money, and departs.

Recent work on Quechua religion supplements Mishkin's findings. In addition to the *alto mesayoq,* who communicates directly with the supernatural beings, and the *pampa mesayoq,* who has less power, there are three other magico-religious specialists: the *layqa,* or sorcerer; the *hanpeq,* or curer; and the *watoq,* or diviner. Actually these titles appear to refer to specialized activities of shamans rather than to mutually exclusive practitioners, since there is much overlap between them. A generic title for the shaman, regardless of his power and specialty, is *paqo.* (See Nuñez del Prado, 1970: 104-106; Casaverde, 1970: 211-25; Marzal, 1971a: 257-66; Garr, 1972: 169-72; and Gow and Condori, 1976: 71-80, for discussions of traditional religious specialists.)

Relying on information collected in the town of Kuyo Grande, near Cuzco, Casaverde (1970: 212-13) describes the selection of an *alto mesayoq* by lightning. The lightning is sent by the *apus* (mountain spirits) who become the shaman's protectors. The supernatural selection occurs in an isolated place out of sight of other people; otherwise the lightning would take the life of the candidate. The first charge is believed to kill him, the second reduces his body to small pieces, and the third reassembles his body. This is a classic example of the ritual death and resurrection involved in shamanic selection, especially among the Central Asian and Siberian peoples, where lightning is one of the media of selection used by the supernatural beings (Eliade, 1964: 19). During Inca times some curers (Molina, 1959: 29) and shrine priests (Arriaga, 1968: 36) were selected by lightning.

After being struck, the candidate awakens a long way from the scene of the accident with a wound in the form of a cross on his chest. Next to him he finds a strangely shaped stone mixed with the blood of the mountain spirits, the *qhaqya mesa* (lightning *mesa*).* This stone contains supernatural power that lasts about three years. After this time the stone is believed to lose its power—as does the shaman, who becomes a common magician. For a week after his initiation by the lightning, the future *alto mesayoq* is kept in the larder of the kitchen, where he is regularly censed, and kept on a diet that excludes salt, peppers, and other condiments. When he emerges he may seek formal training as an assistant to a competent *alto mesayoq* or begin curing people on his own initiative.

---

*Marzal (1971a: 258) reports that the novice also receives the *mesa* cloth, a crucifix, a bell, square stones representing the different *apu* sponsors, and three stones called *llamp'us* used in preparing infusions for patients (data from the town of Wanqara near Cuzco).

David Gow (1976: 241–42), working in the towns of Pinchimuro and
Lauramarca near Cuzco, describes a formal shamanic initiation as follows:

> The *pako* [*paqo*] is divinely appointed by *Apu Ausangate* on the First of
> August, the day on which the *Pachamama* lives. The aspiring *pako* ascends the
> lower slopes of *Ausangate* the previous day in the company of an established
> *pako*, who acts as teacher and witness. The night is passed bathing in a lake,
> reading the *coca* leaves, making offerings to *Ausangate*, and waiting to see if the
> *apu* will appear. If he does, dressed in white on a white horse and wearing a
> helmet, then this means that the aspirant has been chosen to be a *pako*. Should
> the *apu* stop and talk, this means that the aspirant has been chosen to be an
> *Altomisa* [*alto mesayoq*]—a magico-religious expert who can talk directly to
> *Ausangate* and the other *apus*. This attribute distinguishes him from the *pako*
> [*pampa mesayoq*] with whom he shares the ability to divine, cure, and perform
> sorcery. It appears that the *altomisa* . . . is becoming rarer and rarer and is
> only to be found in the very isolated areas of the *puna* [high pastures].*

Our data on Quechua beliefs and practices now permit us to define the
stages of the *mesa* ritual and the paraphernalia used by Quechua shamans.
The order in which the phases of a session occur varies according to the individual shaman and the particular purpose of the ritual. But as a general
rule the ritual begins with prayers and libations (*t'inka* or *ch'alla*) of alcohol
in the four corners of the room, which may then be censed. This is followed
by divination with coca leaves.

Next comes the preparation of the *mesa* proper (also referred to as *pago*,
payment; *despacho*, dispatch; *ofrenda*, offering; or *alcanzo*, reaching). On a
wooden box covered with a white cloth (*mesa*), or on a special white alpaca
skin (*unkuña*) spread on the floor—in either case oriented to the east—the
shaman places a sheet of white paper. The paper has a cross printed on it,
the head of which is also oriented to the east. A bed of cotton is laid over the
paper. Clusters of coca leaves (*k'intus*) are placed on the cotton in sets of
three, often arranged in twelve pairs. The shaman lifts each set, dips it in
alcohol, breathes on it, and offers it to a mountain spirit (*apu*). Then he
places other ingredients on top of the coca leaves: llama fat, silver-colored
paper, gold-colored paper, bits of candy, bread, wheat, barley, beans, herbs,
white cornmeal, carnation petals, mint, lead figurines, and so forth. All
these items have been removed from a package, also called a *mesa*, which
was purchased in the herb section of the local market. When the shaman has
assembled all the ingredients he folds the white paper, thus forming another
package (*mesa*), which is tied with silk ribbons. Sometimes a llama fetus is
placed in the package before folding. Once the *mesa* is ready, it is usually
censed. Often at this time the shaman performs ritual libations with alcohol,
followed by a break until about midnight. Frequently the foregoing rituals
are punctuated by coca chewing, consumption of alcohol, and ritual embraces of forgiveness.

*For another description of this type of initiation, see Gow and Condori (1976: 76–77).

After divining with coca leaves, the shaman instructs his two assistants to prepare a bonfire. When a strong blaze has been achieved, they must place the *mesa,* oriented to the east, on the fire to be consumed. While the offering is burning, the shaman often instructs the participants to embrace ritually and offer pardon to each other. Once the package has been completely consumed, the shaman checks the ashes. If they are white, the ritual has been successful; black ashes indicate that the offering has not been accepted by the *apus* and another *mesa* must be performed before tragedy strikes the shaman's client. The ashes must be buried before dawn.

In fertility rites performed on behalf of livestock (alpacas, llamas, sheep, cattle) every year during Carnival (in February or March) and in August, this ceremony is performed in a special ritual corral (*señal kancha*). Once the package is prepared, it is burned or deposited in a hole located in the eastern corner of the corral or in the center (*allpapa sonqon,* "heart of the earth"), covered by a huge flat stone called a *mesa.* Rituals involving *incaychus* (images of livestock) are performed on these stone *mesas.* They are also associated with a ritual "marriage" of a male and female of the species for which the rite is performed.*

Two recent ethnographic studies give some insight into the Quechua ideology relating to *mesa* rituals. The first (Flores, 1976: 119) focuses on the ritual objects used in animal-increase rites performed by herders of southern Cuzco. Of particular interest is a detail that at first seems relatively insignificant. In describing the blanket or cloth containing a herder's ritual paraphernalia, which is opened during fertility rites, Flores points out a weave pattern delineating three divisions: *paña* (right), *lloque* (left), and *pampa* (plain). Apparently the enclosed power objects are positioned according to the three zones of the textile once the *mesa* is set up for rituals (Flores, personal communication). This is an interesting parallel to the three fields of Eduardo's *mesa.*

The second report (Gow, 1976: 205) complements the information provided by Flores. Working in the towns of Pinchimuro and Lauramarca, Gow discovered that the people believe that everyone has two stars, a left and a right. Given to them on August 1 by *Apu Ausangate,* the most important indigenous deity of the region, the stars embody the concept of duality that seems to be the central theme in Andean ideology. The star on the left is considered to be female and malevolent, the right male and benevolent. These stars are not physical entities; "rather they are symbolic metaphors for the

*For specific details of Quechua paraphernalia and rituals see: Aranguren, 1975 (rites for the entire native year); Boltons, 1976 (theft); Casaverde, 1970: 144-49, 164-66, 211-36 (livestock, fertility, theft, curing); Custred, 1973 (fertility, tribute to mountain spirits); Dalle, 1969, 1971 (livestock, native New Year); Delgado, 1971 (livestock); Favre, 1968 (curing, livestock, tribute to mountain spirits); Flores, 1976 (livestock, native ideology); Garr, 1972: 145-59 (land and house blessings, livestock, curing); Gow, 1976 (fertility, native ideology); Lira, 1969 (removing bad luck); Marzal, 1971a: 273-76; 1971b (earth "payment" or tribute, livestock); Nachtigall, 1975 (llama sacrifices); and Quispe, 1969 (livestock, see pp. 92-100 for a synthesis of literature on livestock rituals).

protective power of the *apu*." The dualistic ideology that they express is manifested in *mesa* rituals performed on August 1, the day when the earth is reborn. Gow points to parallels in Inca times—for example, Cuzco was divided into two halves: Upper Cuzco (associated with the right) and Lower Cuzco (associated with the left); an Indian chronicler, Santacruz Pachacuti-Yamqui, depicted the Inca cosmos as divided into female left and male right, with respective star associations. Later in this chapter, when we discuss Inca cosmology, we shall return to these pre-Columbian antecedents.

Cosmology

The work of Nuñez del Prado (1970) in the town of Qotobamba and of Casaverde (1970) in Kuyo Grande—both in the vicinity of Cuzco—has done much to clarify our knowledge of Quechua concepts regarding the supernatural. The universe is believed to be divided into three major realms:

Hananpacha (Upper World). This is a region of plenty inhabited by God, Christ, the Virgin Mary, the saints, and the spirits of the dead who led good lives on earth. Human beings can reach it only after death. They arrive by crossing a river, *jordan mayu*, on the back of a dog. Once there, they live and work just as they did on earth, except that everything is abundant and free of strife. The spirits of children cultivate gardens of flowers for God; unbaptized children go to a section called *Limpu* (Limbo). Animal spirits go to Animal Towns.

Kaypacha (This World). On this level is the earth, a hierarchy of mountain spirits (such as *apus* and *aukis*), evil spirits, man, animals, plants, and objects. Some informants describe it as a flat platform supported by four columns that rest on the world below. Others say it is like a bowl floating on the ocean. A more acculturated version describes it as a top floating in space with man occupying the upper portion and the inhabitants of the Lower World on the lower portion.

Uku Pacha (Inner World). The Underworld, or Inner Earth, is inhabited by little people whose activities are similar to those of the people in the world above them. When it is day on the earth it is night in the world below, and vice-versa. Sometimes this region is identified as the Hell of Catholicism, the domain of the *Supay* (Devil), which is reached through the craters of volcanoes.

The sun is considered to be masculine and is married to the moon. When it sets on This World, it passes through the firmament of the Lower World. Lightning, the sponsor of shamans, is male and has two brothers, snow and hail. Another atmospheric phenomenon, the rainbow, is a malevolent being who inhabits springs in the form of colored threads that are spun in the sky after it rains. Springs, rainbows, and malignant winds all cause supernatural ailments that are treated by shamans.

Roal and Pachamama. According to Nuñez del Prado (1970: 69),

Quechua cosmology is structured around two principal deities, *Roal* and *Pachamama*. "The former is the creator spirit (*camac*) who occupies the top of the hierarchy, while the latter permeates the system from top to bottom, being linked with femininity and fertility." *Roal* "governs the forces of nature and maintains their equilibrium" (1970: 71), assigning supervision of specialized activities to the mountain spirits of lesser rank, the *apus* and *aukis,* who originated from him. Nuñez del Prado feels that *Pachamama,* who predominates in agriculture, may "have a position similar to *Roal,* since her powers are not subject to him nor have they been delegated by him as in the case of the great *apus.* She may well be, rather, a being of pan-earthly powers who intervenes as the feminine factor in the origin of things." (1970: 73)

Although the system exhibits a degree of syncretism with Christianity, for the most part "there is a clear dividing line between the native structure and the coexistent one, since the native specialists cannot establish contact with or propitiate the Occidental deities and, equally, the priest who propitiates the latter cannot communicate with the native supernatural beings." (1970: 116)

Wamanis. Research in the Ayacucho region of southern Peru complements the information from Cuzco. Here the mountain spirits are called *Wamanis.* Billie Jean Isbell (1976) gives an idea of the spirits occupying the three levels of the Quechua universe through the innovative use of children's drawings collected in the village of Chuschi. At the top of the Upper World is the sun, with his wife, the moon, to his left (a spatial relationship recognized by men and women of the community in all ritual interaction). Below the sun and moon are two stars called grandfather and grandmother — Venus of the morning and Venus of the evening, respectively. The *Wamanis,* who live in gold and silver homes inside the mountains, manifest as condors, men, crosses, or mountain peaks from which flow irrigation canals. They are the owners of all animals and give shelter to the leader of the herds, a four-horned sheep called the *Inca,* and to the progenitor of the sheep, a bisexual animal called the *Wari* (or *Mari*). The Underworld, which is reached through springs (*puqyos*), is inhabited by the dangerous non-Christian ancestors (*gentiles*), a supernatural cat (the *ccoa* of the Cuzco region), and a hairy snake known as the *Amaru,* who occasionally has two heads. This lower world also nurtures a special tree called *mallqui.*

A fine monograph by Quispe (1969), dealing with *mesa* rituals for livestock in the communities of Choque Huarcaya and Huancasancos in the Ayacucho region, supplements the work of Isbell. Quispe (1969: 102–103) offers an explanation of the relation between the native deities who are propitiated: the *Wamanis, Pachamama,* and *Amaru.* The *Wamanis* are associated with the mountains, the highland pastures, the sky, livestock, and man. *Pachamama* is associated with the earth, agriculture, and woman. Thus there is an opposition between these two divinities. But they are related to each other through the mediation of the *Amaru,* who inhabits the springs and lagoons of the high pastures. From there he circulates to the valleys through streams and irrigation canals, for his principal element is water. Offerings from *mesa* rituals are deposited in the springs found at the foot of the mountains in the high country. Then the *Amaru* emerges from the Underworld to sweep the gifts of man down to the valleys below. In this fashion the *Wamanis* (sky) communicate with *Pachamama* (earth) through the mediation of the *Amaru* (water). Once again, we find a basic dualism underlying Quechua religious ideology. But, as in the case of Eduardo's *mesa,* it is a "mediated" dualism in which complementary opposites are brought together in a meaningful interaction that sustains life.

AYMARA

Shamanism and *Mesas*

The first major source for the Aymara Indians is Tschopik (1946, 1951), who studied the Peruvian village of Chucuito, located on Lake Titicaca. Here diseases are thought to be caused by seeing ghosts, soul kidnapping by evil spirits or witches, other types of soul loss, dreams, the glances of evil spirits, the intrusion of a foreign object into the body, the evil eye, and mutilation of one's effigy in witchcraft. "*Chullpa* sickness" is caused by the intrusion of a fragment of human bone into the body—performed by evil spirits inhabiting ruins or by witchcraft.

Sacrifices to the supernatural beings are restricted to rites performed (mostly at night) by white (*paqo*) and black (*laiqa*) magicians who use elaborate ritual paraphernalia, much of which shows marked similarity to the artifacts of the *mesa* used in northern Peru. Tschopik (1951: 262n.) states that the general structure of the séance in northern Peru reported by Gillin (1947) is similar to that of Chucuito. The term *mesa* is actually used by the Aymara for certain elements of their ritual complex—for example, the cloth on which the artifacts are placed, large and small stone "spirit seats" on which the spirits are supposed to rest during the session, and a square modeled lump of shaved llama fat coated with gold and silver paper, which is the major offering to the spirits. Tschopik (1951: 252n.) offers a suggestion that might shed some light on the concept of the *mesa*: "It seems not unlikely that the term *mesa* may be a corruption of the Spanish word *misa,* 'Mass.' "

Mesa spirit seats are only a few of the numerous Aymara amulets and talismans. In Bolivia these power objects (mostly of alabaster or soapstone) are referred to generically as *khochqas* or *waqanquis.* They are subdivided into *sepjas,* mainly stones with geometric incisions (including *mesas*), and *illas,* mainly livestock figurines (Haley and Grollig, 1976; Frisancho, 1973: 89-97; Oblitas, 1963: 202-29; Paredes, 1963: 99-102; Tschopik, 1951:

237–40). *Illas* are the equivalents of the Quechua *incaychus* mentioned in chapter 5. The Chucuito Aymara studied by Tschopik acquire many of these magical charms from traveling doctors (*qollahuayas*), a cultural subgroup of the Bolivian Aymara with a distinct dress and dialect who travel all over the Andes and are famous for their knowledge of herbs, amulets, ritual, sorcery, and curing. (See the next section on Aymara cosmology for detailed information on these people.)

The feline concept seems to play an important role in the symbology associated with Aymara artifacts. When not in use the artifacts are wrapped in a jaguar skin. Also, two puma paws and two stuffed wildcats are included among the major artifacts used for animal-increase rites practiced on behalf of livestock breeders (Tschopik, 1951: 243, 276).

Divination is considered a necessary accompaniment to every conceivable act. Omens are sought in nearly all natural objects and phenomena. In addition, the Aymara have special diviners (*yatiri*) who ascertain the future through the medium of coca. This same technique is used by practitioners of white and black magic and by doctors (*qolasiri*), who have additional professional techniques. The *yatiri* may locate lost or stolen property, divine the outcome of a marriage or trading venture, discover infidelity, or tell whether a sick person will live or die. Much attention is also paid to dreams.

Although the Aymara distinguish between white and black magicians, some practitioners perform both kinds of magic. Both types of supernatural power come from the same source: lightning. To practice magic, a man must be struck by two successive bolts. It is believed that the first bolt kills him while the second restores him to life. When the novice recovers he undergoes a period of training in either the black or the white art, during which time he serves as his teacher's assistant and makes payments to him of food, alcohol, coca, and small amounts of money.

The chief functions of the black magician seem to be to kill people with magic, to send disease at the bidding of his clients, to cause accidents, and to destroy victims' livestock. Apparently he also performs love magic, discovers and punishes thieves through black magic, and cures some diseases. He divines by using coca, interpreting dreams, and invoking the spirits of the dead, of owls, and of demons. Spells are performed by the standard techniques of imitative and contagious magic.

The white magician cures diseases, performs weather and love magic, offers sacrifices for the benefit of the crops and flocks, apprehends thieves, finds lost property, and counteracts witchcraft. His methods of divination include the use of coca and the interviewing of spirits. Sickness is cured by counteracting witchcraft and by placating the spirits who either sent the disease or seized the patient's soul. The healer summons the spirits in a séance to discover the cause of the ailment, after which the appropriate offerings are made. The white magician always has extensive recourse to herbal remedies in addition to employing supernatural cures. Seven directions are recognized in all rites: the four cardinal points of the compass plus the zenith, nadir, and central earth.

Tschopik documents the arrangement of ritual gear for four different kinds of *mesa* ceremonies: (1) summoning the spirits (see figure 7-1; note especially the caption listing of objects and the particular positions of each), (2) house dedication (including llama sacrifice), (3) offering a *mesa* (the most common, used in curing and in countering sorcery), and (4) animal-increase rites. Like the Quechua Indians, the Aymara wrap the ritual equipment in bundles consisting of a ground cloth (*inkuña*)—that is oriented to the east in all rituals—amulets, seashells, crucifixes, a rosary, religious medals, libation bowls, an incense burner, brass bells, brass spheres (symbolizing lightning), red beans, stuffed wildcats, and a piece of glass with a silver coin on it (symbolizing Lake Titicaca). Offerings include coca, alcohol, smoke (from incense or wild tobacco), llama fat, mint, candies, ají (hot chili peppers), salt, food, flowers, lead figurines (offered in pairs), a gold leaf, a silver leaf, and a llama fetus.

The phases of a session are almost identical to those of the Quechua

Figure 7-1. Aymara *mesa* used to summon spirits. Key: 1. Small brass bell. 2. and 4. Scallop shell, with a small bottle of red wine placed inside it. 3. Two small bone crucifixes. 5. Old rosary with two crucifixes and three religious medals. 6. Small square stone *mesa* with iron pyrites, representing gold, on top of it. 7. Small stone *mesa* to serve as a spirit seat. 8. Small square stone *mesa* with galena ore, representing silver, on top of it. 9. Piece of mirror glass covered by an old silver coin, representing Lake Titicaca. 10. and 11. Perforated round brass balls, representing lightning. 12. Three large scallop shells, each with a smaller one placed inside; these also serve as spirit seats. 13. Bivalve shell with the halves closed, containing a seed and a snail shell. (After Tschopik 1951: 263. Courtesy of American Museum of Natural History.)

ceremony: libations of alcohol (*t'inka*); arrangements of clusters of three coca leaves (*k'intu*), sometimes in groups of twelve totaling 144 (*p'awaqa*); preparation of the offering (*mesa*) until about midnight; burning of the offering; reading of the ashes, et cetera—interspersed by consumption of alcohol, coca chewing and divination, and ritual embraces of forgiveness. Andean dualistic ideology is implied in the fact that the right side of the *mesa* is associated with gold and is interpreted as good, while the left side, related to silver, is evil (Tschopik, 1951: 231, 253).* Also, in preparing the offering, the *mesa* for the spirits is divided in half by scratching a line down the center and arranging pairs of lead figurines along the sides, opposite each other (1951: 252). Another manifestation of dualism is indicated by the fact that during the session women are seated to the left of the *mesa*, and men to the right, all facing the doorway, which is oriented to the east (1951: 236, 253).

Recent ethnography among the Aymara of southern Peru documents the *mesa* as a symbolic expression of "mediated dualism" reminiscent of Eduardo's division of his *mesa* into three fields. Mayorga, Palacios, and Samaniego (1975) show that power objects on the right side of the *mesa* are associated with the sun, gold, day, human culture, and the present, while those on the left are associated with the moon, silver, night, nature, and the past. Also the right is related to the east (sunrise) and the north (the sun's position directly overhead at noon; the heavens); the left is related to the west (sunset) and the south (midnight and the Netherworld). A middle zone contains paired objects from both culture and nature, as well as a cross, a star (Venus), a snail shell, and lead figurines representing human couples. The writers interpret this central section as a mediating region containing the *Axis Mundi* (World Axis) of the *mesa*. In the section on the Incas we shall see that the expression of mediated dualism through the tripartite zoning of icons is derived from Inca cosmology.

Aymara shamans frequently claim to have been called to their profession by being struck by lightning. Hans and Judith-Maria Buechler (1971: 94-95), working in the Bolivian community of Compi, report on another way in which the shamanic "call" can manifest: through prolonged illness. Quintín, a shaman from the neighboring community of Capilaya, became a magician when he was well into his forties. Previously, while living in La Paz, he had become ill. He was hospitalized and experienced moderate improvement. Shortly thereafter his *compadre*, a diviner, revealed that Quintín's ailment was caused by supernatural forces, a sign that he should become a shaman. Quintín went to Compi and asked a magician to intercede on his behalf with the *achachila* (mountain spirit) of Kakape, a peak near Compi, in order to obtain permission to become a shaman. Too weak from his illness to walk,

---

*This is confirmed by the Bolivian Aymara themselves in an excellent ethnographic film about them, *Magic and Catholicism* (1975), made for the American Universities Field Staff by Hubert Smith.

Quintín began his journey up the mountain on a donkey. Halfway up he began to feel better and continued on foot. At the top of Kakape he was initiated with a sacrifice to the *achachila*. After that it was suggested that the new shaman confirm his position by making a pilgrimage to Oje, whose patron saint, Peter, is endowed with miraculous powers. However, the trip became unnecessary, for Quintín successfully performed a ceremony to protect the crops of Capilaya from hail. According to the Buechlers (1971: 95):

> Apart from the process of becoming a magician, Quintín's case also illustrates how modern medicine (represented by the La Paz hospital), Catholicism (the desirability of the magicians' endorsement by the image of Saint Peter in Oje), and magic are not considered to be incompatible but instead have complementary or reinforcing functions in an individual's life. Saint Peter may be called upon like any powerful mountain spirit to bestow magical powers on the individual. The fact that Quintín's health improved in the hospital did not lead him to doubt his *compadre*'s verdict that supernatural forces had brought about his illness.

For more information on Aymara beliefs and practices see Bandelier (1910), Bolton (1974), Frisancho (1973), La Barre (1948), Monast (1972), Oblitas (1963, 1971), Otero (1951), and Paredes (1963).

Cosmology

The work of Joseph Bastien (1973) in the Bolivian community of Kaata has done much to delineate the Andean model of the universe and the way in which it finds expression in ritual and ecological adaptation. The community of Kaata is the center of *ayllu* Kaata, a vertical land mass divided into high, center, and low ecological zones, each containing several communities. The highland communities of *ayllu* Kaata are inhabited by Aymara-speaking pastoral herders of alpacas, llamas, sheep, and pigs. The central communities are occupied by Quechua-speaking farmers who produce potatoes and barley. The lowest communities are inhabited by Quechua-speakers who grow corn and wheat. Ecological interdependence and resource exchange bind together the different levels of land and distant social groups of the *ayllu*. But since Inca times the people of this region, the *qollahuayas*, have been famous throughout the Andes as ritual and medical specialists. Bastien focuses on the ritual life of Kaata relating to a symbolic ordering between high, central, and low levels of land. He demonstrates that "ritual serves to make visible the connection between the levels, groups, and Kaatan history in such a way that the participants not only understand their *ayllu* but also create their *ayllu*." (1973: 16)

Kaatans conceptualize their *ayllu* as a metaphorical body, with the highland communities forming the head, the central communities composing the heart and bowels, and the lowest communities making up the legs. The highland head is *uma* ("head" in Quechua, "water" in Aymara)—the place of origins and return, where the dead go to complete the life cycle. It is the self-contained part from which many things in the *ayllu* originated, such as herbs and llamas. Sacrificial llamas come from the head and return there after their blood (life) and fat (power) are circulated through ritual to the other body parts. The sacrifice occurs in April during Fresh Earth Breaking, an agricultural ritual for the entire *ayllu* that brings together participants from the head (highlands) and legs (lowlands) at the heart and bowels (center—the two organs essential to blood and fat). Although the rite is mainly concerned with the crops of the central fields, the growth of the lower fields and the fertility of highland livestock are symbolically included. Bringing the llama from the place of origin, *uma,* and sprinkling its blood on the central fields symbolizes life being pumped from the center to the other body parts. A body with parts sharing the same blood and fat is the symbolic metaphor that holds *ayllu* Kaata together. Kaatans experience the wholeness of their social body the same way that they experience the wholeness of their physical bodies. As Bastien (1973: 218-19) puts it:

> The ritual shows that the individual's corporeal life is dependent upon the environmental life. The ritual symbolically circulates the blood to the ecological parts of the *ayllu* body, which in return assures the life within [the inhabitants'] own bodies by providing a good harvest. . . . Kaatans realize that they must physically, ritually circulate the fat and blood through all the parts, or they may wither just as plants do.

Kaatan curing ceremonies symbolically unite the three levels of the *ayllu* by bringing together ritual items obtained from each level and then "feeding" the spirits and *ayllu* shrines of each level with these offerings. The rites are governed by the path of the sun over the *ayllu,* which "constitutes a whole just as much as the reciprocity between the communities and ecological zones." (1973: 133). Since the *ayllu* faces the eastern slopes of the Andes, Kaatans conceptualize the sun as being born in the lower level, passing over the central level, and dying in the higher level. Bastien (1973: 133) explains how this orientation to the sun affects the ritual:

> The health mass will order its ritual activity first to the place where the sun dies, which is associated with the high level as well as the dead ancestors buried in this direction. The health mass feeds the dead ancestors in the west before midnight. From sunset to midnight, the sun is dying and passing underneath the *ayllu* Kaata from the top to the center level. For the second part of the ritual, the health mass will feed the *ayllu* shrines in the east and north after midnight, when the sun is passing underneath the *ayllu* from the center to the low level where it will be born. The high level is associated with the claim to land, and the low level is associated with the supply of food and birth of children. The two parts of the ritual symbolize two periods of time divided by midnight.

The dead ancestors are fed by spreading out three wads of black llama wool on a cloth. Twelve leaves of coca are placed on the wool and then covered by pig fat. The ingredients are wrapped by pulling the attached yarn ties tightly into a ball. The three balls are then placed in a fire on the west side of the house facing the ancestor-mummy sites and the place where the sun dies.

After midnight the shaman places four piles of cotton on another ritual cloth. They are dedicated to the lord of the inside of the house (female), the lord of the outside of the house (male), the lords of the season (governors of the agricultural year), and the lords of the *ayllu*. Twelve coca leaves and llama fat are placed on each pile. The four piles are then wrapped and placed in a fire burning in a rectangular adobe hole at the side of the supply house.

The last *mesa* is spread beginning about 2:00 A.M. At that time a staff and llama fetus, associated with the high areas, are placed at the head of the *mesa;* coca and carnations, associated with the low areas, are placed at the foot; bread and eggs, associated with the central region, are placed in the corners; and a coin, also associated with the central lands, is placed in the center. Then the shaman places shells dedicated to specific *ayllu* lords on the *mesa*. Each shell is filled with cotton, twelve coca leaves, carnation petals, llama fat, incense, dried ferns, lead figurines, candies, confetti, sugar, coin scrapings, and eggshells. In filling each row of shells the shaman moves from west to east, symbolically following the path of the sun as it dies in the west, is buried in the earth, and travels underneath the *ayllu* for rebirth in the east. Alcohol is poured into each shell, but this time the shaman moves from east to west along the rows in imitation of the sun's movement during the day. Once the shell offerings are prepared, they are consecrated to the *ayllu* lords and burned in a fire pot; the remains are placed in the adobe hole at the side of the supply house. The ritual terminates with entrail divination performed with a guinea pig.

Rituals to change bad luck are performed at the river, which is believed to wash away misfortunes and restore whatever is lacking. Bastien (1973: 251–52) explains how this works:

> The river is associated with different geographical places, periods of time, and social groups, as well as sickness, feuds, and loss of land. Another set of meanings is, however, associated with the river in the form of a continuous stream originating from and flowing to the original time and place (*uma pacha*). The river makes the body complete not only by washing it but by defining its boundaries. The river is forever returning what has been removed to make the body complete. . . .
>
> The river is a symbol of division, dissolution, and linear time, as well as a symbol of completeness, self-contained place, and restitutive time. The river is the exchange between this earth and the original time and place.

Kaatan cosmology is also reflected in the beliefs relating to funerals:

The burial rite emphasizes the journey of the dead to the *uma pacha.* The dead are merely traveling within the earth, the reverse of the fact that every living Kaatan is traveling above the earth. The living travel down the three levels of the *ayllu* in life, and they climb back up the *ayllu* in death. The sun goes above the *ayllu* during the day, and it travels underneath the *ayllu* during the night. As a result, both the living and the dead are actively involved in the processes of the universe. (1973: 263)

Once a year on November 2, the Feast with the Dead, the dead return to the *ayllu.* They are called back by the living at the end of the dry season when most of the decay and rest phases of the year are finished and the growth and work phases are about to start. At that time all beings and levels of the *ayllu* come to the center. Everyone prays for the dead, but the most effective prayers are those offered by the people from the highlands, who receive bread, made at the center, and *chicha,* made in the lowlands, for their prayers. The feast is conceptualized as a gathering of the dead from the lowlands with the ritualists from the highlands at the center. The dead are returning to the *Uma Pacha,* while the ritualists are originating. They meet at the center, where the higher and lower inhabitants are coming together for ritual and agricultural activity.

After death a person's soul must be fed by his relatives for the next three years during the Feast with the Dead until he completes the cycle by climbing up the three levels to the *Uma Pacha.* His relatives set up a *mesa tumbolo* (table for the dead) for him in the kitchen, where his soul can come to eat and visit for twenty-four hours from noon on November 1 to noon on November 2. The table, covered by a large black cloth, has three levels. The table's surface, representing the lowlands, holds typical produce of this level such as coca, apples, oranges, bananas, candy, and a glass of *chicha.* A platform placed on the surface of the table—covered with potatoes, other Andean tubers, beer, and breads—symbolizes the central level. A square wooden box holding a wicker basket from which protrude bread figurines of birds, llamas, ladders, fish, cows, babies, and flowers forms a third level, which symbolizes the "head" of the *ayllu.* Above the table is a cross decorated with flowers and a string of oranges, the latter representing suns journeying across the sky. The decorated cross symbolizes the heavens of the saints and the sun. Drawings possibly associated with the dead or the Devil are attached to the cloth and extend over the edges of the table. On the morning of November 2 the whole table is taken to the cemetery and placed over the grave, suggesting an association of the legs and underside of the table with the Netherworld.

The *mesa tumbolo* is a concrete representation of Kaatan cosmology, which views the world as divided into three places (*pachas*): Heaven (*Janaq Pacha*), This World (*Kay Pacha*), and the Netherworld (*Ura Pacha*). The heavens are inhabited by the sun, the staff (representing the Inca), gods, saints, and angels (the last three symbolized by the cross). Kaatan pictographs depict the cyclical sun with the staff, cross, and little sun within it, symbolizing the historical epochs of the *ayllu,* which are originating and returning to the *Uma Pacha.* The Netherworld, a region associated with shadows, the lowlands, and darkness, contains inhabitants from different epochs: the past dead associated with the ancestor mummies; the Devil of the Christian epoch; and the present dead of the last three years, who are climbing back to the *Uma Pacha.* The Feast with the Dead symbolically brings together the three worlds of the universe by dramatizing beliefs regarding the Devil, the ancestor mummies, the angels, and the saints.

Finally, Bastien (1973: 278) offers a summary statement that is particularly relevant to a clear understanding of Andean *mesa* symbolism in general:

> The dead [person's] table not only brings together the three levels of *ayllu* Kaata but also the heavens, this world, and the netherworld. The cosmological levels reinforce the *ayllu* levels, adding peripheral areas which symbolize a larger cosmology.

Enrique Oblitas (1963: 121-26) discusses the divinities inhabiting the *qollahuaya* cosmos. According to him the "Supreme Being who embraces all existence, visible and invisible," or the "compendium of the opposites," is *Tutujanawin.* The next major deity is *Pachaqaman,* "supreme day or light," who Oblitas compares to *Camac Pacha* (Lord Earth) of the Incas. *Pachaqaman's* son is *Pacha Tata* or *Inti,* the sun, whose main attribute is life-giving warmth. *Pachaqaman* has two daughters: *Pachamama,* Earth Mother, the wife of *Inti,* who governs life and movement; and *Oqa,* the moon, governess of the night, cold, and death. *Uwaro Khocha,* a culture hero and son of the sun, is compared to the Inca culture hero *Viracocha.* There is also a benevolent dwarf-god of happiness, the *Eqeqo,* who is contrasted with his dwarf-brother, the malevolent *Anchancho* (1963: 81-91). Oblitas (1963: 42, 90) suggests that the *Eqeqo,* governor of good luck and abundance, may be the mythical representation of the *machulas,* or mountain spirits (also known as *achachilas, chchalis, apus, auquis, jawaris,* and *jïrk'as*). Finally, there is the underworld demon or dragon, the *Supay,* who is engaged in a constant struggle against man, *Pachamama,* and the mountain spirits (1963: 60-63).

Regarding *qollahuaya* ideology, Oblitas (1963: 50) explains what he calls "the doctrine of the opposites," which is yet another example of Andean dualism:

> The *qollahuaya* concept of existence resides in the equilibrium produced by the opposing forces that constitute the universe. If the world were not dominated by the two forces or currents that produce its stability, it could not exist. . . . Therefore, good opposes evil; the day, the night; health, sickness; integration, disintegration. According to this doctrine, two forces constantly struggle in the universe: one that tries at all costs to maintain the stability of matter and another that tries to destroy it.

INCA

Shamanism and *Mesas*

Discussing shamanic practitioners during Inca times, Rowe (1946: 302–304, 312–14) describes the specialists associated with divination, curing, and sorcery. Divination was used to diagnose disease, locate lost property, identify hostile sorcerers, and settle doubtful questions. In addition to the specialists mentioned above, there was a class of shamans (*omo*) who claimed to speak directly with the spirits at night and were consulted to find lost or stolen articles or to learn what was happening at a distance. Some of these shamans were reported to mix *vilca* (*Anadenanthera colubrina*) with *chicha* (fermented corn beer) to induce trance. Other methods of divination involved the use of fire, coca, and sacred stones, as well as observation of the movements of animals and interpretation of omens and dreams. Finally, it was believed that stumbling, twitching of the eyelid, lip, or another body part, or humming in the ears indicated that the affected person was going to receive a message: good, if it was on the right side of the body, bad if it was on the left.

Disease was believed to be caused by supernatural beings angered by sin or neglect of their cult; by sorcery; by exposure to evil forces residing in certain springs or winds; or by soul loss resulting from sudden fright. Sickness could take the form of a foreign object lodged in the body, displacement of the organs, or poison. A wide variety of herbal remedies was known and applied, but always for magical reasons.

Curers were called *hampi kamayoq* (medicine specialists), *kamasqa* ("cured"), or *sonqoyoa* (heart men). They were also diviners, and some may have practiced sorcery in secret. Curing power was acquired in a vision or by making an unusually quick recovery from severe illness (as in the case of the *kamasqa*). The curer treated a patient with the help of the spirit which had appeared in his vision to give him the necessary power and instruments.

In treatment, the curer first divined the cause of the ailment. In a case of religious neglect the patient was given several colors of maize flour mixed with ground seashells to blow in the direction of the *huacas* (religious shrines) with a prayer. Then he offered coca to the sun and bits of gold and silver to *Viracocha*, the Creator. If the patient's ancestors were angry, he was ordered to set food on their tombs and make a libation of *chicha*. If the sick person could walk, he was expected to wash himself with white maize flour at the junction of two rivers. When illness was caused by displacement of internal organs or intrusion of a foreign object, the healer massaged and sucked the injured area until he produced the causative agent by sleight of hand. Shamans were consulted in cases of poison and black magic. There are reports of surgery with crystal knives. Trepanning of the skull was also practiced. Shamans used the principles of sympathetic and contagious magic—

that is, production of an image containing something that belongs to the victim which is subsequently cursed and abused, or burial of a tortured toad in a place where the victim is likely to sit. Shamans also provided love charms for a price.

A special class of shamans, the *ichuri* (grass men) from Collao (home of the ancestors of the Aymara), heard confessions of sin, imposed penances, and purified those who sought their services. Sin had a community connotation throughout ancient Peru, for unconfessed sins were believed to exert a blighting effect on the social group. Thus these practitioners were consulted frequently. Penance and purification took place on riverbanks. The penitent confessed in secret into a bunch of *ichu* grass. Then he transferred the sin to the grass by spitting on it. The grass (and the sin) were thrown into the water, to be carried far from the reach of humanity. A ceremonial bath in the water completed purification.

Finally, mention should be made of an Inca precursor of the modern *curandero*. According to Father Martín de Murúa (1946: 155-56), who wrote in 1590:

> The Incas had some doctors or philosophical diviners called *Guacacue* who went around naked in isolated, gloomy places of the region . . . and walking alone in the deserts without rest or tranquility they dedicated themselves to divination or philosophy. From sunrise to sunset they looked at the solar disk with great firmness, no matter how fiery it was, without moving their eyes. . . . They said that in that splendid fiery disk they saw and attained great secrets. . . . All day they stood on the burning sands without feeling pain; and they also suffered with patience the cold and snow [of the highlands]. They lived a very pure, simple way of life . . . and they did not covet anything beyond what reason and nature demanded. Their sustenance was very easy, they did not pursue what sagacity, covetousness, and appetite look for in all elements — only what the earth produced without being mistreated by iron [sowing and reaping]. . . . [T]hus they carried their *mesas de manjares* [tables of refreshments which recruit the spirits]; and as a result of this, among them there were no ailments or diverse sicknesses, rather they had perfect health and died at a very old age.

This gives us the first inkling of a pre-Columbian concept of *mesa*, the pivot of Andean *curandero* therapy today in Peru. It appears that the *Guacacue*, like spiritual ascetics the world over, lived on wild roots and herbs. Although Murúa — in typical sixteenth-century theological style — seems to be referring to food of the soul when he mentions *mesas,* the fact that he says that these philosophers "carried" their *mesas* seems to imply a physical artifact or artifacts of ritual or symbolic import. Even if this is not the case, it is still significant that the word *mesa* is used to denote the concept of spiritual food.

Cosmology

Scattered elements of contemporary Andean *curanderismo* are directly traceable to a pre-Columbian aboriginal world view, the last systematic version of which was formulated by the Incas and recorded by the Spanish chroniclers. Valcárcel (1959: 136–38) gives us an insightful summary of Andean cosmology as inherited by the Incas, drawn from the ethnohistorical sources. The world (*pacha*: space, time) was divided into three vertical planes: the Underworld or Inner World (*Uchu Pacha*) of the dead and of seeds, both referred to by the term *mallqui*; the earth's surface (*Cay Pacha*), inhabited by human beings, animals, plants, and spirits; and the Upper World (*Janan Pacha*), occupied by the deified Sun and Moon (considered to be married siblings, like the Inca and his wife, *Coya*), the stars (which were the guardians of humanity, animals, and plants), the lightning, the rainbow, and other gods. Communication between the surface of the earth and the Underworld was achieved through the *pacarinas*—caves, volcanic craters, springs, and lagoons—which were the places of origin of all life in this world. Within the Inca Empire communication between earth and the Upper World was realized through the Inca, son of the sun but born on the earth, which made him an apt intermediary between the human and the divine. His means of communication was the rainbow, which was represented on the royal coat of arms.

Valcárcel relates an ancient legend referring to two mythical serpents who operated on all three levels of the universe. They both began in the Underworld. When they reached this world one of them, *Yacu Mama*, crawled and was converted into the Ucayali River, mother of the rivers. The second serpent, *Sacha Mama*, had two heads, walked upright, and was like an aged tree. Upon reaching the Upper World, the first serpent turned into lightning; he was now called *Illapa* and was god of the storm, thunder, and rain. The two-headed serpent turned into the rainbow (*Coichi*), the deity that fertilizes and gives color to the earth and all living things. Thus the three worlds were united by these serpent gods of water and fertility.

Another myth inherited by the Incas, and one that supplemented the legend of the two serpents, described the activities of *Viracocha*, the Creator. After causing a great flood to destroy his first creation (earth and sky without light, and giants fashioned from stone), *Viracocha* brought forth the sun, moon, and stars from an island in Lake Titicaca, the primordial *pacarina* (place of origin). After fashioning men and animals out of clay, he is said to have traveled north, accompanied by two sons and following the main chain of the Andes (actually this would be northwest), calling forth the people from their *pacarinas*. When his work was finished he disappeared across the Pacific "like foam on the sea," promising to return. Zuidema (1971: 39) demonstrates the relationship between the legend of the two snakes and the solar myth of *Viracocha*:

> *Viracocha* created in the East, from a lake high in the mountains; he went over
> the Earth to the Ocean and disappeared in the West. His movement was like
> water in a river from a lake in Heaven to the Ocean under the Earth. . . .
> *Viracocha* was the prime Mover in the Cosmos of the Sun's daily route through
> Heaven and through the Underworld back again. Water was the symbol of this
> movement, especially the water from Heaven that went back to the Ocean.

It seems that the sun also provided the model for the horizontal dimension
of the world, as reflected in the division of Cuzco (meaning navel or center)
and the empire (Tahua-ntin-suyo, "Land of the Four Parts") into four
ceremonial "quarters": Antisuyo, eastern (approximately); Chinchaysuyo,
northern; Contisuyo, western; and Collasuyo, southern. Religious shrines
(*huacas*) located along lines (*zeques*) radiating out from the Temple of the
Sun were assigned to each quarter. According to Valcárcel (1959: 109-110),
anti (as in Antisuyo) refers to the region where the sun rises, and *conti* (as in
Contisuyo) to the region where it sets. Chinchaysuyo received its name from
the Chinchay constellation to the north (believed to be a feline that
periodically devoured the sun and moon). Collasuyo was named after the
Colla peoples of the south (the contemporary Aymara), but it also means
"thing come out of the water." This is most appropriate since Lake Titicaca,
the place where the Creator, *Viracocha*, brought forth the sun, moon, and
stars, falls in Collasuyo. In addition, this region is the source of many major
rivers. It is interesting to note that Cuzco, following the Andes as did
Viracocha, is built with its long axis running roughly southeast-northwest.
Thus it appears that the biannual journey of *Viracocha*, "the Sun behind the
sun," from sunrise in the southeast (site of the "thing come out of the water")
during the December 21 solstice to sunset in the northwest (where the ocean
and the Chinchay feline "swallow" the sun prior to its return journey) during
the June 21 solstice established the mythic paradigm for the solar cosmology
of the Inca "children of the sun."

Some support for this contention is provided by the fact that the Temple of
the Sun (*Coricancha*, Golden Enclosure) in Lower Cuzco was located near
the southeast end of the southeast-northwest axis along which the city was
aligned. Also, the Indian chronicler Guaman Poma (1966: 119-20) informs
us that the Incas viewed the sun as following a circular route, starting at its
southern "seat" at the beginning of the year, taking six months to its northern
seat, and returning to its starting point in another six months. Thus we see
that for the Incas each solar year was a reenactment of the cyclical "return to
origins" as first performed by *Viracocha* in the beginning.

On the back wall behind and above the main altar of the Temple of the
Sun was a graphic depiction of the Inca cosmos, drawn by the native
chronicler Juan de Santacruz Pachacuti-Yamqui (see figures 7-2-a and
7-2-b). Lehmann-Nitsche (1928) analyzed this drawing, providing us with
an interpretation of the cosmology portrayed on the wall of the *Coricancha*.

In the Inca cosmogram, cult objects were arranged along three vertical

lines. The right line (from the point of view of the actors, in this case the
deities) was composed of masculine icons. From the top of the wall to the bottom these were: the golden sun; grandfather Venus (the morning star); the
stars of the clear night skies of the dry summer season; Lord Earth (*Camac
Pacha*), including the mountains and inner earth (*Pacha Mama*), encom-
passed by the rainbow and drained by the Pilcomayo River (the legendary
place of origin of the Incas), with serpentine lightning off to one side; and
seven "eyes of abundance" (the Pleiades) protecting the granary (*colca*). The
left line was made up of feminine icons: the silver moon, wife of the sun; the
clouds of the rainy winter season; grandmother Venus (the evening star);

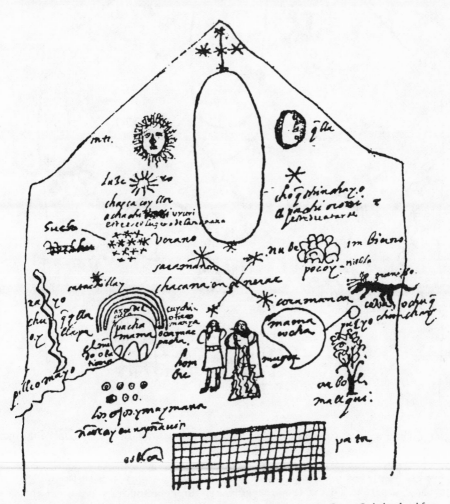

Figure 7-2-a.   Inca cosmology as depicted in *Coricancha*. (Original. After
Pachacuti 1950: 226.)

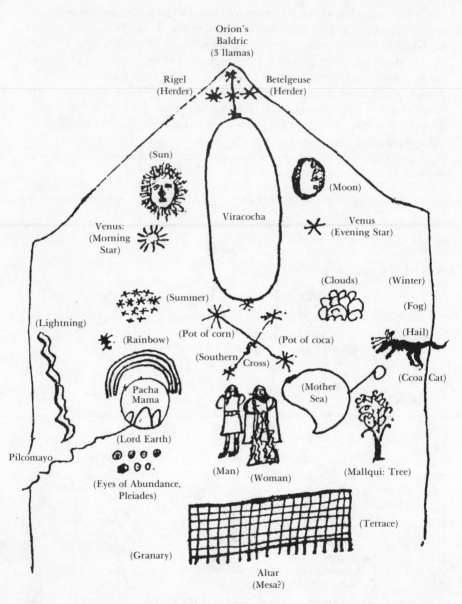

Figure 7-2-b. Inca cosmology as depicted in *Coricancha*. (Redrawn with translations.)

Mother Sea (Lake Titicaca), connected to a spring (*puqyo*), with the hail-causing supernatural cat (*choquechinchay*, the contemporary *ccoa*) off to one side emitting hail from his eyes; and a *mallqui* tree or seedling (symbolizing the ancestors) growing out of the agricultural terrace (*pata*).

At the top of the central line were five stars in the form of a cross. There were the three stars of the baldric of Orion accompanied by Rigel to the right and Betelgeuse to the left. The five stars were interpreted by the Incas as a train of three male llamas with a herder on each side. Below the stars was a golden ovaloid disk representing *Viracocha*—the bisexual supreme Creator, as well as a culture hero. Under the "cosmic egg" of Viracocha was the Southern Cross, regarded as a hearth of crossed poles. It may have provided the pattern for the four quarters of Cuzco and the empire. Two stars at the ends of the long diagonal axis of the cross were labeled by Pachacuti: The one in the upper right was a pot of corn, the other in the lower left was a pot of coca. This union of food plants and magical flora dominated the central portion of the entire cosmogram. Below the Southern Cross was another union, this time between man (on the right) and woman (on the left). Finally, at the bottom of the central line was the *mesa*-like main altar of the temple, which symbolized both the storehouse of agricultural produce (*colca*) and the agricultural terrace (*pata*) referred to earlier. Thus opposite poles (sky, earth) were depicted at the top and bottom of the drawing. Androgynous *Viracocha*, source of the male and female hierarchies, assured the fertility of the herds, the human realm, and the plant kingdom (agricultural and medicinal). Also, in addition to establishing the celestial yearly journey of the sun, the Creator governed the end points (sowing and reaping) of the terrestrial agricultural cycle. As Isbell (1976: 40) expresses it: "The creator god is the origin and generator of all and the *colcas* are the end product of the procreative process. Together they form a closed system—the beginning and end of the reproductive cycle."

Zuidema (1969: 20, 22) discusses three mediators in Pachacuti's version of Inca cosmology: (1) the *choquechinchay* cat, an aspect of Venus, who emerges from the Underworld and ascends to the heavens to secure abundance from the Upper World; (2) the lightning, another aspect of Venus, who descends from the Upper World to the earth (and, we might add, as the *Yacu Mama* serpent flows back to the Underworld in the form of the Pilcomayo, red river); and (3) the two-headed *Sacha Mama* serpent-rainbow mediating between the earth and the sky. Since the rainbow emerges from springs (*puqyos*), entrances to the Underworld, it probably also communicates with this lower region. Thus these three supernatural entities unite the three levels of the Inca cosmos. In addition, as Isbell (1976: 40) points out, the female elements are associated with upward movement whereas the male relate to downward movement. Also "movement (the lightning) is a manifestation of male energy, while a still body of water (a lake or the sea) and the inside of the earth are feminine nurturance concepts."

John Earls and Irene Silverblatt (1976) offer an insightful interpretation of the different levels of Pachacuti's drawing. First, *Viracocha* expresses the entire universe, totality, eternity, the unity of all spatial and temporal dimensions. The separation of the sun and the moon creates a dualistic cosmos at the highest level, establishing the basic order of space and time. Then the two manifestations of Venus establish the celestial order in greater detail on the level of the stars, the constellations of which provide the patterns for all natural and social life, such as plants, animals, and social classes. The next level, the terrestrial, is manifest through the interaction of earth (Lord Earth on the male side) and water (Mother Sea on the female side). The union of man and woman establishes the family, the basic unit of the social sphere. Finally, the interaction of the natural and social domains results in agricultural production symbolized by the *mesa*-altar at the bottom of the diagram.

In order to explain the dynamic of the terrestrial level of the universe, Earls and Silverblatt refer to the contemporary conceptions of the *amaru,* which, as we saw in the section on Quechua cosmology, manifests as water, the mediator between sky and earth. They contend that the *amaru* is an ambiguous underworld deity, a bridge between categories capable of taking on a variety of forms: bull, pig, cat, snake, lightning, and probably the rainbow. It provides a metaphorical explanation of the annual hydrographic cycle in the Andes. Today it is believed that during the rainy season the *ccoa* cat emerges from highland springs (*puqyos*) in the form of clouds. Near the end of the dry season the *amaru* serpent gushes forth from the springs and into the irrigation canals in the form of a flow of water, mud, and stones. It also manifests as the lightning that announces the arrival of the first downpours of the rainy season.

The authors show that these concepts are depicted in Pachacuti's diagram. On the left side the *choquechinchay* cat is seen arising from the *puqyo* in the form of clouds during the winter (rainy season). On the right we see lightning in association with a flow of water (the Pilcomayo) and the summer (dry season). Also on this side we see how the rainbow unites *Camac Pacha* (the contemporary *Roal,* who is called *Camac*) and *Pacha Mama*. As the authors express it:

> On this . . . terrestrial level . . . the "parents" of humanity . . . seem to represent a concept of "Viracocha" on a minor scale. In general, particular mountains are masculine concepts (*wamanis, apus,* et cetera) and the earth in its totality (the *Pacha Mama*) is feminine. . . . [I]t is the circulation of water from the inside toward the outside to return inside again that unifies them in a total dynamic. (1976: 15)

From this we can see that the Inca cosmogram depicted the diurnal, seasonal, and stellar rhythms of nature and the elements, along with their negative and positive effects on the interdependent network of life shared on this earth by human beings, plants, and animals.

As we noted at the beginning of this review of Inca cosmology, fragments of this unified world view can still be found in contemporary Andean folk healing. Among both the Aymara and the Quechua, lightning is the medium by which the shaman receives his call. In the case of the Quechua shaman, the *ccoa* cat, whose eyes emit hail like the Inca *choquechinchay* cat, is the supernatural being who strikes the novice with lightning. Also, the cat is closely related to fertility in Aymara shamanism, as evidenced by the numerous feline symbols used in animal-increase rites. We have seen how the supernatural cat and serpent unify the three levels of the cosmos today much as they did among the Inca. One of the most graphic examples of the survival of pre-Columbian cosmology can be found in the ritual artifacts set up by Aymara diviners from Chucuito, as reported by Tschopik (figure 7-1). If we view this ceremonial layout from the point of view of the actors (the deities), there is a pattern that approximates the Inca cosmogram as follows:

CHUCUITO		*CORICANCHA*		
Crosses (3)*		Cross		
Rosary (5)		Sun	Viracocha Oval	Moon
Gold (6)	Silver (8)			
		Lightning	Lake Titicaca	
Lightning (10,11)	Lake Titicaca (9)			

*Numbers correspond to figure 7-1.

This correlation is not too surprising, for many of the Incas' cosmological concepts were borrowed from their southern neighbors, the Colla or Aymara.

The most striking parallel between Inca cosmology and contemporary *mesas* is in the tripartite zoning of icons to express an ideology of mediated dualism. We find the dualistic philosophy of benevolent right/malevolent left among both the Quechua, where it manifests as right star/left star, and the Aymara, where it is found as golden sun/silver moon. (The latter dichotomy is also implicit in Quechua *mesas.*) However, among both peoples it appears that in *mesa* rituals the opposites are rendered complementary through the mediation of a "third term"—whether it be the *pampa* between the *paña* and *lloque* of Quechua *mesas* or the central mediating section of the Aymara. This seems to have been the case in Pachacuti's drawing, in which the central line mediates between male icons headed by the golden sun disk on the right and female icons headed by the silver moon on the left. Isbell (1976: 38) argues, in fact, that the central line depicts "the realization of the combination of male and female elements—the necessary synthesis for procreation and regeneration." Her work describes the principle of "sexual complementarity" as an essential and enduring element in Andean cosmology manifesting in contemporary children's drawings, social organization, and concepts of time and space. As we saw in the last chapter, Eduardo's power objects also give expression to a complementarity of opposites manifest through the three fields of his *mesa*.

⊹ ⊹ ⊹

From the foregoing we can see that the *mesa* complex is found throughout
Peru and Bolivia, and seems to be a ritual expression of Andean cosmology.
The comparative data summarized in appendix A show that *mesas* are found
in many parts of highland Latin America. Appendix B synthesizes our
knowledge of the native cosmologies in this region. A review of the latter information shows a remarkable similarity, which I believe is due to the fact
that aboriginal New World cosmologies are rooted in what Americanist
scholars refer to as an archaic substratum, forming the underlying basis of
American Indian ideology and perhaps ultimately traceable to shamanistic
Old World Paleolithic and Mesolithic hunting and gathering religion. There
is probably much yet to be discovered in the ethnohistorical literature that
can help Americanists define more precisely the nature of the archaic
substratum. A great deal can be retrieved by careful ethnographic studies in
Indian (and even *mestizo*) communities, and by ethnological comparison.
But one thing is certain: Today, wherever a shaman sets up his *mesa,* the
place it occupies is not just another patch of ground. It is *the* sacred space on
the cosmic terrain. To the casual observer it may appear ephemeral and temporary; but to the native practitioner it is perennial and rooted.

8

Sacred Time: The Seasons
of the Séance

APOCALYPSE: CHARTER MYTH
FOR POWER BALANCE

A night healing session provides the proper environment for the activation of the *curandero*'s "vision" and his manipulation of the forces of the *mesa* in order to solve the patients' problems. There are two parts to the session: ceremony and curing.* The ceremonial division lasts from about 10:00 P.M. until midnight and consists of a series of prayers, rituals, and *tarjos* (songs interspersed with whistling) performed to the rhythmic beat of the *curandero*'s rattle. At periodic intervals, as explained previously, a mixture of boiled San Pedro cactus and black tobacco juice is "raised," or imbibed through the nostrils, first by the *curandero* and his two assistants, later by patients and accompanying friends or relatives. In addition to "clearing the mind," the raising ritual activates the symbolic zones ("fields") and associated magical numbers of the *mesa* as well as the San Pedro brew itself and the curing powers of the healer.

The first division of the séance terminates at midnight, when all present drink a cup of pure San Pedro infusion. The purpose of this ceremonial division of the session is to invoke the forces of nature and guardian spirits, to balance the opposing forces operating within man and the cosmos, to make the patients susceptible to therapy, and to focus the *curandero*'s "vision" on the problems at hand.

The phases of the ceremonial division of the séance can be summarized as follows:

Opening prayers and invocations lead to the activation (by raising) of the

---

The first subsection of this chapter was originally presented as a paper read at the Ninth International Congress of Anthropological and Ethnological Sciences, Chicago, 1973.

*Appendix B provides a detailed description of the entire séance based on my observations and Eduardo's explanations of taped replays.

"center," or "axis," associated with the number 7—the crucifix. The raising is done by the *curandero* and his two assistants.

Next, the right side of the *mesa*, associated with the forces of good and the number 12, is activated, again by the curer and his assistants.

Then the mediating Middle Field, associated with the number 25, is activated by the two assistants. In this process the smaller left side of the *mesa*, associated with the forces of evil and the number 13, is also brought to life.

After this the two assistants and all participants activate the energizing forces of the San Pedro brew through a raising ritual. Then the assistants raise the *curandero*—that is, imbibe San Pedro and tobacco, taking positions on either side of him. This allows the shaman to give the San Pedro brew a final raising himself and to initiate its consumption at midnight.

Finally the *curandero* cleanses all participants in the séance, including himself, by rubbing his rattle over their bodies.

Eduardo's shorthand formula for the linear, numerical build-up of power involved in activating the "accounts" of the *mesa* is: 3 + 4 = 7 + 5 = 12 + 12 + 1 = 25. He gives the following explanation for this formula:

> The number 3 [represents] the Trinity of Christianity, the three planes of the cosmos (Hell, Earth, and Heaven), the pyramid, the triangle, and the tripartite division of man into body, mind, and spirit; 4 [represents] the four winds [the four cardinal points], the four roads [the diagonal lines crossing the *mesa* through its central crucifix], and the four elements of nature [earth, water, air, and fire]; 7 [represents] the seven justices [miracles] of Christ, the seven seas, the seven rungs of Jacob's ladder, the seven virgins, the seven churches of early Christianity, the seven seals on the book of life mentioned in Revelation, the seven angels, the seven planets, the seven martyrs, the seven metals, the seven capital sins, the seven spirits, the seven hours required for the preparation of San Pedro before the session, the seven somersaults [I] perform to exorcise attacking evil spirits in serious crises during the curing acts. [The number] 5 [represents] the five senses of man and the four corners of the *mesa* united to the crucifix by means of the four roads; 12 [represents] the twelve disciples (with Judas replaced by Paul), the twelve hours of the day, the twelve signs of the zodiac, the twelve months of the year, "completion," unity, and the *Campo Justiciero;* 13 [12 + 1 in the formula] [represents] the eleven loyal disciples plus Paul and Judas, and the *Campo Ganadero;* 25 [represents] the twenty-five accounts of the *Campo Medio* [in which polar opposites are united].

In phase 9 of the ceremonial acts (see appendix B)—raising the twenty-five and the two hundred fifty thousand accounts of the *Campo Medio*—the balancing of the forces of evil or darkness included in the number 25 involves a skillful power play. According to *curandero* folklore, Saint Paul—the great lawyer of Christianity who replaced Judas, thus restoring balance to the "incomplete" ranks of the eleven disciples by making their number the "complete" 12—gathers the positive forces of the *Campo Justiciero* (particularly the Virgin of Mercy, patron of the military forces of Peru, and Saint Michael, commander of the celestial armies). Then, through the balancing power of the *Campo Medio,* he moves into the *Campo Ganadero* to remove Judas temporarily from the domain of Satan. The rationale behind this process is that Judas, as one who has fallen from grace, has a certain affinity with the forces of light despite his residence in hell. This makes him the most likely candidate to serve as "informer" regarding the evils performed in the *Campo Ganadero,* which he knows so well. But the power of the number 12, by itself and as part of the number 13 that governs the *Campo Ganadero* (i.e., 12 + 12 + 1 = 25), is required to concentrate enough force to perform this balancing act.

At the same time that the Middle Field and the sinistral side of the *mesa* come to life, something is happening to Eduardo. For, as we recall, the *mesa* is a projection of his inner power. A clue regarding this psychological transformation is provided by the fact that Eduardo abstains from raising the all-important number 25. His abstinence occurs because one of the most important mediating artifacts of the *Campo Medio,* Eduardo's spiritual alter ego (the herb jar), is activated as a result of the raising performed by his two assistants. By abstaining, Eduardo is able to be on guard throughout the dangerous process of activating the negative forces of the *Campo Ganadero.* Another reason for abstaining is that the operation involves the raising of his own soul. This vital activity can be best accomplished by his assistants, since they are capable of being more objective about a process which includes the activation of the *curandero*'s own capacity for evil as projected onto the *Campo Ganadero.* This part of his being is kept under control by the balancing action of the *Campo Medio.*

But control is not enough. The *curandero*'s capacity for evil must be recognized and integrated into his personality. This is symbolically achieved later in the session (phase 12) when the two assistants raise their master's corporeal self as he holds his activated alter ego. They thus "center" the *curandero* and establish their capacity to do this for the patient later on in the curing rituals.

Once both his alter ego and his corporeal self are raised, the *curandero* is finally in a position to "complete," or integrate, himself by raising the San Pedro infusion and then drinking it at the twelfth hour of clock time, midnight. At the same time he "charges" the San Pedro, which is the energy source of the *mesa.* This culmination of events leads to activation of all his personal powers at the birth of a new day, realized by balancing the opposing forces of the microcosmic *mesa* and—by extension—of his own psyche.

There seems to be an apocalyptic undertone to this number symbolism and repetitive increase of sacred power. A review of the mystical experiences of St. John the Divine contained in Revelation (the New Testament) confirms this. For example, the idea of the four winds and the four cardinal points, although it has Indian antecedents, probably received some reinforcement from the following passage:

> And after these things I saw four angels standing on the four corners of the earth, holding the four winds of the earth, that the wind should not blow on the earth, nor on the sea, nor on any tree. (Rev. 6:1)

In Revelation there are also four beasts—a lion, a calf, an animal with a man's face, and a flying eagle—corresponding to the Four Evangelists around the throne of God, which provides a central fifth point, like the crucifix of the *mesa* in relation to the four cardinal points. We also have the Four Horsemen of the New Testament Apocalypse: war, destruction, hunger, and death.

The number 7 is found throughout Revelation: the seven churches of early Christianity symbolized by seven golden candlesticks surrounding Christ, seven stars in Christ's right hand symbolizing the seven angels of the seven churches, the seven seals on the book of life as held by the seventh angel, the seven angels with seven trumpets who usher in the Millennium, seven plagues, the red dragon with seven heads and crowns, and the seven-headed beast from the sea. But the following passage gives us a clear indication of the number's use in association with Christ, the sacrificed Lamb of Christianity:

> And I beheld, and lo, in the midst of the throne and of the four beasts and in the midst of the elders, stood a Lamb as it had been slain, having seven heads and seven eyes, which are the seven spirits of God sent forth into all the earth. (Rev. 5:6)

The following passage may indicate where the idea of multiplying the accounts of the *mesa* by thousands comes from (see appendix B):

> And I beheld, and I heard the voice of many angels round about the throne and the beasts and the elders: and the number of them was ten thousand times ten thousand, and thousands and thousands. (Rev. 5:11)

Twelve is very clearly an important number associated with "completion" or salvation, for Jerusalem, the holy city in Heaven promised to the elect after the Millennium, embodies the number: twelve gates (three at each cardinal point), associated with twelve pearls, guarded by twelve apostles, and named after the twelve tribes of Israel; twelve foundations of twelve precious stones named after the twelve apostles; and a wall twelve thousand furlongs in length, height, and breadth. In addition, at the end of Revelation the Tree of Life, nurtured by the water of the River of Life flowing from the throne of God, has twelve fruits that are replenished every month. A power build-up is associated with the number 12 when it is squared (12 × 12) and multiplied in reference to the 144,000 elect (see appendix B). This is the number of servants of God, marked on their foreheads with the seal of the living God by a fifth angel ascending in the east from among the four angels at the four corners of the earth just before the destruction of the world. Finally, we have twenty-four elders surrounding the throne of God, who provides the central, "balanced" number 25, the sacred number governing the Middle Field.

Thus the Apocalypse provides the charter myth for the ceremonial division of the séance, which consists of a linear, balanced power build-up. The power accumulated is then applied to patients in the second part of the session, the curing division, which lasts from midnight until about 6:00 A.M. This phase of the séance consists of cyclical curing acts.

During the curing division, each person present must take a turn before the *mesa* while the *curandero* chants a song in his or her name. Then everyone concentrates on the staffs and swords placed upright in the ground at the head of the *mesa*. One of these artifacts is supposed to vibrate, since it embodies the forces affecting the patient. It is given to the patient to hold in the left hand over the chest while the *curandero* chants the song of the staff to activate its account and cause its powers to manifest. While everyone now concentrates on the patient, the *curandero* begins a long divinatory discourse in which he relates what he "sees." Sometimes others present see the same things. According to Eduardo, the purpose of the discourse is to allow the patient's subconscious to release whatever blockages are causing the problem. Once the discourse is terminated, two assistants (one on each side of the patient) "raise" the patient from foot to waist, waist to neck, and neck to crown with a liquid provided by the *curandero* (usually the San Pedro and tobacco mixture, but other liquids—often a perfume—may be chosen). While this is going on, the curer chants a final song. Then the patient must nasally imbibe a liquid provided by the *curandero* while holding the staff by one end over his or her head. (This is called "raising the staff.") Finally, an assistant or the *curandero* rubs the patient with the staff, sprays it orally with a perfume, and returns it to the head of the *mesa*.

After all present have had a turn before the *mesa*, the *curandero* closes the account with a final invocation to the four winds and four roads combined with a ritual purification of the *mesa*—performed by spraying it twelve times with substances from the *Campo Justiciero*. Thus the number 12 associated with Christ can be seen as an apt symbol for completion ("I am Alpha and Omega, the beginning and the end"—Rev. 1:8). Before departing, each person is orally sprayed with a mixture of water, lime, white cornmeal, white flowers, white sugar, and lime juice. The *curandero* collects his artifacts, then makes the form of a cross in the ground where the *mesa* stood, and sprinkles the four corners of the area and the outlines of the cross with the same white cornmeal mixture.

Analysis of the structure of the curing séance reveals the symbolic expression of Eduardo's major goal: balance of power. Through ritual and the mediation of the Middle Field, the opposing forces of the *mesa* — and of the *curandero* — are activated and brought into meaningful, balanced interaction. The power generated by the ritual manipulation of power objects is then applied in solving patients' problems. The creative synthesis of aboriginal shamanism and Christian symbolism manifest in Eduardo's art seems to be directly relevant to those who seek his services.

THE METAPHYSICAL CLOCK

An important aspect of every séance Eduardo conducts is the manner in which he handles time. As we have noted, each session is divided into two carefully delineated divisions, each of which has its allotted time. Watching Eduardo move systematically through the phases of the night ritual and through his solitary vigil, one forms the impression that he is ticking off the hours on an inner "metaphysical clock." Discussion of this matter with Eduardo elicited the following comments:

> In every curing act or *mesa* or session . . . *curanderos* activate the accounts at 10:00, when they begin to work, until midnight, when the accounts begin to work. Then one "accounts" from midnight until 3:00 A.M., when the "charms" begin to work, and on through 6:00 A.M. under the eye of the sun, to noon, when the account turns over in following the path of the sun. The reason for this is that the session equals the cycle of life of the day. For the passage of a day is a cycle of life that is departing, a cycle of life that has to be borne in mind in order to work and live and reproduce the "charm" of intelligence and the future of the accounts. . . . One accounts according to the hour. . . . Even mathematics enters into this, for all time and the excursion within time is mathematics.

In further conversation, Eduardo elaborated on the above. He said that a new account begins at noon, the time when the San Pedro brew is put on the fire to simmer for seven hours. Sometimes Eduardo takes a nap before a session, during which he may experience dreams that provide hints for therapy in the forthcoming séance. As a general rule he sets up the *mesa* on the ground between 9:00 and 10:00 P.M. Eduardo says that the power build-up from 10:00 P.M. to midnight "charges" the *mesa,* while curing rituals "discharge" the *mesa.* The "charms" begin to work sometime between 2:00 and 3:00 A.M. Between 4:00 and 6:00 A.M. the ritual ends and Eduardo must pick up his *mesa.* The rays of the morning sun must not shine on the "deactivated" *mesa,* since the hours from 6:00 A.M. until noon are a dangerous period during which Eduardo maintains a vigil. Usually he stays awake during this vigil, but occasionally he may sleep in order to be guided by his dreams. Thus for Eduardo a séance consists of more than the night session participated in by assistants, patients, friends, and relatives. It is a complete

24-hour cycle, beginning and ending at noon, when the sun reaches its zenith. In short, it is a cyclical dramatization in time of aboriginal cosmology, just as the *mesa* artifacts are a demarcation in space of the native *imago mundi*. The fact that the word *mesa* refers to the spatial conglomeration of ritual power objects as well as to the temporal ritual itself reflects one of the major characteristics of aboriginal cosmology, noted in chapter 7: Time and space (*pacha*) are intimately related.

Obviously, the sun provides the celestial model for the "metaphysical clock." But that is only half of the story. It must be remembered that all the most important phases of the 24-hour cycle occur at night, when the sun is not visible, and that the *mesa* artifacts must not be touched by the "eye of the sun." The earthly model for this vital half of the metaphysical clock is provided by the magical plants, especially *the* major plant, the night-blooming San Pedro.

The important position of the magical plants in *curandero* lore is revealed by the many ways in which plant analogies are used to express vital concepts. For example, the ritual bath at Las Huaringas (discussed in chapter 10) is referred to as "sowing one's shadow [soul] in the lagoon." Here the soul is nurtured just like the many magical herbs that are only found in the "magical gardens" watered by the lagoons. During shamanic initiation at the lagoons and at the famous hills of Chaparrí and Yanahuanga, the herbs of "good" or "evil" select the novice, determining whether he will be a *curandero* or a *brujo*. But, most important of all, the main object of a séance in *mesa* therapy is to make the accounts and the participants "bloom" at night, in imitation of the night-blooming San Pedro. The blooming process is symbolized by perfumes, sweet lime, and sugar, which possess the aroma and sweetness of purification and flowers in bloom (many of the magical herbs, as well as San Pedro, produce flowers). The process is achieved by raising visionary San Pedro and falcon tobacco and by using medicines made from those plants that "talk" to the *curandero* during divination, when the patient's subconscious "opens like a flower." Divination is further aided by the spiral-like "unfolding" of the shaman's personality and the realization of his alter ego, appropriately contained in the herb jar of the Middle Field. Finally, the crucifix dominating the axis of the *mesa* is carved out of *pial*, a woody vine.

In terms of the passage of time, a *mesa* or session replicates the growth cycle of the magical plants. Much of this plant lore is pre-Columbian in origin, as attested to by the fact that the center of the Inca cosmic ideogram in the Temple of the Sun at Cuzco (see chapter 7) contained representations of a pot of corn, which feeds man's body, and a pot of coca, which feeds his spirit. The adoption of Christ as the model for man in contemporary *curandero* syncretism is not out of place, for Christianity was shaped by the ancient tradition of the young dying and resurrecting vegetation god of the circum-Mediterranean peoples.

Christianity's concept of liturgical time is one of the mythical elements that rendered it amenable to syncretic blending with Indian cosmology and ritual. For, as Eliade (1960: 3) points out, Christianity has preserved

> one mythic attitude—the attitude toward liturgical time; that is, the rejection of profane time and the periodical recovery of the Great Time, *illud tempus* of "the beginnings." . . . The religious experience of the Christian is based upon an *imitation* of the Christ as *exemplary pattern*, upon the liturgical repetition of the life, death, and resurrection of the Lord and upon the *contemporaneity* of the Christian with *illud tempus* which begins with the Nativity at Bethlehem and ends, provisionally, with the Ascension. [The reader is reminded of the objects depicting all the phases of the life of Christ on Eduardo's *mesa*, the *tarjo* of the life of Christ, and the imitation of the mass during a session.] The imitation of the transhuman model, the repetition of an exemplary scenario and the breakaway from profane time through a moment which opens out into the Great Time, are the essential marks of "mythical behavior"—that is, the behavior of the man of the archaic societies, who finds the very source of his existence in the myth.

Danielou (1961: 124) discusses some beliefs held by the early Christians which, along with Apocalypse number symbolism, may have contributed to *curandero* ritual. The twelve apostles symbolized the twelve hours of daylight and the twelve months of the "Lord's year." The four Gospels symbolized the four divisions of the day and the four seasons of the year. The disciples' abandonment of Christ during the Passion was referred to as the time when "the hours of the day became the hours of the night." And, by his betrayal of Christ, Judas "maimed the clock . . . of the apostles."

Since, for the *curandero*, the session begins and ends at noon, the apparent linear progression of time observed by participants in the curing séance, from about 10:00 P.M. to 6:00 A.M., tends to mask an overall cyclical process. Figure 8-1 is a diagram that attempts to pull these patterns together into one paradigm that simultaneously depicts time concepts and the theme of spiritual rebirth in north Peruvian shamanism. It must be borne in mind, however, that the therapeutic value of the séance lies in its juxtaposition of seemingly unrelated elements. If the *curandero* is perceived as a sacred being bringing light into darkness, the model can be considered to reflect the dynamics of a séance quite well.

Consideration of the séance in terms of a 24-hour cycle (and the passage of the four seasons), during which the shaman dramatizes the theme of death and rebirth, reverses "normal" concepts regarding the progression of the hours of the day and seasons of the year. For example, in a séance "autumn" and "winter" occur during the day, while "spring" and "summer" occur at night, instead of vice versa. Also, "birth" occurs at midnight and "death" at noon, instead of at sunrise (6:00 A.M.) and sunset (6:00 P.M.), respectively. However, this reversal does not seem so unnatural if we conceive of sunrise and sunset as the equinoxes between the light of day and the darkness of

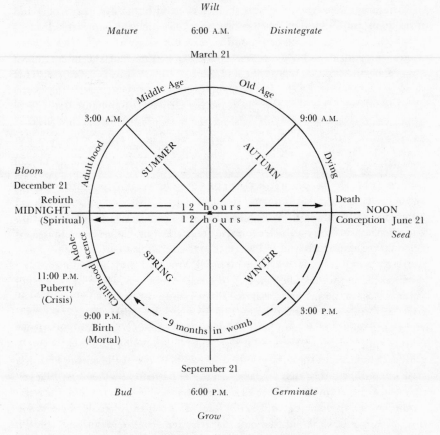

Figure 8-1.   The metaphysical clock.

night (reminiscent of the "crack between the worlds" concept of Castaneda, 1968: 195–96), with noon and midnight as the solstices, instead of establishing the equinoxes and solstices simply in terms of the light of the sun only—that is, seeing noon and midnight as equinoxes and dawn and sunset as solstices. (The reader is reminded that northern Peru is located in the Southern Hemisphere, so that September 21 and March 21 correspond to the spring and autumn equinoxes, respectively, whereas June 21 and December 21 correspond to the winter and summer solstices, respectively.)

Correlating these cosmological rhythms with the 24-hour cycle of the session can best be done by making an analogy to the growth cycle of a seed. From conception at noon until 6:00 P.M., the seed begins to grow. From 6:00 P.M. until midnight is the spring season, during which the plant buds. At midnight it blooms. From midnight until 6:00 A.M. the summer season occurs, during which the plant matures. At 6:00 A.M. it begins to wilt. Finally, from 6:00 A.M. until noon it disintegrates and dies.

Correlating these rhythms with the life cycle of humanity, the nine hours from noon until 9:00 P.M. (in the first seven of which the San Pedro brew is prepared) can be seen to correspond to nine months in the human mother's womb. At 9:00 P.M. birth occurs, at the same time that the microcosmic *mesa* is born. Childhood is replicated from 9:00 P.M. until 11:00 P.M. This phase is exemplified by the Christ Child on the *mesa,* who carries the world in his hands as if it were a toy. (In using his rattle the shaman actually picks up, or "raises," the world by its axis, for the body of the rattle is conceived of as the world, with the handle as the world's axis. The body of the rattle is also conceived of as the human head, in which the life principle resides, so that the rattle symbolizes the oneness of man with the cosmos.) The mass performed at 11:00 P.M. dramatizes the crisis of puberty, for the transformation symbolized here is vicarious—made possible by Christ's sacrifice to redeem humanity—and emphasizes the need for one's own personal ego to mature and then die in order to achieve salvation or metamorphosis. At midnight personal redemption is realized when the transcending shaman is reborn as a spiritual being. This is the time of breakthrough from the secular to the spiritual plane through the "unity," or "completion," achieved by balancing polar opposites, permitting "magical flight" along the center, or World Axis. In essence the shaman is integrated; he *becomes* the center. Thus from midnight until 3:00 A.M. he can perform the curing rites as a fully integrated and mature spiritual adult. From 3:00 A.M. until 6:00 A.M. he is in middle age, a period of balance in the life cycle that allows him to end the curing acts in a state of equilibrium, which he passes on to the patients. By 6:00 A.M. the session must be terminated, because from 6:00 A.M. until 9:00 A.M. the *curandero* is experiencing "old age"—that is, a return to secular or profane time. From 9:00 A.M. until noon, sacred time comes to an end for the *curandero* and the curing cycle is completed; he dies as a sacred being and returns to the profane world of humanity.

That Eduardo recognizes the theme of death and rebirth underlying the structure of the séance can be seen from the following remarks, offered in reply to a question asking if a ritual death and resurrection were implied in the session:

> Symbolically, yes. . . . Unconsciously it exists because when one drinks the potion, drinks the brew, the body is submitted to a slight drowsiness and then afterwards returns to consciousness. In other words, in that moment the spirit has "unfolded" in order to go and commune with the spirits of exterior worlds, of other planes, of other dimensions; and matter remains in a state of symbolic death. . . . There is an "unfolding" and it is symbolically an attitude of death.

To summarize, the ritual of the curing séance dramatizes the manipulation of sacred time in order to transcend the tension of opposites and the barriers of profane time and space, thus permitting a spiritual rebirth. The ap-

Figure 4-1. Eduardo observes tall stalks of San Pedro cactus growing on the Peruvian coast. (Reprinted from *Archaeology*, vol. 30, no. 6, 1977.)

Figure 4-2. Sections of San Pedro cactus being sliced in preparation for boiling.

Figure 4-3. Boiling the San Pedro over an open fire. (Reprinted from *Archaeology*, vol. 30, no. 6, 1977.)

Figure 4-4. Eduardo with the power objects he uses in curing, including the can of San Pedro infusion. Note the piece of San Pedro stalk at the left. (Reprinted from *Archaeology*, vol. 30, no. 6, 1977.)

Figure 4-5. Floripondium *(Datura arborea)* growing on the Peruvian coast.

Figure 4-6. Chavin stone carving (ca. 1300 B.C.) of a mythological being holding a stalk of San Pedro cactus. (Photo courtesy Abraham Guillen. Reprinted from *Archaeology*, vol. 30, no. 6, 1977.)

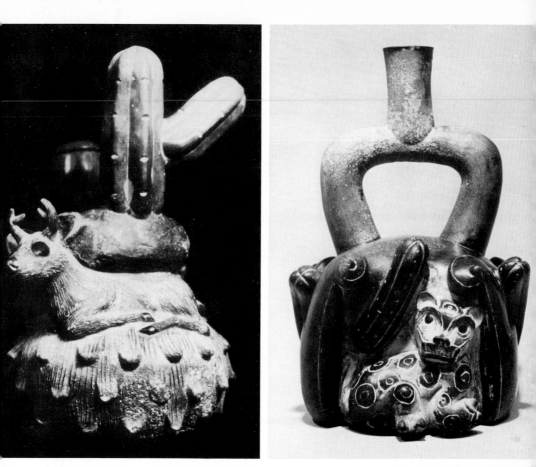

Left:
Figure 4-7. Chavin ceramic bottle representing a deer and San Pedro cactus. (Photo courtesy Donna McClelland.)

Right:
Figure 4-8. Chavin ceramic bottle representing a feline, San Pedro cacti, and volutes. (Photo courtesy Andre Emmerich. Reprinted from *Archaeology*, vol. 30, no. 6, 1977.)

Left:

Figure 4-11. Chimu ceramic bottle representing a female curer holding San Pedro cactus. (Photo courtesy Alan Sawyer.)

Right:

Figure 4-12. Eduardo's staffs, with the owl figure at the left, a female curer on the center staff, and the serpent on the right-hand staff.

Figure 6-1. Eduardo's *mesa*. See Appendix A for the key to the artifacts.

parent linear progression of the twelve hours of clock time is embedded in a more comprehensive 24-hour cyclical process that includes every phase of the spiritual life cycle. The mythical model for the metaphysical clock governing the session is provided by the movement of the sun, the life cycle of the magical plants, and the mystical imitation of the life of Christ, the contemporary culture hero who embodies and mediates between the celestial and terrestrial cycles.

9

Full Bloom: Ecstasy
and Psychic Unfolding

ECSTATIC "MAGICAL FLIGHT" AND "VISION"

With the unfolding of Eduardo's ritual into cyclical fullness comes the
metamorphosis of a new being. Set free from matter, his spirit may now soar
to realms of knowledge and vision that defy the uninitiated. The best and
most complete definition of shamanic magical flight comes from Eliade
(1960: 101-102), for whom it is

> the ability of certain individuals to leave their bodies at will, and to travel "in
> the spirit" through the three cosmic regions. One commits oneself to
> "flight"—that is, one induces ecstasy (not necessarily involving a trance)—either
> to bring the soul of a sacrificial animal to the highest heaven and offer it to the
> God of Heaven, or to go in search of the soul of a sick person . . . supposed to
> have been decoyed or ravished away by the demons . . . or . . . to guide the
> soul of a dead person to his new dwelling-place. . . . By his ecstasy the shaman
> renders himself equal to the gods, to the dead and to the spirits: the ability to
> "die" and come to life again—that is, voluntarily to leave and to reenter the
> body—denotes that he has surpassed the human condition.

Eliade also points out that regardless of the socio-religious system supporting the shaman, the novice must undergo an initiation involving magical
flight to the celestial spheres (ascent) and/or to the Underworld (descent). In
addition to being conceptualized as a symbolic death and rebirth, the flight
may include spiritual shape-shifting. The experience of becoming a crow
reported by Castaneda (1968: 168-84) is an example of such an initiatory
flight.

Magical flight and transformation were among the reputed feats of Peruvian Indian shamans shortly after the Conquest. This was noted in the mid-
sixteenth century by the *corregidor* of Cuzco, Licentiate Juan Polo de
Ondegardo (1916: 29), who wrote:

> Among the Indians there was another class of wizards, permitted by the Incas to
> a certain degree, who are like sorcerers. They take the form they want and go a

long distance through the air in a short time; and they see what is happening, they speak with the devil, who answers them in certain stones, or in other things that they venerate a great deal. They serve as diviners and they tell what is happening in remote places before the news arrives or can arrive.

In his *Crónica Moralizada* (1638: 631–33), portions of which document seventeenth-century coastal Chimu culture, Father Antonio de la Calancha, citing Father Teruel, reports that one shaman rubbed himself with powder (probably made from *Datura)*, went into a trance, and upon awakening claimed that while he was unconscious he had been to a place of detention for shamans two miles away. In addition to naming most of the shamans held at the site he claimed to have visited, he also divined the capture by the authorities of a shaman (his brother) for idolatry, an event that came to pass shortly thereafter. Three priests were witnesses to these events.

Ecstatic magical flight, the hallmark of the shaman, is no mystery to Eduardo, as we saw when discussing his plant lore and *mesa*. We have noted Eduardo's capacity for magical ascent to the lagoons and descent into the mountains or to the bottom of the ocean. We also saw that Eduardo considers San Pedro ingestion a type of symbolic death.

Here is how Eduardo describes San Pedro-induced flight, which involves spiritual shape-shifting or transformation:

San Pedro is a cactus that contains an ingredient which, upon ingestion, produces the opening of the subconscious and the sixth sense of the individual—that is, the telepathic sixth sense of the individual [which allows him] to transport himself, to sublimate himself across matter, time, and distance. One can spiritually transport oneself in a rapid fashion to the place where one wants by concentrating on one's goal. San Pedro is very powerful in the sense that I have explained, but it is not like other "potions"—for example, the hallucinogenic mushrooms, peyote, LSD, *ayahuasca*—which are too strong. Also *misha* [*Datura*] can be added to San Pedro to produce greater visual force. [Although Eduardo prefers not to use this powerful and toxic plant, sometimes he adds small dosages to his San Pedro brew.] One is transported across time, matter, and distance in a rapid and safe fashion in conjunction with the artifacts also. San Pedro is an aid which one uses to render the spirit more pleasant, more manageable.

(Question: Does the spirit separate itself from the body to make flights of vision?)

Yes, it separates itself. It separates itself and is materialized in other beings, in a saint, a mountain, an ancient shrine, and so on. In a series of manifestations in agreement with the "charm" or spell or place of the task or the symbology of which one is thinking: a lion, a tiger, a horse, a bird, a mountain, a lagoon, a stream, a saint, an herb, possibly even a demon.

Because of his mastery of magical flight, Eduardo is able to provide guidance for patients in avoiding the dangers of a "bad trip" during therapy:

> There are cases where the *curandero* has to control the spirits of the patients, to form a telepathic chain in order to be able to control their flights. Because it is very dangerous that an "axial" individual, that an axial *curandero* allows the spirit of a patient to fly by means of the charms through the different "charmed mansions" of the field of esoteric magic. Because misfortune can occur causing the spirit not to return from the ecstatic trance state and leaving the individual dead. Death can occur as well as insanity or blindness. One has to control the patient in the magical field through the whole manifestation of his problem, along his entire path, throughout his task—control him in a continuous fashion. Otherwise chaos can get the upper hand. It can exert itself in insanity, in hysteria, in sickness, in pain, in death.
>
> (Question: In other words, the *curandero*, with his experience of flight, with his control, can guide patients and carry them, take them out of the evil in which they find themselves?)
>
> Yes. The *curandero*, with his experience in this work, is especially prepared to act as a guide, a spiritual guide in this case. For example, if the patient has to walk through a "mansion," an ancient shrine in which his spirit is captured, is "accounted," the *curandero*, since he knows all of the "cabalas," has to guide the patient through the shrine just as Virgil did with Dante.

In our conversation Eduardo made frequent reference to an ecstatic trance state. I pressed him for a description of his trances, pointing out that he manifested no dramatic outer indications when one was occuring—no hysteria, lack of consciousness, epilepsy, or dancing, such as are recorded ethnographically for shamans in many different cultures. Here is how he described his ecstasy:

> According to the experiences that I have had, the drug first of all produces a feeling of drowsiness, a sort of dreamy state and a feeling of lethargy. This is the first symptom. But, as one begins to concentrate, the movement toward the end that is sought accelerates. It is rather smooth, like a kind of removal of one's thought to a distant dimension, to another "mansion," to a far-off place. It is something like a feeling of tranquility, of sweetness. There is nothing abrupt or painful or bothersome about this experience. It is sort of like a feeling of relief, do you understand? It is exclusively related to what one is really looking for, with the end that one is seeking. It relates to one's goal, nothing else.

The practical nature of Eduardo's ecstasy is further underscored by the fact that this highly subjective inner experience does not blot out objective, conscious perception:

In the state of trance, according to the general concept of everyone, the person is in a semiconscious state. . . . In actuality, semiconsciousness does occur, but not permanently. It occurs in an initial momentary form, as a type of dizziness during which one is in a state of vigil. This passes, it passes, and the conscious field becomes more alive. It is a kind of drowsiness—let us say, nonintellectual, semi-drowsiness, a minimal thing. But very possibly during this state there occurs the passage from consciousness by means of the unconscious toward a far superior state.

(Question: Are the five senses included in this state?)

All of the five senses and a "vision" much more remote, separated, more remote in the sense that one can look at things that go far beyond the ordinary or that have happened in the past or can happen in the future.

In chapter 5 we briefly noted the relationship between shamanic power and ecstasy. The latter seems to be the spark that activates power touching off the entire process of shamanizing. For the ecstasy accompanying the trance state is momentary; its main purpose is to prepare the spirit for flight:

Ecstasy occurs in a very tenuous, simple fashion and almost instantaneously. That is, it lasts seconds. Ecstasy serves to predispose the spirit for flight. In other words, it prepares, it is the preamble of the flight.

(Question: But the flight is an experience of ecstasy, right?)

Yes, in part it is an experience of ecstasy, but in a very light fashion. It is not a prolonged ecstasy. It is light. In other words, the ecstasy prepares one. Ecstasy is the preparation of the spirit for the flight. One passes through ecstasy before the flight.

In short, ecstasy must not get out of hand. The flights constitute sacred activities conducted in the service of Eduardo's fellow man. The highly pragmatic, functional nature of the vision that accompanies ecstatic trance and spiritual flight and its relationship to the patient's needs and faculties are outlined by Eduardo as follows:

"Vision" is the act of "visualizing" the scenes related to the life of the patient and as a consequence the problems that present themselves in his life. That is to say, [it occurs] as much with the effects of the "account" or the power of concentration of each individual [as with the effects of the brew]. For example, after having ingested San Pedro one automatically begins to feel the effects of the opening of the sixth sense, or the power to visualize things—the power, for example, to "see" a person who sends his object, his handkerchief; to see the sickness from which he suffers. He lives in such and such a place, and there one directly visualizes the individual through this object; the same individual who has sent the object is seen by means of the handkerchief. In other words, San Pedro relates itself with the radiation emitted by the "humors" of the individual in the handkerchief.

(Question: Exactly what does the *curandero* see when he is visualizing the patient or his ailments?)

The *curandero* sees what is related to the *daño* that has been done, the manner in which the sorcery or witchcraft originated.

(Question: In other words, he sees actual things and people, not symbols?)

No. Symbols also present themselves in a direct manner to the *curandero*. For example, he might see a bouquet of flowers accompanying the patient. That is a symbol. What does it mean? These magic flowers are a living symbol signifying forlornness, sorrow; in short, a grievance. Or he can also see how the very person suffering from *daño* was afflicted and who did it to him. The scene presents itself to the *curandero:* the house, the people, the godparents, the brothers, the parents, and the "pact" — over what and with what. He sees all those things. They are not just symbols, lights, and things like those seen with peyote and other substances. . . . [He sees] real life as if it were a scene on television.

(Question: In other words, he sees real things from life and symbols also?)

Yes, symbols as well, which one must know how to decipher. For example, one makes a comparative reference of the symbolism with the color, stature, form, manner, defects, and marks of the one who performed the *daño*. You don't know the person, for example, but you see him because he is "transmitting." Then they [those participating in the séance] begin to realize, or they might also see. If they have adequate vision to see, they observe the person directly and say "Yes, he's the one," and they see him as a result of the effects of the brew, the visualization, the concentration of the *maestro* in a telepathic chain with the whole group and the whole cosmos.

(Question: In other words, the brew together with the accounts of the *mesa* gives one an opportunity to "unfold" oneself?)

Yes, to unfold oneself across time, distance, and matter.

(Question: In other words, to make a connection with the cosmos?)

Yes, with the cosmos.

(Question: I suppose that to be able to interpret the symbols requires a great deal of time, experience, and practice?)

Well, there are certain people who have the potential force, but unmanifest, who have the capacity. Then what happens? The first session that they go to, all of a sudden they are seeing. They already have the inherent power, but not realized, not realized with the things of the moment. But the first time they attend a session, they drink San Pedro, and suddenly it develops. Others need more time. Others never see. Others need a serious preparation of attempts and exercises in this system. That's the way it is.

Finally, Eduardo provides some insights into the psychic processes involved in shamanic vision:

In reality the visual sense is not sight as we commonly refer to it. You do not see with the eyes, but you see cerebrally, you see internally. The eyes in that moment are "turned off." You are looking at another thing, but what you are looking at is not related to what I am talking about, which the eyes do not see. It is the internal eye. Your eyes can be looking at another thing—for example, what is happening in that moment, like a mouse or cat running by—but the other thing you are seeing is not seen by the eyes; the internal eye sees it.

(Question: In other words, physical sight is half interrupted, asleep?)

Yes. It's asleep, it's working within its physical field; but the other things that are manifest are being visualized with the other eye, the internal eye.

(Question: In other words, physical sight continues functioning, but in a less dominating fashion?)

Yes. All of the five physical senses manifest themselves internally—not in a physical fashion, but within: smell, vision, all of them.

(Question: But to do this one must stimulate all five senses in a pleasant fashion?)

Yes. It is what we commonly call entering the "account," the "charm."

(Question: Then, when the five senses are concentrated or, more correctly, relaxed, the sixth sense begins to open?)

Yes, the sixth sense is general so that one can absorb all those faculties. If one doesn't dominate that sixth sense nothing is achieved. All remains null. Thus the *maestro* has to be well prepared. He begins to concentrate and to enter the account by means of the San Pedro, the chants, the music. Then the man begins: *sssssssssssssss*. He unfolds himself, he unfolds his personality. Then the "other I" jumps. In other words, there is a reflection of the "I," of the "internal I" of the man toward the outside, the unfolding of the personality of the man.

(Question: In other words, is it necessary to jump out of the rational, conscious "I" in order for the superconscious or superior "I" to come out?)

Yes. It is necessary. All of the manifestations that are realized in that moment are related to what is superconscious, not to the physical. All of the great mystics, more so the magicians of the esoteric, have realized the unfolding of their personalities in order to be able to transport themselves from here, let us say, to the United States or Mexico. In their work they unfold themselves, or make themselves sublime; they depart: *sssssssssssssss*. In a second you visualize. You look out front, for example, at what is happening in a certain site, but you are not looking there; your spirit, your double, your personality has unfolded and you are elsewhere. Your being is not seeing from here.

Thus we see that Eduardo, the modern shaman, has much in common with his shaman forefathers and with shamans in other cultures. For visionary, ecstatic magical flight is the mark of the true shaman of all times and places.

THE SPIRAL OF PSYCHIC UNFOLDING

In an effort to probe deeper into Eduardo's subjective trance states I briefly described to him the use of the Indo-Tibetan mandala (a circular pattern often divided into four parts) as an aid to concentration and meditation, the object of which is to find one's own "center." Since I had often observed Eduardo's long silences during séances, when he concentrated on his power objects in order to divine for patients, it occurred to me that his artifacts might have a function similar to that of the Eastern mandalas. After my explanation, I asked if Eduardo had previous knowledge of the mandala or if he experienced anything similar to it in applying his *curandero* practices. He answered:

No, I do not know it. I know the symbol of the *remolino* [whirlpool] —that is, the symbol of the spiral, yes. It was taught by a great mystic, Aurobindo [a Hindu sage who died in 1950]. He said "As above, so below" and "From a point of departure is born and delivered the point of origin." One adopts this concept as a base, since from one point all is born and contained. In other words, man, he says, is endowed to take everything from its origin and embrace and absorb all, all that the universe contains.

The spiral is Eduardo's most important symbol. Its great value to him is indicated by the fact that it is engraved upon his rattle, the sacred instrument that activates all the accounts of the *mesa*. The dictum "As above, so below" is taken by Eduardo to mean that the spiral, in a vertical position and seen from the side, looks like a cone. Under the base of the upper part of this cone there is a "lower" cone; it is a mirror-image of the first, with its apex pointing downward. In other words, the two cones forming the spiral have a diamond or egg shape.* The region where the bases of the two cones meet corresponds to the middle- or earth-plane and the sacred space delineated by the *mesa*, or, more correctly, around the *mesa*.

The *remolino* had great significance for me since it corresponded to my

---

*This is similar to the Quechua concept of a top-shaped world mentioned in chapter 7. The Kogi of northeastern Colombia believe in an egg-shaped cosmos (see appendix D). Their temples are microcosmic models, with the conical roofs representing the Upper World and an invisible cone under the floor representing the Lower World (Reichel-Dolmatoff, personal communication). The same cosmological structure can be implied from the initiatory symbolism of Waika (Yanoama) shamans in Venezuela (see *A Shaman's Initiation*, 1970, a UCLA Latin American Center film made by Inga Steinvorth-Goetz, M.D.).

subjective experience after ingesting San Pedro during séances with Eduardo (see Sharon, 1972a: 133-34). I asked Eduardo about my experiences:

(Question: I remember that last year, when I first started to see with San Pedro, the first thing I saw was a *remolino* of colors—red and yellow, I believe they were. Is this something that always happens at the beginning with everybody?)

Yes. Always. That is the beginning for the person when he experiments with concentration, with visualizing. . . . That *remolino* is a symbol; it is the unfolding of the "other I." San Pedro begins to penetrate or to give rise to concentration toward the unfolding of the "other I" of the person.

Thus it appears that the *remolino* is Eduardo's personal symbolic center (as opposed to the external center of the *mesa*, the crucifix), which manifests itself at the beginning of his visualization, or realization of his "other I." The whirlpool also seems to be experienced by those with whom he works, the anthropologist not excluded. This experience does not appear to be peculiar to Eduardo and his associates. Paleolithic rock paintings from Rhodesia depict spirals, and spirals are also found in a Neolithic relief from Tarxien, Malta (see Jung, 1972: 37). Campbell (1959: 65-66) points out that the spiral "appears spontaneously in certain stages of meditation, as well as to people going to sleep under ether." It is found at the entrance and in the passages of New Grange, the ancient Irish royal burial mound. For Campbell

> these facts suggest that a constellation of images denoting the plunge and dissolution of consciousness in the darkness of non-being must have been employed intentionally, from an early date, to represent the analogy of threshold rites to the mystery of the entry of the child into the womb for birth.

We have seen that the stylized spiral (volute) was associated with San Pedro and jaguars on pre-Columbian Peruvian ceramics of the Chavín period (ca. 700-500 B.C.). The spiral was one of the recurring geometric motifs etched on the deserts of the south coast by the Paracas and Nasca cultures (ca. 400 B.C.-A.D. 500). Reiche (1969: 282) reports "at least a hundred" spirals ranging from 12 to 250 feet in diameter.

In Colombia among the Tukano Indians of the northwest Amazon, Reichel-Dolmatoff (1972: 94-95, 109) reports that the spiral is associated with sacred flutes and incest, the latter being a metaphor for hallucinogenic intoxication with *yagé (Banisteriopsis caapi)*. The spiral is also an important religious symbol among the highland Kogi, where it is associated with temple architecture (Reichel-Dolmatoff, personal communication).

Referring to the work of Max Knoll, Reichel-Dolmatoff (1972: 111; 1975: 174, figures 39, 40) shows that the spiral is one of fifteen basic motifs based on phosphenes that apparently are triggered by hallucinogens. Recent clinical research at UCLA (Siegel, 1973) seems to indicate that the "tunnel perspective" is a visual-imagery constant associated with the use of many hallucinogens. Most interesting of all, note the following description of the *remolino* as experienced by a Caucasian, urban Chilean during clinically controlled experiments with harmaline (the active ingredient in *yagé* or *ayahuasca)* and mescaline, conducted by the ethnopharmacologist Claudio Naranjo (1973: 182):

> I saw tiny dots, like those on a television screen, transparent dots that agitated and turned (when I fixed the gaze on one point) around a cone forming a sort of funnel, like the whirlpool that is formed when one removes the stopper. They turned, rather slowly, and this funnel opened upwards from the floor I was gazing at, and extended to the sides into my entire visual field. . . . And in this swirl of particles lies all my visual experience. It all comes from it, this is the foundation of the scenes I saw, this was their spirit. [E]ven the meaning of this incessant turning was in everything. . . . Something of a sardonic joke was in all this, these changing situations confronting the spectator (me), these images in incessant transformation, never permanent, meaning nothing but change as such, like the whirlpool that twined and carried in it all these visions.

Naranjo refers to this experience and others like it as the "center." His comments are particularly instructive since they coincide with Eduardo's interpretation of the *remolino* as a manifestation of the "other I" (1973: 183):

> From the subject's experiences and associations, as from the context in which these images appear, I definitely believe that this contraposition of center and periphery, the core and the surface, the immobile and the incessant turning, the source, beginning and end, and the ever-changing flow, is that of the deeper self and the multiplicity of experience, and it encompasses but transcends the duality of mind and body. More precisely, it is that of being and becoming, and it matches the traditional Hindu symbol for *samsara* and *nirvana:* the wheel of incessant death and rebirth, and its hub. Or, according to a remarkable passage of the *tao-tê-ching,* the practical materiality of a jar and the enclosed void that constitutes its essence.

However, the spiral can be used by a veteran shaman to stimulate nonordinary perceptions in an apprentice without the aid of hallucinogens, as in the following incident reported by Castaneda (1974: 102):

> Don Juan lifted his hat. Underneath there were spirals of ashes. I watched them without thinking. I felt the spirals moving. I felt them in my stomach. The ashes seemed to pile up. Then they were stirred and fluffed and suddenly don Genaro [Castaneda's "benefactor," responsible for helping him experience power] was sitting in front of me.

Jung (1971: 450–51) discusses mandala symbolism in the visions and dreams of a patient who successfully discovered his inner self, or center, in the process referred to in Jungian therapy as individuation. His remarks concerning mandalas as symbols of the self are particularly helpful because of the insights they give into spiral symbolism:

> We can hardly escape the feeling that the unconscious process moves spiralwise round a centre, gradually getting closer, while the characteristics of the centre grow more and more distant. Or perhaps . . . the centre . . . acts like a magnet on the disparate materials and processes of the unconscious and gradually captures them as in a crystal lattice. . . . [I]f the process is allowed to take its course . . . then the central symbol . . . will steadily and consistently force its way through the apparent chaos of the personal psyche and its dramatic entanglements. . . . Accordingly we often find spiral representations of the centre. . . .
>
> [I]t seems as if all the personal entanglements and dramatic changes of fortune that make up the intensity of life were nothing but . . . excuses for not facing the finality of this . . . crystallization. . . . [O]ne has the impression that the personal psyche is running around this central point . . . always in flight, and yet steadily drawing nearer.

More information regarding the spiral as mandala is provided by Jungian psychologist M. L. von Franz (1964: 247–48). He points out that the spiral represents the creative aspect of the mandala, which gives expression to something new and unique in psychic development. The spiral manifestation contrasts with the conservative circular aspect of the mandala, which restores a previously existing order in the psyche. Thus the *remolino* is very much in harmony with Eduardo's highly individualistic and creative temperament as an artist and a *curandero*.

It does not seem to be accidental that Eduardo the visionary shaman is also an artist. Lommel (1967: 148), who sees shamanism as intimately related to man's earliest artistic works, contends that "without artistic creation in some form or other, there is no shaman." Eduardo himself is not unaware of the intimate connection between artistic sensibility and shamanism. Here is what he has to say on this topic:

> The power of artistic sensibility in *curanderismo* is . . . , according to my evaluations, essential. In general the artist is sensitive, extremely sensitive in this field. Because by being sensitive he also possesses a special gamut of fantasy, which is the supreme essence of the artist. In order to create, the artist has to have fantasy. On the contrary, in doing things he would be nothing more than a mechanical person. . . . All that the artist effuses toward the outside in his expressions is of a character which is not intellectual, but spiritual. For this reason it goes without saying that within *curanderismo* artistic appreciations are essential, very essential, because the symbols are perceptible only to persons who really note a line, a trajectory of appreciation, in order to be able to dominate the distinct phases of

a curing scene. In this manner for example, the famous Mochicas [and] the Chimu are introducing something from mysticism in their plastic manifestations, in their symbology. . . . Those individuals always related art with mysticism, with the esoteric, with the mysteries.

Although Eduardo is speaking here in the abstract, it is evident that he has used his artistic perception to articulate himself and his mission.

10

Metamorphosis: Regeneration at the Sacred Lagoons

During my conversations with Eduardo in the summer of 1970, a recurring topic was the importance in north Peruvian *curandero* lore of a series of sacred lagoons, called collectively Las Huaringas, located near the highland town of Huancabamba (population about ten thousand) close to the Peru-Ecuador border. The symbolism governing some of Eduardo's most powerful artifacts as well as the wording of some of his *tarjos* referred directly to the lagoons. Eduardo told me that near each lagoon lived a powerful *curandero* who was considered to be the guardian of that region, including the surrounding mountains which nurtured a large variety of magical herbs used in therapy. Some of the healers to the north of Trujillo (with whom Eduardo had worked while an apprentice) had been initiated into folk healing by *curanderos* at Las Huaringas after making a pilgrimage on foot, tracing a sacred geography that terminated at these lagoons.

The Peruvian author Camino Calderón, in his novel *El Daño* (1942: 177), relates some of the folklore surrounding these powerful healers (translation by Gillin 1947: 126):

> Every year Narciso Piscoya [a *curandero* from Salas] . . . went to purify himself and to receive new training at the Gran Huaringa de Huancabamba, where Quintin Namuche lived, an almost mythological person who was the Pope of witchcraft and the owner and distributor of the *pajas* [herbs] which originated there: the *misha rey*, the *simora*, the *huachuma* . . . divine plants whose alkaloids awoke supernatural spiritual powers and with which the *curandero* acquires a double sight extending beyond all scientific notions of time and space. In this chilly *paramo* [wilderness] whither he had had to flee from the *Guardia Civil*, Quintin Namuche—the repository of the therapeutic tradition of the Incas—uncontaminated by *maleros* [evildoers] and humbugs, led a life of an anchorite, receiving the homage of the neophytes, initiating them in the secrets of the *pajas* which must be employed for the welfare of mankind and exercising an absolute power over the *brujos* for 100 leagues around.

In recent years the fame of the *curanderos* at Las Huaringas has spread. People from all walks of life and from all over the Andean region travel to the lagoons for treatment of ailments that do not respond to modern medicine. Pilgrimages of the sick and the faithful to Las Huaringas have long been common knowledge in Peruvian gossip and folklore, but recently public information has seemed to be circulating more overtly among Peruvians. For example, several newspaper reports (see especially Carnero Checa, 1971) document some of the events occurring at the lagoons. The flow of patients appears to be growing larger and more noticeable. It is conceivable that this apparent renaissance of lagoon lore correlates with social and psychological disruptions brought on by rapid cultural change since World War II.

Although Eduardo said that he could "see" the lagoons when focusing his "vision" during a session, he had never actually been to Las Huaringas until the summer of 1970, when, at the end of field work, I invited him to accompany me on a trip to the major lagoon in the group, called Shimbe, the White Lagoon. Although we met the *curandero* of Shimbe, don Florentino García, and were able to participate in a ritual bathing ceremony (an essential part of lagoon curing ritual) in Shimbe at midday, we were not invited to a night session at this time and did not feel that we had won the *curandero*'s confidence. But we did observe at first hand and participate in some of the local ritual, in addition to noting that large numbers of people were indeed visiting don Florentino. We had been part of a group of twenty people who bathed in the lagoon, and others were arriving as our group departed from don Florentino's house in the small hamlet of Salalá, two hours from Shimbe. Eduardo and I returned once again in fall 1971, accompanied by our photographer, Dave Brill. Before narrating our experiences, a word is in order regarding the Huancabamba region.

VALLEY OF THE GUARDIANS

Huancabamba is an Aymara word meaning "Valley or plain *(bamba)* of the stone-field guardian *(huanca)*." As we have noted, stone was sacred in pre-Columbian Peru. Narrow, pointed stones *(huancas)* placed in the fields embodied the spirits of the clan ancestors who protected the crops and the people caring for them. Thus it seems that in pre-Columbian times this pleasant, sheltered valley, situated at an altitude of about six thousand feet, was believed to have a magical protective quality. Today the magical nature of the valley seems to be confirmed for the inhabitants by the fact that the town of Huancabamba, located on an incline bordering the plain, actually "walks." Built on loose soil infiltrated by water from numerous irrigation ditches and embraced by a bifurcating fissure running from a hill above the town to the river below, Huancabamba is gradually sliding into the Huancabamba River—which in turn has its source in the Shimbe Lagoon. Before the geological reasons for this phenomenon were discovered, the townspeople thought it was the work of the Devil. It almost seems as if the ancients are reaping their revenge on Spanish culture.

The word *huaringas* is formed, in part, from the Aymara word *huari,* meaning "god of force" or "thick water." We know that a god named Huari, one of the first giant-ancestors and founder of ancient communities, was invoked by Indian shamans during curing rituals in the early colonial period (see Valcárcel, 1959: 146, 158-59). The other root of *huaringas* is the colonial Spanish version of the word "Incas" (*Ingas,* meaning "lords" or "kings"). Originally the term "Inca" referred only to the ruling aristocracy of the Inca Empire. Gow (1976: 198-200) argues that *inca* also means archetype and life force. Thus "Las Huaringas" means something akin to "place of the archetypal lords of life force and water" or, more prosaically, "bath of the Incas."

The lagoons, considered sacred to this day, are located at an altitude of approximately thirteen thousand feet, eight hours by rugged mule trail from Huancabamba. Though it is close to the equator, the altitude and exposure to moisture-laden winds make this a barren, cold region of marshes and coarse grasses often obscured by fog or buffeted by wind and rain. But these same conditions make the area propitious for the growth of an immense variety of herbs, many of which have definite medicinal properties, discovered through millenia of empirical experimentation. Along with San Pedro, the magical herbs *misha blanca* (floripondium), and black tobacco are employed extensively in *curandero* therapy, which is passed on from father to son among the isolated shamans inhabiting farms between Huancabamba and the inhospitable heights around the lagoons.

Von Hagen (1964: 143-44) has summarized the scanty knowledge available about the Huancabamba region prior to the Spanish Conquest. He informs us that it formed the major axis of one of the pre-Columbian trade routes of the Moche (ca. 100 B.C.-A.D. 700) and Chimu (ca. A.D. 700-1475) kingdoms, which cultivated the irrigated desert oases of the north coast. Von Hagen goes on to say:

> The second and most important trade route was the Serran-Huancabamba-Jaen route, which followed the upper Río Piura. . . . Only thirty-seven miles in length, it could be walked in three days by an Indian loaded down with seventy pounds of trade-goods. The Huancabamba was a tribe of considerable magnitude which occupied the arable lands of a sharply pitched valley formed by a river (Río Huancabamba) which, flowing into the Marañón, was thus one of the affluents of the Amazon. Little of its pre-Inca history is known, only that it was one of the myriad of tribes which peopled the Andes.

In addition to obtaining gold from the jungle peoples to the east (for subsequent trade to the Moche and Chimu peoples, who were noted metallurgists and artisans), the Huancabamba peoples passed on various plant substances to the coast. A sixty-mile trade route led from Huancabamba to Jaen, located near the Marañón and in the heart of the jungle milieu of the Shuaras, who traded

> rubber, chicle, *chonta*-wood (an iron-hard palm wood for spears and pipes [and staffs]) and such narcotics as coca, *guayusa* (an ilex holly . . . which was used as an emetic to make one vomit out the food not digested during the night), as well as *guaraná* (a nerve tonic), *niopo* snuff (which was inhaled into the nose through the shank bone of the oil-bird), and *caapi* (a vine which, when drunk in an infusion, caused hallucinations and which was in great demand by the witch-doctors). Besides these, there were bird feathers and animal skins, and, when wanted, *curare*, which when tipped on arrows caused death. (Von Hagen, 1964: 144)

After conquering the region in about A.D. 1475 the Incas built a fortress, a temple to the sun, and a convent for the virgins who attended to the rites of the state sun cult. These structures were built in the valley, where political control over the surrounding arable lands could be consolidated. The Incas also improved upon the Huancabamba trade route, making it into a stone-laid lateral road connecting the parallel Andean and coastal Inca highways. Very little archeology has been done in this area, but it does not seem that the Huancabamba culture prior to Inca conquest had developed large-scale stone architecture or a centralized state cult. Thus, if lagoon lore was well developed at the time of the Inca takeover (as it was at this time among the Chibchas of Colombia), it could have easily escaped the notice of the official Inca state sun cult—as it certainly did during the colonial period, when the Church was busy trying to "extirpate idolatry." Or the lagoon cult may have been elaborated by the Incas themselves.

That is the extent of our knowledge of the Huancabamba region prior to the Spanish Conquest. Unfortunately, our knowledge of the ethnohistory of religious practices during the colonial period is similarly sparse. We can only surmise the contours of the general socioeconomic history of the area, which seem to parallel the pattern traced in chapter 3.

At the present time the Huancabamba area, like the rest of northern Peru, is dominated by a particularly rustic, provincial version of *mestizo* culture. No Indian dialects, garb, or social patterns have survived here as they have in southern Peru near Cuzco and Lake Titicaca. Religious beliefs and practices are the one area of aboriginal culture in which survivals from the past are still very strong, but merged with Christianity in a syncretic form that often makes it difficult to separate the two traditions. This is true throughout northern Peru, but there is a definite pattern of increasing sophistication and accommodation to Catholicism and the twentieth century as one moves south along the coast. It appears that a combination of factors—inconspicuousness, isolation in rugged mountain terrain, and a degree of resistance to acculturation—has maintained the lagoon lore of Las Huaringas relatively intact and capable of resisting clerical and socioeconomic pressures.

THE *CURANDERO* OF THE SHIMBE LAGOON

In September 1971, when Dave and I took up quarters in Eduardo's house—in the same room set up as an altar for Maximón—one of our first concerns was to make a return trip to the White Lagoon with Eduardo. The two Maximón masks (mine had been placed beside Eduardo's on the altar) looked on sagely as I explained the need to travel before the rainy season, which often occurs there sometime in September, and thus avoid the near-impassible muddy trails it produces. Eduardo was ready to go at a moment's notice, but there was one problem: Before leaving don Florentino the previous year, we had promised that if we returned we would bring him two swords for his *mesa*. Almost three weeks passed before we could locate these swords. We finally packed them with the rest of our gear, along with the two manifestations of Maximón, which were to be "accounted" in the lagoon with other talismans.

Two days later, when we got off the bus in Huancabamba, I was relieved to see that there had not been any recent rain in the valley where the town was nestled. Once we had settled in our hotel, we began to make arrangements for mules for the next day and to inquire about don Florentino. We discovered that he had just returned from a trip to Ecuador and was planning to leave Huancabamba the next day in order to attend to several patients who were waiting for him at his home in Salalá. What luck! If we had come earlier in the month, as originally planned, we would have missed don Florentino. (Eduardo remarked that Maximón was working for us!) We learned that don Florentino was staying with a *compadre* in town, so we decided to see if we could talk to him.

I was very apprehensive about an interview, remembering our experience the year before. On that first visit we had arrived in Salalá as don Florentino was preparing to depart for Shimbe with a group of about twenty people. We had had some difficulty getting him aside to ask for permission to go along. He kept excusing himself abruptly whenever we tried to approach him.

While waiting for his next appearance, we sat on a bench in his back yard, with Eduardo to my right. When don Florentino appeared, he went over to a hammock slung between two posts about twenty feet to the right and slightly in front of the bench, so that Eduardo was between us. I noticed that this time Eduardo did not try to approach don Florentino, so I decided to sit still and let him handle the situation. He did absolutely nothing; he was in another man's territory and was letting that man take the initiative. In the meantime I caught glimpses out of the corner of my eye of don Florentino swinging back and forth on the hammock. No one said a word, and I felt like a schoolboy during his first day of classes.

My curiosity almost made me itch! Finally, I leaned forward, looking straight ahead as if taking in the scenery, and then strained my eyes to the sides of their sockets to get a view of don Florentino swinging in his hammock. I saw that he was taking us in from head to toe with the most intense, penetrating look I have ever seen on a human face. Suddenly he stopped swinging and left us. A little later one of the men who was saddling mules for the journey told us that mounts would be found for us. I began to protest that we still did not have don Florentino's permission, when Eduardo interrupted me, saying "It's all right now. Don Florentino has 'seen' us." And that was that!

We ascended to the White Lagoon with the group and participated in the ritual bath. I forgot to throw the offering of silver coins and sweet lime sprinkled with white sugar into the lagoon while I was in the water, so I had to return to do it. I was told that I had to go out further this time to make up for my error. My mistake must have provided some comic relief, for don Florentino's attitude seemed less forbidding during our return to Salalá. Once there, he told us that we did not need to attend a *mesa* and then disappeared. I was somewhat relieved, for although I was curious about don Florentino's practices, I had heard that lagoon healers mixed the highly toxic *misha (Datura arborea)* with San Pedro in preparing their brews. But I went away wondering if I would be welcome should I happen to return. This same preoccupation haunted me as we approached the house of don Florentino's *compadre* a year later.

Don Florentino's *compadre,* a local schoolteacher, turned out to be very hospitable. When don Florentino arrived, a few minutes later, Eduardo stood, shook his hand, and told the healer that we had brought the two swords we had promised the year before. Eduardo then explained our mission and asked me to show our letter of introduction from the National Geographic Society. He said that we hoped to take photographs of don Florentino and his work. Eduardo also talked about my experiences with the *ajkúnes* in Guatemala, including an account of Maximón and how the saint was working in his home. The conversation went on in a relaxed mood for about an hour.

Don Florentino told us about his recent treatment of a European priest. The priest had undergone extensive medical therapy and was actually being cared for by a doctor when he went to the *curandero*. Don Florentino was worried about the risk involved in applying "pagan" therapy to a minister of the Lord but finally consented to take the case. When he terminated his ministrations, the priest was completely cured. Apparently there must have been a community of belief between the priest and the *curandero*, for don Florentino said the priest had told him that envy (considered one of the prime causes of witchcraft) is a universal evil and that to this day in isolated parts of Europe there are *curanderos* who treat people who have been be-witched by envious enemies.

We also got an idea about don Florentino's working schedule. During the dry season he frequently makes two or three trips a week up to the Shimbe Lagoon, taking twenty or more patients each time. He can accommodate a maximum of about thirty people in each session. When he has a group larger than thirty, he usually splits it in two. Often people come only for the bath in order to "raise" their luck and do not require a session with the *mesa*.

During our conversation don Florentino asked me if I had worked with a *mesa* yet. I told him that I was still a student with much to learn and that my university studies did not give me much chance to practice. He advised me to remain with one teacher, since numerous tutors can confuse an initiate and cause great harm. He told me that he does not trust assistants and always works alone, except when he has to handle a case of insanity, which often re-quires assistants to help restrain the patient.

Eventually we invited don Florentino to our hotel, where we presented him with the two swords for his *mesa*. His last pair had been broken during a par-ticularly violent session, and he had not been able to replace them. The presentation of the new swords warranted a celebration, and we all went out for dinner. Late that night when we returned to our hotel, its name, El Dorado, seemed to match our good fortune.

PILGRIMAGE TO THE POWER LOCUS

When we arrived at Salalá at about 5:00 P.M. the next day, there were already some fifteen patients in don Florentino's front yard. One patient, a boy in his late teens, stood out from the rest because of his agitated and troublesome behavior. He was muttering senseless phrases to himself and oc-casionally shouting insults and obscenities at the assembled group. As our mules entered the front yard, he directed his insults at our party and struck the neck of the lead mule. Then he leaped up on a terraced incline and con-tinued to hurl invectives at the group.

Once we had dismounted and unpacked our gear, we learned from the boy's father that his son had suddenly gone crazy a week earlier for no ap-parent reason. The father added that the boy had been quiet on the way up to Salalá, but once they arrived the presence of so many people seemed to have scared him and precipitated another outburst. The father asked me to help him catch the boy and tie him up. I told him I thought a chase would only stir his wrath more, that if we ignored him he would calm down. How wrong I was!

Suddenly the boy charged the group. Before I knew what was happening he had hit me on the side of the head with an empty can he found in the yard, and was running on to hit someone else. Eduardo was the next person in line—unfortunately for the enraged youth. In the time it took me to turn my head Eduardo had jumped to his feet, tripped the boy, and was holding him down to be tied. Others joined in to hold the boy's arms and legs.

The boy was unharmed but dazed by the speed with which Eduardo had acted. Eduardo took a very calm, casual attitude toward the whole matter: He felt sorry for the boy and wished him no harm, but he could not permit him to bother and possibly injure others. The boy jabbered on about how he was Jesus Christ and we were Jews who should ask forgiveness, spitting and swearing all the while at the group. But everyone recognized that a man of action was present who knew exactly how to handle a crisis.

As we stood in the front yard, one of the group came over to us and began speaking English. He turned out to be a naturalized American citizen who had left Peru fourteen years earlier, at age seventeen, to seek his fortune in the United States. He had served in the armed forces in Korea and at the Bay of Pigs in Cuba. This was the first time he had returned to Peru since his departure. He told us that he suffered from a nervous disorder he had developed after a car accident. In addition, he had had arguments with his employers that cost him several jobs. He said that he had made a great deal of money in the past but had nothing to show for it because of his ailment and the general bad luck seemingly related to it. He had been treated by specialists in the army as well as by many civilian practitioners, but none of them had been able to help him. While visiting his family in Peru, he de- cided to come to Las Huaringas to seek relief.

We agreed to meet subsequently to compare notes, and three months later, in Los Angeles, I contacted him. He assured me that his condition had been alleviated and that he had new confidence and willpower to cope with his situation. He attributed his improved state to his faith in don Florentino.

To get back to Salalá: We retired early in quarters provided by don Florentino's brother. The next morning at 10:00 A.M., after much delibera- tion regarding the bad weather and many problems obtaining enough mules for everyone, we finally departed for the Shimbe Lagoon. There were seven- teen pilgrims in the group. One of my fears became a reality, despite Max- imón's help. It had been raining around Salalá for several days prior to our arrival and was still drizzling, making the trail a veritable sea of black mud. Our mules slipped and slid over hill and down dale, occasionally getting bogged down in mudholes up to their stomachs. Sometimes it was necessary to dismount until the mule dislodged itself, which meant that the poor rider had to wade through mud up to his knees until the animal regained its footing.

Close to noon we had to leave the mules on the slopes above the lagoon and walk for about half an hour, since the spongy marshes around the lagoon would not support a mule's weight. In local folklore, approaching a highland lagoon is considered, in any case, to be a very dangerous business. Tales of people who have been "enchanted" (encantada) by being turned to stone when approaching sacred lagoons are common. Possibly to prevent such a mishap, don Florentino began to invoke the lagoon during our approach. This procedure consisted of blowing on his *seguro* so as to make a whistling sound. Once at the water's edge, he dipped his new swords in the lagoon and began to brandish them while continuing his invocations.

After the opening invocation, don Florentino approached all the participants and poured a small portion of herbal remedy from his *seguro* into their palms. This was imbibed through the nostrils by all present. As it passed through the nasal passages and into the back of the throat, it stung and caused all of us to cough. Next don Florentino instructed us to prepare for the bath. Undressing to our underwear, we entered the water, tossing offerings of silver coins and sweet limes sprinkled with sugar into the lagoon. We were next instructed to wade ashore briefly and then return to the lagoon for a quick final dip. As we came out of the water for the second time, the *curandero* blessed each of us and then instructed us to jump up and down and wave our arms in order to get warm. Once dry, we were allowed to dress.

The temperature must have been near freezing, for we could see our breath. My body was numb with cold. It was impossible to get completely dry, since the drizzle continued throughout the whole ceremony. Our clothes also got damp as we pulled them out from under the rain ponchos where we had placed them before the bath.

Once dressed, each of us picked up the amulets and good luck charms we had brought with us and bathed them in the lagoon. Then, one by one, we took a turn before don Florentino for a "cleansing," or rubbing with his large sword. Then an assistant blew white powder over our chests, and the curer sprayed us orally with liquid from his bottle of magical plants. Then each participant orally sprayed perfume and sweet wine over the lagoon. To end the ceremony, we brought our artifacts before the *curandero* to be blessed in the name of the lagoon—a process that consisted of invoking the lagoon, calling out our names, and then orally spraying the artifacts with the herbal liquid from the *seguro*.

Then came the return to Salalá through that abominable bog. One man got off his mule to retrieve his hat and the animal went on without him. The man ahead stopped the mule for him, but to turn it around and send it back in the mire at that narrow point in the trail was unthinkable. So our hardy pilgrim had to wade through the muck back to his mule. When he arrived, he looked like a monster from the black lagoon!

Ahead of me an animal took a serious fall, but the rider managed to jump clear and avoid being pinned under it. Going around a slippery corner in a clay embankment, a mule which began to slip stiffened its legs and slid for about ten feet. Then Eduardo's cinch broke, and down he came. The cinch could not be replaced, so he cut a section from the animal's hitching rope and, with a sailor's skill, tied the saddle back on the animal. When we finally reached Salalá, every member of our party was wet and muddy.

THE GOLDEN SERPENT

But more was in store for us; this time we were invited to a night session. Another guest that night was the crazy boy, who had not gone with us to Shimbe. Don Florentino had given us permission to take pictures of the session, and Dave accordingly set up his strobelights, which would be required to capture the action once the candle was blown out. One of the crazy boy's first acts was to make a beeline for the nearest strobe. Fortunately, Dave's trigger finger was fast. He flashed the strobe, blinding the boy long enough for his father to stop him. The boy was tied around the waist to a pole, but one of Dave's strobes was taped above him and he kept grabbing for it. Then don Florentino told us that the strobes were going to get in the way, since everyone would be moving around most of the night.

While Dave was having his adventure with the strobes, don Florentino had invited Eduardo to set up the artifacts from his *mesa* along with talismans belonging to clients, and to share the honors in conducting the session. He also asked Eduardo to keep an eye on the crazy boy and give him whatever attention might be required during the evening.

The session began at 9:00 P.M., and don Florentino immediately served the brew. (In his session this constituted the opening act.) The pint cup which was handed to me contained a black liquid. I could smell the San Pedro in it, and Eduardo told me that it also contained *misha (Datura arborea)*, so I surmised that we were in for a rough trip. Instant confirmation came as someone who had taken the brew before me rushed out to the edge of the group and began to vomit violently. Then I realized why everyone was going to be moving around a lot that night. Purgative plants must have been included in don Florentino's brew because *Datura* alkaloids, such as scopolamine and atropine, are antispasmodic.

Our only source of light up till now had been a candle. It was blown out at 9:30, and at 10:00 P.M. don Florentino began his *tarjos*. At about this time I began to hallucinate. My head felt giddy and ached slightly. When I looked around I felt dizzy. I was totally conscious of my surroundings and of the people around me, but at the same time I saw a rapid series of visions. It was almost like watching a sped-up motion picture. At first I saw faint whirlpools of light spinning before my eyes; they became steadily brighter and then gave way to an incredible array of lights, designs, forms, and colors. At one moment a series of angular geometric designs would be parading before my eyes. Then suddenly the visions would become organic and curvilinear, twisting and turning into undulating shapes and colors. Sometimes the visions were realistic, such as a series of human faces, some of them wearing sunglasses. Many of the faces were those of highland Indians. Another realistic image was that of a series of Greek columns, which suddenly turned into a huge photographic negative. One recurrent image was of a shiny golden snake, writhing slowly, which suddenly burst into a curvilinear form of many colors and shapes. This image occurred three times. Another theme was a series of mechanical designs, some of them commercial signs, which passed before me as if on an assembly line. In addition, a quick succession of kaleidoscopic symbols gave way to pulsating and spiralling colors and twisting, rope-like forms. I could see the visions with my eyes open or closed, although closing them made the hallucinations stronger and clearer. There did not appear to be any order or reason to the scenes I viewed — they flowed freely and spontaneously with no apparent relation to the world of cause and effect. It seemed as if my unconscious was releasing an uninhibited stream of images and impressions.

At about 11:00 P.M. don Florentino went out to a patio beyond the roofed area where the session was taking place and began a ferocious sword battle, cutting and slicing the air. Occasionally he struck the sword on a rock, bringing forth sparks. (I suddenly understood how his other two swords had been broken!) All the while he directed a tirade against the "spirit of evil" and the "Devil," which he was attacking.

When he finished the battle, he called each person forth to imbibe a mixture of San Pedro, *misha*, and black tobacco through both nostrils, with Eduardo helping to serve the patients. This brought on a general spell of coughing followed by a chain reaction of vomiting. Throughout the session don Florentino imitated the sound of vomiting in order to keep everyone's stomach active. At about this time I had my first vomiting spell. It came almost without warning.

Dave had started to vomit earlier than I and was already in total misery. Now I joined him. To add to our problems, the crazy boy acted up intermittently all through the night. He kept getting loose and bothering people. Once he ran away but got sick — allowing his father time to catch up to him and bring him back. Since the post he was tied to was right in front of us, I kept wondering when another fist was going to come flying at me out of the darkness. So there we sat between fits of vomiting, shivering in the cold night air, anticipating assault, and asking each other what kind of insanity had got us into this predicament.

At about 2:00 A.M., with Eduardo's help, don Florentino had us all imbibe another dose of San Pedro, *misha*, and tobacco. At regular intervals he chanted his *tarjos* or invited Eduardo to chant his. The music had a soothing effect during moments of low vitality when one felt like sleeping because of weakness from vomiting and the lateness of the hour. I recall drifting back from half-remembered landscapes at the edge of a dark, bottomless pit of nothingness.

The vomiting continued throughout most of the session until 4 A.M., by which time most of us were completely purged. The visions decreased in direct proportion to the vomiting spells. At approximately 5:30 A.M., don Florentino instructed Eduardo to "refresh" everyone, by orally spraying a mixture of lime juice, sugar, white flowers, and tea in our faces and on the backs of our heads. Then each of us drank the mixture, which had a soothing effect on the stomach. We were also instructed to spray white wine in the four directions: toward the lagoons, hills, and *mesa*.

When the session ended at 6:00 A.M., our stomachs were settled and we felt quite well, despite the ordeal we had undergone. Our bodies and our psyches had been thoroughly purged. Even the crazy boy had become very civil.

Before departing later that morning we had a final, brief consultation with don Florentino, during which he provided herbal medicines, talismans, and advice to each patient. While chatting with us, he showed us several power objects. The one that caught my eye was a beautiful gold-colored serpent staff. I recalled the serpent theme that had been so prominent in my visions the night before. I also remembered the ancient Chibcha legends of Colombia that associated serpents with highland lagoons. Colombia was also the place of origin of the legend of *El Dorado* — the fabled city of gold — which is Spanish for "gilded man." The term originally referred to the Chibcha ceremony in which a chief coated with a vegetable gum and sprayed with gold dust jumped into a lagoon from a raft in order to offer the gold on his body to the gods. The theme of this ritual act seems to have been a symbolic shedding of the skin or metamorphosis — just as it seems to be today in the ceremonies at Las Huaringas. Gold is where you find it. Greedy treasure hunters have always thought *El Dorado* was in the Amazon Jungles. They never thought of looking closer to home.

PACHAMAMA AND METAMORPHOSIS

It seems feasible to me, from personal experience and my observation of approximately forty Peruvians during two pilgrimages, that the basic theme underlying the pilgrimage to Las Huaringas is spiritual metamorphosis. Note how the first ritual bath affected Eduardo:

> I felt as if I had come out of a wrapping. At first I felt apathetic, heavy, as if something was pulling me downwards. But when I was in the lagoon it seemed as if the world was spinning in a thousand different forms. I felt the spiral again in my mind, internally. I saw myself spinning like a top, physically, but also internally as if coming out of a tomb. I saw the world, the mountains, spinning . . . *ffffffffffffff* . . . The bath was very good for me. It was a purification.

If metamorphosis is the goal of the pilgrimage, what is the religious matrix or world view supporting this transformation? In order to answer this question a summary of basic pre-Columbian religious concepts — still very much alive today — is necessary.

In one of the best interpretations of the basic forms of pre-Columbian Peruvian religion, Brundage (1963: 42-58) indicates that the principal deity underlying all Peruvian religion was *Pachamama*, the Earth Mother, despite the fact that she hardly figured in the Inca imperial pantheon. For the Peruvian Indian she was the earth itself. She was seen in a tilled field *(chacra)* and in the soaring Andes (where she was called *Coya*, or Queen). The mountains were regarded as her breasts, and the numerous streams and rivers rushing down the mountainsides as her milk. In the Inca legend she took the form of *Mama Huaco*, who was mysteriously born without a begetter and was associated with serpents and rocks. In her avatar as *Mama Sara* (Corn Mother) she appeared at one of the four major ceremonies of the Inca state. Throughout Peru, *Mamacocha*, Mother Sea, seems to have been but another manifestation of the Earth Mother, who fed the coastal peoples as abundantly as *Pachamama* provided for the children of the *sierra*. The peoples of the Lake Titicaca region venerated the lake as their mother and claimed to have sprung from her body. Everywhere in Peru springs were considered to be "daughters of the sea" and received offerings of conch shells after the crops were sown.

Brundage (1963: 46) explains the persistence of Pachamama as follows:

> In all her various forms the Earth Mother is to be found in the basement of all Peruvian religion. She was the Holy Mother *(Mama Ocllo)* and is at times indistinguishable from Moon Lady *(Mama Quilla)*. Not only was she a deity, or rather a series of deities, and therefore capable of being mythologically and humanly understood; she was also a prodigious religious abstraction. She was "the experience" of the Peruvian Indian as he moved wonderingly, humbly, delightedly, and fearfully from the cradle to the grave. . . . [C]onsequent upon the discovery of empire as a mode of organization by the Inca state, with its political demands, she seemed to sink deeper into the folk consciousness; serenely as always, because sure of her power, she could allow the architecture of a state pantheon to arise in noble and masculine proportions over the preserve of Nature, whose mistress she yet remained.*

A basic concept of Peruvian religion was the idea of *huaca*, the creative manifestation of *Pachamama* (see chapter 5). In particular, mountains, the home of storms, were *huaca* and were scarcely distinguishable from the storms to which they gave birth. In the *sierra* the storm was the most pervasive and dynamic of all the male *huacas*, envisaged as a heroic figure in the heavens armed with rain, hail, and thunder; the flash of his golden sling was lightning. All male children born in the fields on a thunderous day were considered to be his sons and were dedicated as future shamans. Among the Incas he was *Illapa* (the Flashing One); in the northern province of Huamachuco, site of a famous oracle, he was *Catiquilla*, who was worshipped on a sacred peak. After the Spanish Conquest he was transmuted into St. James, mounted (the hoofbeats were his thunder) and brandishing a glittering Spanish sword (his lightning). The serpents that are often associated with the sky-god are not difficult to identify as his lightning. As we

---

*In the Inca cosmogram discussed in chapter 7, she is enclosed within *Camac Pacha*, Lord or Creator Earth.

saw in chapter 7, the ancient form of the sky-god lingers on today among contemporary Quechua Indians as *ccoa,* the sponsor of shamans, a vicious catlike figure residing in the heights of the Andes and commanding the storm and hail. In function he is interchangeable with Saint James the Thunderer.

Stars possessed the powerful *huaca* of sustaining all the species of animals and birds on earth by providing the fertilizing powers that multiplied them. The Pleiades, which represented a generalized form of this power for all living beings, including humanity, received special sacrifices and were called Mother. The festival of the Pleiades was celebrated by many Peruvian tribes with confession and purification. On the coast the moon was *huaca,* superior to the sun, holding sway over the thunder, the sea, the whirlwind, and fertility.

Brundage (1963: 50) explains the duality of stellar and earthly expressions of *huaca:*

> It is significant that the Peruvian Indians saw the heavens in the same terms as the earth, radiating holy influences. Stars and stones differed not at all in the intensity of their respective powers. One real difference, however, can be perceived on closer inspection between the stellar and the chthonic, namely that the stellar *huacas* served more as repositories for the basic ideas and categories in creation, as blueprints and sources of all forms and shapes, whereas stone and earth possessed in a higher degree the vital element that infused these forms. No stone *huaca,* for instance, was thought to be the progenitor of all mankind; it was rather the ancestor of a particular tribe, more specific and less ideal. No star, on the contrary, was known as the ancestor of any specific tribe of men.

The *huaca* manifest in the earth and in stone had a special significance, for it was the very flesh of the Mother. As opposed to the stellar concept of a supreme creator-god, the cult of stones was a more basic, persistent form of religious expression.

Another aspect of Peruvian religion was the prevalence of oracles and of pilgrimages to the sites where they were located. Such sites were visited by peoples from a large number of distant communities—even though the visitors and hosts may have been engaged in some conflict. The oldest and most famous of these sites was the temple of *Pachacamac* in the Lurin valley on the coast south of Lima. Here the oracular god was the *huaca* of origination of the surrounding community, a wooden post or tree trunk believed to have created the people of the area. An oracle on the Apurimac River, high in the Andes, contained a multitude of sacred wooden female posts, of which the principal idol was *Apu* (Great One). Here we might have a survival of the World Tree mentioned by Eliade (1964: 269–74), of whom the shaman "asks the 'future' of the community and the 'fate' of the 'soul.' "

Brundage (1963: 55) points to a "fundamental shamanism . . . behind all sacred offices in ancient Peru." He presumes that there was some sort of hierarchical connection linking the minor shaman of the community who consulted his personal *huaca* (pebble, spring, or tree), the diviner of a provincial *huaca,* and the formal priesthood of *Pachacamac* or *Inti* (the sun). All of these different offices continued to exist at the time of the Inca Empire.

For the ancient Peruvians, men evolved from the living rock, and the concept of *huaca* embodied the capacity for infinite self-multiplication, the very secret of nature. Inca mythology and religion simply built a political superstructure over this foundation without eliminating it. Unfortunately, the Spanish did much to alter the *imago mundi* of the Peruvian peoples, but the *Axis Mundi* of the Andes has remained as solid as the rock, the flesh of *Pachamama,* of which it is composed. As one student of contemporary Andean religion expresses it:

> The *Pachamama* is the point where time and space meet. The past, the present and the future are born from her and all return to her. She is the universal and eternal matrix. The *apus* [mountain spirits], the ancestors, and the various spirits are all born from her, controlled by her, and protected by her. Contemporary man, too, with his family and all his possessions—land, house, and animals—is born from her, nurtured and raised by her, and finally drawn back within her when he dies. (Gow, 1976: 209-10)

Gow adds that she "is regarded as the fount of all life. She has always existed outside time and place, as an elemental life force . . . who symbolizes the seamlessness and continuity of peasant life." (1976: 267)

Thus it should come as no surprise that modern middle-class Peruvians—that is, urban Christians—are flocking to the Andean Shangri-La in order to heal the wounds of the twentieth century. Here it is possible to return to nature or Mother Earth (through a ritual bath or return to her womb, the *pacarina* or place of "origins") after realizing a "dangerous passage" (the slippery, narrow trail to the lagoons). Emergence from the lagoon is only the beginning of the process of rebirth, for there still remains the perilous journey down the trail and out into the everyday world. The "incomplete state" of those who have arranged to participate in a night séance is symbolized by ritual taboos that must be observed before the session: for example, abstinence from salt, ají, bathing, and sex, and a sanction against looking at a hearth fire. Birth is a painful process, and this is dramatically experienced by the pilgrim during the violent purge and catharsis of the séance and the return by mule to don Florentino's house. The fact that the participant exerts his entire being (physical, mental, and spiritual) through rugged exercise, visions, regurgitation, exposure to the cold and the elements, and lack of sleep reinforces the resurrection of consciousness and self-integration that are the goals of the ritual. When the pilgrim returns to the "plain of the guardian ancestors" he is truly a new person; no longer an alienated statistic of the metropolis, he has encountered the customs and traditions of his past and has been reunited with his ancestors.

11

Metaphysical Equilibrium:
Transcending Opposites

THE DIALECTIC OF GOOD AND EVIL

The problem of good and evil has plagued philosophers for millennia. No doubt, thinking humanity for further millennia will keep on trying to resolve the conflict between these two opposed and apparently irreconcilable forces. In the meantime, the moral dilemmas faced by the individual will always upset the lofty formulations of the philosophers. What is right at one particular time or place often turns out to be wrong at another time or place. The sheer futility — and relativity — of the problem seems to argue against our even considering it in the first place. But consider it we must — each one of us at some time in our lives — for it crops up in the events and actions of our daily existence and is intimately related to our inner psychic beings.

Eduardo is a man who has grappled with his problem and continues to do so. Thus, although he understands the philosophical implications of the problem of good and evil, he also recognizes the need for a less abstract philosophy of action that can guide his relationships with others in the world of affairs. In short, his ideology and way of life reflect a great deal of common sense and a realistic appraisal of human nature. In view of the militant undercurrents and apparent dualism in much of his *curandero* lore, I asked whether he saw the world and human life as a struggle between good and evil. His answer:

Constantly. Man by nature is the fiercest enemy of man. Always. Given the cultural scales found in this life, man is always fighting. The majority of men are selfish. They always have to establish, to monopolize, to be absolute. And this struggle will never end.

Good and evil have to be harmonized in the world, by all means, because if these things did not exist it would not be complete. By all means, there has to be good and evil so that things exist on their side, within their term, within a framework. There has to be ambiguity, there has to be the duality of things. There is a saying that goes like this: "In the world there is, and has been, a little of everything: joy and sorrow; if there was only celestial sweetness there would be no world." It is logical that within the human environment there will always exist evil and there will always exist good. Because with all creatures some tend toward good and others tend toward evil. And even one who tends toward good is always influenced to think, to desire [evil], to falsify his problems, his wants, because selfishness always exists.

(Question: In other words, it is the interaction between good and evil that makes this world and its functioning?)

Yes, by all means. To function, this world requires the existence of good and evil. Don't you see how the nations hate each other for supremacy? They want to have more power within the economic field, others in the military field, and so on—supremacy, race, and so on. In any case, all of humanity is forced to live and not to be exempt from the truth of things while there is no intervention between these elements that are inseparable in the world, in the life of man: good and evil.

In order to explore Eduardo's personal philosophy a little further, I asked him to explain his concept of good:

Good is a force much more powerful than evil. Evil has its adepts, but the majority of them fight among themselves. On the other hand, this does not happen with good. Good is much more secure, less treacherous. Cooperation among the good is much more frank. Among the evil it is not, because they are people of the same malevolent disposition and they envy each other since this rage is in their blood, in their lives, in their hearts. No matter how much they try to get along, they are of the same temper and they end up hating each other, doubting each other.

It is obvious that Eduardo identifies with the forces of good:

My orientation, my goal, is to look for good without prejudice, to do good more than anything because I feel that good is necessary. There are people who suffer too much, who are in chaos, in life as in death. Thus it is necessary to give them relief without prejudice, without discriminating against a particular disposition; to dispense good in an absolute fashion without condescension, without selfishness, without restrictions.

His identification is due to the fact that he distinguishes the necessary interaction between amoral forces in nature from the moral judgments regarding good and evil in human conduct. This is revealed by his concept of evil:

Evil is all that is contrary to good, by logic. It is all that exists that is contrary to frank things. Evil is a necessary thing, very necessary. If an individual is too good, automatically people—no matter how kind—turn against him. Thus evil is one of the forces that serve to restrain certain extremes. But in its extension as a major force in the esoteric field of magic, evil is no longer necessary. Yes, the world needs both things from both fields; but, in reality, humanity suffers from the influence of harm, evil, malevolence, the bad thing, the black. In the world as a whole it is necessary, yes; but it is not necessary on the individual level.

(Question: In other words, the key lies in the equilibrium between these two forces?)

You are right. Equilibrium is necessary. If there is no equilibrium between these two forces, between good and evil, the thing changes aspect. It is necessary that equilibrium persist, and be influential. . . . If evil exists in a fashion that is much more eloquent, stronger, more expressive, more charged with force, good recedes; just as, when there is too much good, evil is separated. . . . By all means, there has to be this equilibrium, the duality of things, so that all is in accord with this road, with the orientation of this equilibrium in the life of man. One must save individuals, yes; in the esoteric field one must save, by all means, because it was for this that things were made.

As we noted earlier in discussing the *Campo Medio,* equilibrium is the key to Eduardo's entire system. This concept is dramatically actualized at midnight during the session, when oneness with the cosmos is achieved and Eduardo becomes the manifest "center" by transcending the opposites at work in the cosmos and within his own being. But, as we saw in discussing the séance, transcendence is achieved only after the forces of the *Campo Ganadero* and the *Campo Justiciero* are "balanced" through the mediation of the *Campo Medio.* We noted that raising the twenty-five thousand accounts of the *Campo Medio* was performed by the two assistants only, since Eduardo's alter ego, the herb jar, was also being raised in the process.

There is an important lesson here. Since the *mesa* — in addition to symbolizing a microcosmos — is a projection of Eduardo's own being, the *Campo Ganadero* represents his own personal capacity for evil, his own unconscious depths. Paul pulling Judas out of Hell to serve the light is a symbol for confrontation with the dark side, or shadow, of Eduardo's own nature, followed by its integration with the rest of his psyche. In other words, it is an allegory for making conscious the contents of the unconscious, for psychic integration, for realization of the self, as Jung would put it. Since this is a process which Eduardo has actualized in his own life, he is able to dramatize it and to help others face themselves. It is instructive to note, however, the caution with which Eduardo undertakes this quest for the self — that is, his amassing of the militant powers of the upper section of the *Campo Justiciero.* For confrontation with the depths of one's own unconscious is a dangerous task, requiring force and constant vigil. Eduardo maintains the vigil while his two assistants raise the twenty-five thousand accounts. Thus Eduardo can transcend the play of polar opposites at midnight because he realizes their full potential in his inner life. Eduardo has exerted his ego in the exploration of the world of humanity and achieved his identity. He is now in the "balanced" years, or the early autumn of his life, a season when deeper strata of his psyche are being manifested. He is the prototype of the true Hero, who realizes that self-conquest is the only battle in life that really matters.

THE THREE AND THE FOUR

If Eduardo's *mesa* is viewed as a mandala, a spontaneous symbolic projection used to focus consciousness, much can be learned about his personality and ability as a therapist. Through years of research on the unconscious, Jung discovered that quadrangular forms manifested in dreams and visions symbolize conscious realization of inner wholeness, whereas wholeness itself is symbolized by circular forms.

Another form of mandala is the *yantra* discussed by Aniela Jaffé (1964: 267-68), which sheds further light on the symbolism governing the *mesa*. The *yantra* is a geometrical design often formed by two interpenetrating triangles, one point-upward and the other point-downward; this is slightly reminiscent of the division of the *mesa* into triangles. Traditionally, the *yantra* symbolizes the union of the Indian male and female divinities Shiva and Shakti. Interpreted psychologically, it expresses "the union of the opposites—the union of the personal, temporal world of the ego with the non-personal, timeless world of the non-ego." In religious terms this signifies the union of the soul with God. Thus the two interpenetrating triangles have a meaning similar to that of the circular mandala in that they symbolize "the wholeness of the psyche or self, of which consciousness is just as much a part as the unconscious." However, in contrast to the mandala, which represents "wholeness as such, as an existing entity," the *yantra* expresses a "tension between the opposites," which implies "a process—the creation, or coming into being, of wholeness." Jaffé (1964: 278) further points out that one of the central symbols of the medieval alchemists was the *quadratura circuli* (the squared circle), their version of the mandala. Thus the division of the *mesa* into triangles can be interpreted as a concrete expression of the creative process of transcendence by which opposites are united. In other words, Eduardo has all of the symbols and instruments for healing the human psyche quite literally at his fingertips.

As we have seen, Eduardo's quadrangular *mesa* provides the cosmic terrain on which the tension of opposites—psychological and cosmological—is manifested. Ritual, through the mediation of the Middle Field, activates and brings into meaningful interaction the opposing moral forces of good and evil symbolized by the right and left fields of the *mesa*. In the process the *mesa*'s four triangles are also united for action in the cyclical death/rebirth continuum of nature. Thus at midnight, when the *mesa* becomes a fully activated ternary and quaternary whole ($3 + 4 = 7$, the number of the center, which unites spatial opposites), the foundation of the twenty-five thousand temporal or ritual accounts of the entire *mesa*, the psychological structure (three fields: personal projections) and the cosmological structure (four winds: cardinal points) become one.

But until this unity is achieved, there is an underlying tension between the ternary and quarternary structures. The fact that the séance opens and closes with an invocation to the four winds and the four roads seems to indicate that this basic conflict is always resolved in favor of the balanced, cyclical, cosmological dimension—that the limitations of the human condition are transcended. In other words, a human moral dilemma of either/or is re-solved in favor of nature's solution: both. For life is not possible without both sides of the coin: good *and* evil, life *and* death, male *and* female, light *and* dark. Not that the ternary structure of the *mesa* does not include both sides of the coin. They are there, but Christian ideology and a modern ra-tionalistic orientation overemphasize the *Campo Justiciero,* or larger right side of the *mesa.* The *Campo Ganadero* and *Campo Medio* together do not equal the distorted size of the *Campo Justiciero.* And the "center" is to the right of true center, to make sure it is well within the domain of "goodness."

From what we have learned of Inca cosmology (chapter 7), the pattern for these three fields can probably be traced to the three axes (male, female, middle) of the wall above the *mesa*-like altar of the Temple of the Sun. The antecedent for the four winds may have been the center of the Inca cosmogram, which was occupied by a natural cross (the Southern Cross) located at true center, the junction of the four roads. The three fields were symmetrical, not asymmetrical as they are on Eduardo's *mesa.* In addition, the concept of cyclical regeneration was much more explicit, more con-sciously elaborated, in the Inca cosmic ideogram. But the Incas were por-traying an agriculturist's view of the world that still borrowed its models directly from nature and had not experienced the double shock of Spanish conquest and modernization.

Eduardo is influenced by the Indian past, but his projection includes the changes that history has wrought in the world view of the peoples of northern Peru. These changes include Christian ideology and Western rationalism. Although these two trends are very different, both have strengthened Western man's emphasis on the conscious ego while suppressing the develop-ment of the unconscious side of human nature. Thus, if Eduardo's conscious division of the *mesa* into three fields is visualized as a projection of the con-flict between the conscious and unconscious forces of the psyche, it can be seen to reflect the human condition of the people of northern Peru quite well; the unconscious or "pagan" or "evil" artifacts (including the Middle Field) are being pushed off the table to the left, while the conscious or "good" or Christian artifacts are doing the pushing, resulting in the unbalanced, asymmetrical structure of the three fields. But the placement of the "center" to the right of true center counters this push to the left, so that the crucifix really acts as an axis, or pivot, holding the entire system together and making it possible for the Middle Field to mediate between the opposites.

As we noted in chapter 6, Eduardo is quite aware of what he is doing in his construction and activation of the three fields of the *mesa*. However, it is interesting to observe how unconsciously he formulated the quaternary structure of the four roads as contrasted with his conscious and deliberate elaboration of the three fields. Eduardo recognizes that the four roads divide his *mesa* into four equal triangles, but that is as far as his analysis goes. During my last field session prior to finishing this book, when I pointed out that the artifacts of the four triangles are generically grouped, just as those of the three fields are, he indicated that he had never realized this in all his years of practice.

As we have seen, the pre-Columbian pattern for the four roads was provided by the four *suyos* of Cuzco and the Inca Empire. But spontaneous quaternary structuring of mandala constructions is also a universal characteristic of the human psyche during the individuation process. This often grows out of a competition between 3 and 4. Jung (1958: 90–91) explains that the opposition between threeness and fourness, or threeness as compared with wholeness, was known in alchemy as the axiom of María.* Alchemical philosophy, which was concerned with the problem for over a thousand years, developed a lower earthly triad (similar to Dante's three-headed Devil) as a counterpart for the divine Trinity. According to Jung this symbolism

> represents a principle which . . . betrays affinities with evil, though it is by no means certain that it expresses nothing but evil. Everything points rather to the fact that evil, or its familiar symbolism, belongs to the family of figures which describe the dark, nocturnal, lower, chthonic element. In this symbolism the lower stands to the higher as a correspondence in reverse; that is to say, it is conceived, like the upper, as a triad. . . .
>
> Between the three and the four there exists the primary opposition of male and female, but whereas fourness is a symbol of wholeness, threeness is not. The latter . . . denotes polarity, since one triad always presupposes another, just as high presupposes low, lightness darkness, good evil. In terms of energy polarity means a potential, and wherever a potential exists there is the possibility of a current, a flow of events, for the tension of opposites strives for balance. (1958: 91)

Jung goes on to demonstrate how three can be derived from four, by imagining the quaternity as a square divided in half by a diagonal. This produces two triangles with their apexes pointing in opposite directions. Metaphorically it can be said that if one divides the wholeness symbolized by the quaternity into two equal parts, two opposing triads are produced.

Following Jung's analogy further with reference to the *mesa*, drawing two

---

*Jung points out that the opening words of Plato's *Timaeus* provided the earliest literary version of this problem. It was dealt with again in the Cabiri scene in *Faust*, when Goethe reminded us of Plato's formulation of the topic.

diagonals (that is, the four roads) produces two pairs of opposing triads (see figures 6-1 and 6-3 in photo insert). But applying the single diagonal presents a dilemma: Which two of the four corners are to be selected as the beginning and end points of the dividing line? The answer is probably provided by the dynamics of ritual. For example, if a particular account calls for positive input, then the diagonal should be drawn from the upper left corner to the lower right, which places the phallic shell at the apex of the positive-input triad in opposition to the negative-output triangle. However, if the account requires negative input, the diagonal should be drawn from the upper right corner to the lower left, which places the vulva shell at the apex of the negative-input triad in opposition to the positive-output triangle. Thus the tension between 3 and 4 in the structure of the *mesa* also nurtures the interaction of other oppositions—male/female, positive/negative, and so forth.

In chapter 9 we saw that the spiral is Eduardo's inner personal mandala. It first developed in childhood dreams and visions. It is incised on his rattle, with which he activates all of the accounts and charms of the *mesa*. It manifests itself during a séance as the psychic process of "unfolding," when he realizes his "second person," or "other I." And it forms two invisible cones—one above and one below the *mesa*—which assume a diamond or egg shape. After our second trip to Las Huaringas in fall 1971 Eduardo began conducting noon rituals to "charge" his *mesa*. By fall 1973 these rituals had evolved into half-hour divination ceremonies for patients conducted within a triangle (that is, the spiral seen from the side) enclosed within a circle (that is, the spiral seen from the top). These symbols were traced on the ground in white cornmeal, with the base of the triangle to the north. The patient stood facing north inside the apex of the triangle. Thus Eduardo's outer mandala now includes the circle as well as the quadrangle. Both have been elaborated idiosyncratically with ingenuity and originality. As is true of all good shamans, Eduardo's power is ripening with age.

THE *MESA* AS A *TONAL* ISLAND

In his fourth book, Castaneda (1974) reports on the successful culmination of his apprenticeship under his Yaqui shaman-mentor, don Juan.* Shortly before guiding Castaneda through two final mystical experiences, don Juan embarks on an explanation of the concepts of *tonal* and *nagual*.

These terms refer to the two sides of every human being. The *tonal* is the social person, the part that apprehends the individual's order amid the chaos

---

*Even Richard De Mille, who contends that the books of Castaneda are fiction, recognizes that the "trickster teacher" has something to tell us (see *Castaneda's Journey: The Power and the Allegory*, 1976). Since I have not done field work in Sonora or Arizona or met don Juan Matus, I do not feel qualified to judge the ethnographic veracity of Castaneda's writings. In the following pages, through comparative analysis, I hope to apply the didactic, philosophical aspects of his work constructively.

of the world. As such, it is everything we are and know, all that meets the eye. Thus it acts as a guardian that protects our very being. However, as we become more worldly it gradually changes from a broadminded, understanding guardian into a narrow-minded, despotic guard that keeps us from realizing our full potential as human beings. The *tonal* begins at birth and ends at death.

In order to clarify what he means by *tonal*, don Juan draws an analogy. Running his hand over the top of a table at which he and Castaneda are eating, he says that "the *tonal* is like the top of this table. An island. And on this island we have everything. This island is, in fact, the world." (1974: 125.)* According to him, everything we know about the world and ourselves is on the *tonal* island. He adds that each person has an individual *tonal* and that there is a collective *tonal* for everyone at any given time — the *tonal* of the times. Pointing to the tables in the restaurant, he elaborates on this point by indicating that they all have the same configuration and hold the same items despite the fact that they are individually different. Similarly, the *tonal* of the times makes us all alike, although each personal *tonal* is an individual perception.

Don Juan describes the *nagual* as "the part of us for which there is no description; no words, no names, no feelings, no knowledge." (1974: 125.) Castaneda's response is that this is a contradiction, that if the *nagual* cannot be felt, described, or named, it cannot exist. He then probes don Juan for a more precise definition, asking if the *nagual* is the mind, or the soul, or the thoughts of humanity, or a state of grace, or pure intellect, psyche, energy, vital force, immortality, the life principle, or even God. Every time he mentions a different category don Juan insists that it is an item on the table; he takes one of the articles from the table and stacks it up in front of Castaneda. When Castaneda mentions God, don Juan jokingly makes a gesture as if he is going to pile up the tablecloth in front of his pupil.

Finally, taking a different tack, Castaneda asks the shaman where the *nagual* is located. Making a sweeping gesture with the back of his hand as if cleaning an area that reaches beyond the edges of the table, don Juan replies, "There, surrounding the island. The *nagual* is there, where power hovers." He adds that for a while after birth we are all *nagual*. But we sense that the *tonal*, which is needed in order to function, is missing. This gives us a lingering feeling of incompleteness. Then the *tonal* begins to develop, eventually becoming so important that it overwhelms the *nagual*.

Don Juan points out that once we become all *tonal* we begin making pairs, since we sense our two sides. However, we always represent these two sides with items from the *tonal* island. Thus we create false dichotomies such as the soul and the body, mind and matter, good and evil, God and Satan, all the while not realizing that we are pairing things on the island.

Castaneda, trying to achieve a better understanding, asks what specifically

*For a more graphic use of the table as a didactic device, see Castaneda (1977: 282-83).

can be found beyond the island. Don Juan asserts that there is no way to answer such a question. If he answers "nothing," that would only make the *nagual* part of the *tonal*. All he can say is that beyond the island the *nagual* is to be found.

Castaneda counters by rhetorically asking, Doesn't the very fact of labeling the *nagual* and becoming aware of it place it on the island? Don Juan asserts that he has simply named the *tonal* and the *nagual* as a true pair. Then he reminds his pupil about one of Castaneda's own attempts to explain his insistence on meaning. At that time Castaneda had suggested that for children the difference between "father" and "mother" might not be clear until they had become quite advanced in comprehension. In the meantime they might think that such pairs as pants versus skirts or long hair versus short explained the difference. This is analogous to our understanding of the difference between the *tonal* and *nagual*. We feel that we have another side to our nature. But when we try to discover it, the petty, jealous *tonal* interferes and cunningly induces us to suppress any expression of the *nagual* as the other side of the true pair.

Once don Juan has laid the philosophical foundation outlined above, he labors patiently to construct an edifice of meaning for Castaneda, or more correctly, for his *tonal*, in preparation for his confrontation with the *nagual* — or the "ally," as don Juan has referred to it prior to the conversation reported above. He tells Castaneda that for a proper warrior everything on the island — that is, in the world — is a challenge, with the greatest challenge being the bid for power that comes from the *nagual*. To deal with this bid, the warrior first brings perfect balance and harmony to two levels of his *tonal:* decisions and actions. Then he must learn to achieve harmony between his *tonal* and *nagual*. Don Juan says that "one of the balancing acts of the warrior is to make the *nagual* emerge in order to prop up the *tonal*," allowing the latter to be the "protected overseer." (1974: 161.) He calls the process by which the *nagual* props up the *tonal* "personal power."

From the foregoing it should be apparent that don Juan's ideas can be used to understand Eduardo's symbol system. Conceptualized as a *tonal* island, the *mesa* proves to be an excellent prop for therapy. As a psychological projection it graphically illustrates to the patient the subtle intrigues of the personal *tonal* in manipulating pairs — for example, good and evil, positive and negative. As a microcosmos it portrays the same conflict of opposites on the collective level, reflecting the *tonal* of the times, with Christian moralism and rationalism exacerbating the tension of opposites by introducing imbalance into the equation. Charging and balancing the *mesa* demonstrates how the *tonal*, both personal and collective, can become harmonized and truly effective in life by drawing on the cosmic sea of *nagual* that surrounds and supports it. Ritual taps this power in order to "prop up" the *tonal-mesa*, and by extension, the patient's personal *tonal*. But it is only the mediating shaman who "sees" the *nagual*, for only he has learned how to make it operative in his daily life. His excursions into the *nagual* are personal and private. They cannot be described, for, as don Juan wisely notes, the *nagual* can only be witnessed; it is indescribable. The average patient who comes to Eduardo is only concerned with temporarily balancing disharmonies in his personal *tonal*, and is not much concerned with learning how to put the *nagual* to work in his life on a more permanent basis. In this respect his participation in Eduardo's magical world is not much different from his participation in orthodox religion: It is activated when expedient and experienced vicariously.

Another aspect of don Juan's teachings that allegorically sheds some light on Eduardo's system is his use of mandala-like structures as didactic devices. One example—revealed to Castaneda prior to his meeting with his mentor in Mexico City—is a trapezoid* containing eight points connected by lines drawn on the ground with ashes (1974: 98-101). Although the outer form is irrelevant, the points represent the totality of a human being and correspond to certain areas in the body (which don Juan prefers to call "the fibers of a luminous being"; elsewhere he says that man is a luminous egg). The diagram has two epicenters called *reason* and *will*. *Reason* connects directly with a point called *talking* and indirectly to three other points: *feeling*, *dreaming*, and *seeing*. *Will* connects directly with five points, which include *feeling*, *dreaming*, and *seeing*, and indirectly with *reason* and *talking*.

The remaining two points directly connected to will are not named by don Juan, since he contends that Castaneda is not strong enough for this knowledge at the time he is shown the trapezoid. They are revealed only at the last "seminar" conducted for Castaneda by don Juan after their meeting in Mexico City. At that time, after recapitulating the growth process he has put his apprentice through during fourteen years of training, the shaman draws an imaginary circle on a rock and divides it in two by a vertical diameter in order to illustrate what he calls the "bubble of perception," or world view, that we eventually become sealed into after birth (1974: 248). He tells Castaneda that the art of a teacher consists in forcing his disciple to group his world view on the right side of the bubble, the side of reason. This strengthens it and eventually keeps it from being threatened by the *nagual*. As everything becomes reordered on the side of reason, the left side of the bubble becomes cleared so that it can eventually be claimed by will. At this point the novice's "benefactor" (the person who introduced him to "power") is responsible for opening the bubble on the side that has been cleared. This allows the luminous being that has been trapped inside to view his totality by transcending the description of himself and the world reflected on the curved walls of the bubble. After this event the ex-apprentice is never the same. He commands his totality with the *tonal* as the ultimate center of his *reason* and the *nagual* as the ultimate center of his *will*.

---

*In Castaneda's 1974 book (p. 98), this is called a "geometrical figure" only. However, in the typed manuscript (p. 125 of copy 38 of 53, dated May 1974) the phrase was "geometrical figure; a trapezoid."

The seminar continues after a mystical experience during which Castaneda perceives the *nagual* at night while facing north on the brink of one of nature's tables, a flat-topped butte, or *mesa*. At that time don Juan reveals the final part of the "sorcerer's explanation": that the last two points composing the totality of man are the *nagual* and the *tonal*. The paradox of luminous beings is that these two points are outside them, and yet they are not. As don Juan puts it: "The *tonal* of every one of us is but a reflection of that indescribable unknown filled with order; the *nagual* of every one of us is but a reflection of that indescribable void that contains everything." (1974: 270–71.)

Returning to Eduardo's system, although there is not an exact correspondence between the *mesa* as a therapeutic prop and the didactic structures drawn by don Juan, the concentration of all the "good" artifacts on the right nonetheless seems to be a technique for reassuring reason or ego consciousness that it has nothing to fear in a balanced encounter with "power." Eduardo's emphasis on the right side of the *mesa* is very similar to don Juan's reordering of the right side of the bubble of perception. This concentration on the right is reinforced by the ritual avoidance of the left side of the *mesa;* Eduardo's assistants ("benefactors") indirectly activate it (and his alter ego) through the mediation of the Middle-Field. And it takes a magical act of will by Paul to bring Judas (who, along with the number 13, is mysteriously missing from the *mesa*) into the power equation. This act of will culminates the activation of the *mesa* as a totality. After the *curandero* has been raised he also realizes his own totality, which is manifested as the unfolding of his alter ego. This parallels Castaneda's experience, for after he witnesses the *nagual* don Juan tells him that his bubble of perception has opened on the left side—the side of will—and unfolded its "wings of perception," allowing him to touch his totality. The shaman adds that his apprentice has experienced "the double" by traveling back and forth between the *nagual* and *tonal* and realizing that the bubble of perception is a "cluster."

It appears, then, that there is a great deal of structural similarity between the teachings of don Juan and Eduardo's symbol system. In terms of mandala symbolism it is appropriate that both men depict totality-as-process with four-sided structures, while totality-as-reality is depicted with circles. After making allowances for cultural variation, differences in their respective formulations can probably be accounted for by differences in their ages and personalities. For power comes to a man in accord with his individual nature, and once it arrives there are an infinite number of paths to be explored.

12

Closing the "Account"

In analyzing the artifacts and rituals associated with manipulation of the power concentrated by Eduardo's *mesa*, we have noted a basic underlying theme: metamorphosis (death and rebirth). This is achieved through the balancing, or centering, of psychological and cosmological forces in space and time. The medium for this balancing process is a symbolic system of communication triggered by the hallucinogenic San Pedro cactus. Although Christian symbolism is woven into the entire fabric of the *mesa*, we have seen that it is reinterpreted in order to provide a vehicle for the expression of the underlying archetypal images of the shamanistic substratum. Thus the syncretism of Indian and Christian religious forms has become a functional and highly adaptive cultural configuration that is still serving the psychological and social needs of the *mestizo* people of northern Peru. The significance of this fact for northern Peruvian society is aptly expressed by Furst (1965: 75), who, referring to Lévi-Strauss (1950) observes:

> [S]ocieties with flourishing shamanism have suffered far fewer cases of neurosis and psychosis when faced with the pressures of modern technological civilization that those which had weak shamanism or none at all.

This brings us back to the major underlying assumption of this work: that Eduardo "is manipulating a coherent system of symbolic communication" consisting of a nonverbal "code" that finds expression in observable acts and artifacts. From the foregoing it should be apparent that Eduardo's system really *is* a system and that it "makes sense," as shown by his behavior in manipulating matter (power objects) and energy (power) in space (*mesa* as a conglomeration of power objects) and time (*mesa* as a nighttime curing ritual). As we have noted, during a *mesa* Eduardo manipulates acts and artifacts on the psychological and cosmological levels simultaneously; both of these taken together constitute the code behind Eduardo's system.

This process can be summarized as follows:

Code		Behavior	
	Acts	Artifacts	
Psychological (projection)	linear	good and evil	Mesa
Cosmological (identification)	cyclical	death and rebirth	

The psychological level appears to be largely conscious, while the cosmological dimension seems to be relatively unconscious (although, as noted, the psychological level can also symbolize the psychic conflict between ego consciousness and the depths of the unconscious). Ritual *mesa* acts dramatize the expenditure of energy in time, while *mesa* artifacts are an expression of matter in space. But the very fact that act and artifact are both expressed linguistically by the same word, *mesa*, indicates the basic unity behind Eduardo's symbol system as governed by the underlying code. On the psychological level of the three fields, the code is linear mediation or balance (the dialectic of good and evil); whereas on the cosmological level of the four roads and winds, the code is cyclical regeneration (death and rebirth). Thus we can say that the two interrelated themes underlying Eduardo's system are equilibrium and metamorphosis. Together they mediate the tension between opposites symbolized by both power objects and curing rituals. In short, they constitute the message or meaning that is conveyed by the shaman as "transmitter" (although he also receives from the cosmos) and picked up by the patient as "receiver"—a process that includes the activities by which the *mesa* is "charged" and "discharged." The intimate relation of code, act, and artifact in the *mesa* seems to justify my humanistic adaptation of structuralist theory.

Borrowing from Jungian psychology and from Wilbert (1972a), the representational model presented in figure 12-1 summarizes what we have learned about Eduardo's system. The model depicts the human psyche (including its conscious and unconscious divisions) interacting with other psyches and its total environment—that is, the natural and supernatural ecologies and human culture. (The biological organism is considered to be intimately linked with the psyche.) The shaman is seen as the centered, or integrated, man who focuses his conscious and unconscious faculties (including the Jungian four parts of the psyche—ego, anima, shadow, and self—and the four functions of consciousness—thinking, sensation, intuition, and feeling) in a balanced fashion upon other psyches and his total environment. In other words, he walks the "razor's edge," or *Campo Medio*, between the natural and supernatural universes and is therefore capable of entering and leaving them both at will. In this process of equilibrium the tension of opposing forces is transcended or channeled and the shaman becomes one with the cosmos. This implies a symbolic death and rebirth which makes ecstatic magical flight, vision, and conquest of the barriers of space and time a reality. Finally, the shaman's balance provides him with an incredible adaptive

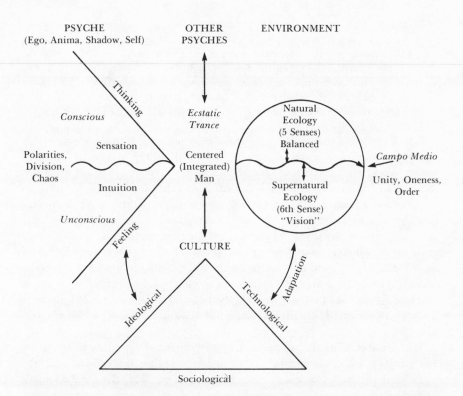

PSYCHE
(Ego, Anima, Shadow, Self)

OTHER
PSYCHES

ENVIRONMENT

Figure 12-1. The balanced shaman interacting with environment and culture.

capacity to assimilate changes in culture along all three of its dimensions: sociological, ideological, and technological. In short, equilibrium is the core of Eduardo's entire way of life.

Eduardo's modern shamanism is simply new foliage on a very old tree. In striving for metaphysical equilibrium Eduardo has much in common with men of other times and places. For the history of religion reveals that symbolizations of the spiritual process of transcending opposites or the *coincidentia oppositorum*—that is, the union of contraries or mystery of the totality (a term coined by Nicholas of Cusa, one of the last of the medieval Christian mystics)—crops up over and over again in myth and symbolism all over the world. After surveying cross-culturally the numerous occurrences of this concept in myths, symbols, rites, mystical techniques, legends, and beliefs, Eliade (1965: 122-23) summarizes the meanings of the union of contraries. He says that it reflects

> man's deep dissatisfaction with his actual situation, with what is called the human condition. Man feels himself torn and separate. He often finds it difficult properly to explain to himself the nature of this separation, for sometimes he feels himself cut off from "something" *powerful,* "something" utterly *other*

than himself, and at other times from an indefinable, timeless "state," of which he has no precise memory, but which he does however remember in the depths of his being: a primordial state which he enjoyed before Time, before History. This separation has taken the form of a fissure, both in himself and in the World. It was the "fall," not necessarily in the Judeo-Christian meaning of the term, but a fall nevertheless since it implies a fatal disaster for the human race and at the same time an ontological change in the structure of the World.

Eliade contends that this reveals a nostalgia for a paradoxical condition in which opposites are reunited and the flux and variety of human life constitute aspects of a mysterious One. Man's desire to recover this lost unity has led him to conceive of opposites as complementary. Historically his need to transcend the tension between opposites eventually resulted in philosophical and theological speculation. But, before being formulated as a philosophical concept, the *coincidentia oppositorum* emerged in myths, rituals, and mystical techniques. In preliterate thought it was expressed in such formulas as evil stimulating good or demons representing the night aspect of the gods. That the union of contraries remains an integral part of human existence is revealed by the fact that this archaic theme survives in folklore and mystical philosophy and in the dream life, imagination, and artistic creations of modern man.

What makes Eduardo unique is the modern, eclectic manner in which he has readapted archaic shamanism in order to realize the *coincidentia oppositorum* within his own age and cultural milieu. But, despite Eduardo's idiosyncratic innovation, the *mesa* concept and related cosmological notions are quite widespread in Latin America and seem to have their roots in an archaic ideological substratum. This may not be so surprising if a suggestion by Furst (1973–74:53) is eventually proved to be correct. As he puts it, in addition to

the shamanistic Asian ancestry of the hallucinogenic-ecstatic complex in American Indian religion and ritual, the striking similarity of much of the American Indian world view as a whole to that of the peoples of Asia, down to a virtual identity of some basic cosmological beliefs and symbols, also suggests that at least some of the intellectual foundations of the great Indian civilizations, beginning with the Olmec about 1300 B.C. may have been present in the shamanistic ideational universe of those self-same "primitive" big-game hunters, and their successors in the North American Archaic, just as certain archaic shamanistic concepts and techniques—revitalization of the bones and animal transformation among them—were still very much a part of thought and ritual in the complex civilization of the Aztecs, as late as the sixteenth century A.D.

In addition to cosmological notions, certain distinctive traits of shamanism appear to be quite stable. In a discussion of the "physiognomy" of South American tropical-forest shamanism, Métraux (1944) specified these traits. He showed that shamanism was dominated by male practitioners; women were not excluded, but they invariably had a modest role in comparison with that of males. Métraux further pointed out that the shaman was often religiously inclined and meditative but could also be of a nervous temperament, restless and unstable. He emphasized the honesty and scrupulousness of shamans in the application of their art.

Supernatural power was often hereditary, but it was derived from contact with the spirits realized by means of a supernatural revelation and/or training under an experienced shaman. This power was conceived of as an invisible substance incorporated within the shaman's body and capable of materializing in the form of magic arrows, spines, and quartz crystals. It was also identified with auxiliary or familiar spirits controlled by the shaman. The extent of his power was conceived to be in direct proportion to the number of spirits he controlled. Métraux distinguished between shamans possessed by the spirits and those who acted more as seers in consulting with the spirits, suggesting that the latter type was more common in the tropical-forest region.

The shaman's major accessories were the gourd rattle and rock crystals, supplemented in some places by a bench or staff. Substances used to induce the shamanic trance state were tobacco juice or smoke, throughout the entire area;* supplemented by *ayahuasca* (*Banisteriopsis caapi*) and *huanto* (*Datura* spp.), in the Upper Amazon basin; and *parica* snuff (*Anadenanthera* spp.), in the Lower Amazon basin.

The essential function of the shaman was to cure sickness chiefly through a séance in which he employed massage, fumigation with tobacco smoke, and suction to extract foreign objects or pathogens, usually sent by a sorcerer. Other functions of the shaman included predicting the future, interpreting omens, protecting the community from destruction by the elements, guaranteeing game, distributing magical force to the needy, and organizing and directing religious ceremonies and dances. Métraux noted the ambiguous role of the tropical-forest shaman; in addition to countering sorcery, he was also capable of performing it, particularly in killing tribal enemies at a distance. As the only specialist in tribal societies without a complex division of labor, the shaman enjoyed a lucrative social position of much prestige and authority, but only among the Guaraní did he exercise actual political power. There was no real distinction between priest and shaman among these peoples, since the shaman performed many priestly functions without requiring the authority of an official cult to support his practices. Finally, Métraux demonstrated the general applicability of his physiognomy by showing that the same notions and practices found in tropical-forest shamanism could be found elsewhere in South America, in North America, in Siberia, and even in Australia.

*In a recent survey of the magico-religious use of tobacco in South America, Wilbert (1975a: 458) concluded that this important magical plant "served as the bond of communion between the natural and supernatural worlds."

Consideration of Eduardo's system reveals many similarities to the shamanism of the tropical forest, despite the great differences in culture and ecology between north-coastal Peru and the tropical-forest region. For example, we have found that Eduardo is religiously inclined, meditative, and characterized by scrupulous honesty in his practices. He could hardly be described as nervous, restless, or unstable, but Métraux did not consider that all shamans were. They may be observed to be this way at the time of their mystical "call," but what sets the shaman apart from psychologically unbalanced individuals is his remarkable will and capacity for self-cure. The following remarks about the tropical-forest shaman of Colombia certainly apply to Eduardo:

> What distinguishes a *payé* [shaman] from others is that he is an intellectual. . . . He is a humanist, in the sense that he is interested in the "pagan" antiquities of his own cultural tradition: in myths of origin, in archeological sites, in long-forgotten place names, and in stories of legendary migrations. (Reichel-Dolmatoff, 1975: 107)

Regarding Eduardo's supernatural power, it seems to have been partially inherited from his maternal and paternal grandfathers and was imparted by divine election and "sickness-vocation." Training under veteran shamans helped him to refine his power. In accord with his modern orientation, Eduardo describes power in semiscientific terminology—as "magnetism," which is incorporated in all human bodies although only the shaman is fully aware of it. But the concept of the "account" of an artifact approaches the idea of an invisible substance capable of materializing in tangible objects. Eduardo, too, has his familiar spirits: the spirits of lagoons, mountains, and archeological shrines, as well as of saints and other *curanderos,* alive and dead. And his power seems to have increased in direct proportion to the growing number of artifacts and associated spirits accumulated on his *mesa* over the years. Eduardo is not possessed by the spirits; rather, he is a seer who controls them during ecstatic magical flight and vision. He is also capable of shape-shifting, or transformation, and acts as a psychopomp, or guide, for the souls of the dead—two other abilities characteristic of tropical-forest shamans but not mentioned by Métraux. (For transformation, see Furst, 1968c, and Reichel-Dolmatoff, 1975; for the role of psychopomp, see Eliade, 1964: 326.)

Like these shamans, Eduardo uses such accessories as a gourd rattle, quartz crystals, and staffs. His narcotics include tobacco and occasionally *Datura. Ayahuasca,* which does not grow on the north coast, is replaced by San Pedro. *Parica* snuff is not used, although we suspect that the plants that produce it grow in northern Peru.*

---

*Snuff trays of whalebone and snuff tubes of bird and fox bones found at Huaca Prieta by Bird (see Wassén, 1967: 256–57) indicate that some kind of snuff was used in the north ca. 1200 B.C. Why its use did not survive with that of San Pedro is a mystery.

Regarding his functions, Eduardo cures by means of a séance that occasionally involves massage, fumigations, and suction to extract pathogens. He predicts the future and interprets omens during séances and when he divines with guinea pigs, cards, and Maximón. On the rainless desert coast of the north, protection against the elements and rites to encourage game increase are not required by the modern middle-class population, but fertility magic is occasionally applied for cases of crop damage produced by a sorcerer's spell; for fishermen; for "raising a patient's luck" (increasing his material wealth); or for undoing a love spell. Although Eduardo does not direct public religious ceremonies (a function reserved for the priest, who is distinguished from the shaman in Catholic northern Peru), he has a great deal of prestige in his community, especially related to the distribution of magical force to the needy, and he recently held a political post. Because of his Christian ideology, Eduardo's role as a "white" shaman is very clear to him and his peers. But ambiguous *brujos* are very common in more tradition-bound areas of the north. And sometimes during divination, especially in the context of a séance, Eduardo is quite capable of playing the "Devil's advocate" or "trickster."

Thus, although it is shaped by his particular society and environment, Eduardo's shamanism is much more than a culture-specific phenomenon. This is not unusual, for as Furst (1973-74: 39) informs us:

> Apart from its remarkable survival value, perhaps the most interesting historical fact about shamanism is this: it may or may not constitute a group's entire religious system, and shaman's may have come to co-exist, or even merge with, sacrificing priests . . . but wherever the system of shamanism manifests itself today, even vestigially, it is apt to do so with a somewhat similar *Weltanschauung* and cosmology, with similar techniques, and sometimes even with similar symbols, if not in detail then at least in underlying meaning. I should not wish to be misunderstood on this point, for as students of shamanism have often noted, the overt manifestations of shamanism can differ even within one more or less homogenous culture area or closely related population. What concerns us here is not so much the specific but some of the fundamental assumptions of shamanism as a system of dealing with universal problems of mankind.

What is the relevance of the study of shamanism for our own society? Part of the answer is given by Furst (1972: xiv) in discussing the ritual use of hallucinogens in other cultures:

> [U]nderstanding the function and the social and physiological effects of the abundant sacred hallucinogenic pharmacopoeia among non-Western peoples may, on the one hand, help lower the level of public hysteria about . . . dangers in the use of hallucinogens and, on the other, make drug users themselves more aware of spurious versus genuine culture. Ideally, it may also help in the formulation of more realistic and intelligent drug legislation. . . . [W]e still know far too little of this important area of the study of

man. . . . There is an obvious need, then, to illuminate the role of the cultural variable in the use of hallucinogens, the important and often decisive parts these drugs have played and continue to play in a variety of sociocultural contexts (especially in religious belief and ritual and the preservation of cultural independence and integrity), and the part they might have played historically in the remote origins of religion itself.

Another part of the answer lies in the fact that modern man desperately needs a better understanding of himself and his place in the Universe. This is required to offset the dehumanization, alienation, and ecological crisis of our world resulting from the failure to balance increased scientific and technological learning with growth in self-knowledge. I believe an understanding of shamanism can teach us much about ourselves.

In this regard Eliade (1965: 14–15) feels that as a result of his encounters with non-Western traditions, Western man will be compelled "to explore very deeply into the history of the human mind and perhaps to conclude that he must incorporate this history as an intergral part of his own being." He states the problem he feels is now emerging—one that will become increasingly urgent for researchers of the next generation—in the form of a question: "By what means can we recover what is still recoverable of the spiritual history of humanity?" He gives two reasons for the increase in importance of this problem:

> 1) Western man will not be able to live indefinitely cut off from an important part of himself, a part that is made up of fragments of a spiritual history the significance and message of which he is incapable of deciphering;
> 2) [S]ooner or later the dialogue with the "others" . . . will have to be conducted, no longer in the empirical and utilitarian language of today (which is ony capable of describing social, economic, political, medical, etc., circumstances) but in a cultural language capable of expressing human realities and spiritual values.

Eliade feels that a dialogue of this type is "inevitable," adding that it would be "tragically naive" to continue to believe that it can be sought indefinitely by the methods in vogue today.

The present study represents an attempt to begin such a dialogue. I hope it has shown that a seemingly peripheral complex within north Peruvian society—*curanderismo*—plays a vital role in the adaptation processes of a culture fully engaged in the rapid social change and modernization typical of most developing nations.

I believe that the current situation in northern Peru verifies an assertion made by Furst and Reed (1970: 280):

> [A]dherents of the scientific world view fondly believe that once people become familiar with Western medicine they will quickly forget "all that supernatural nonsense" and turn their backs on the indigenous healer. Not so.

For in the north we find a Spanish-speaking, Catholic, *mestizo* population with a well-developed and Westernized middle class having access to the benefits of modern medicine. And yet this same middle class is strongly represented among the clientele of the contemporary *curandero*, who often combines the use of modern pharmaceutical products with his use of herbs and supernatural therapy. The majority of Eduardo's patients are middle-class urban dwellers.

It is apparent that the *curandero* is adapting to modernization. At the same time, however, he continues to command respect because his calling is firmly rooted in the cultural history and ideology of his milieu. This is obvious in regard to the tradition of San Pedro use dating back to the very beginnings of Central Andean civilization (some three thousand years ago). It is also apparent in the cosmology underlying *mesa* acts and artifacts that is kept alive, albeit in altered form, among the contemporary Quechua and Aymara peoples of Peru and Bolivia.

There are implications here for applied anthropology that sooner or later, I feel, modern planners are going to have to face. As Eduardo's story illustrates, the *curandero* is a health resource utilized extensively in the communities of the north. His vocation is firmly embedded in their cultural heritage. He is part of a grass-roots network established by the people. He is adapting to modern medicine. On the other hand, doctors and health facilities are in short supply and will continue to be for some time to come, given the high costs and lengthy time involved in modern medical training and the rapidity of population growth. It appears that the only realistic solution to health problems in northern Peru is a paramedical program that builds on available human resources, similar to the Chinese "barefoot doctor" program. We now have good evidence that the combination of traditional and modern medicine in China has been a success (Sidel and Sidel, 1974). But to be successful in Peru such a program will have to be built on an understanding that the transmission process is a two-way street. The doctor has much to learn from the *curandero* and vice versa.

Education offers the key to establishing such an understanding. The members of isolated communities have to be taught the basic principles of hygiene and preventive medicine. And medical personnel must be taught the resources and beliefs of such communities to make their services relevant and acceptable to those they are meant to serve. Given recent efforts to reform the Peruvian educational system (see Drysdale and Myers, 1975), perhaps an additional innovation in medical education might be feasible.*

Reciprocity between traditional and modern medicine is not a new idea in Latin America. The Instituto Nacional Indigenista of Mexico has been applying this principle for many years in its integrated program of community development. And a similar professional opinion is held by the world-

---

*In August 1978 I gave a course on folk medicine at the Universidad Nacional de Trujillo, Programa Académica de Ciencias Médicas, under the sponsorship of the Tinker Foundation of New York City.

renowned Peruvian social psychiatrist Dr. Carlos Alberto Seguin. At the First National Congress of Peruvian Psychiatry held in Lima in October 1969 he had the following to say regarding Peruvian shamans:

> From the point of view of our specialization, I dare say—after many years of experience—that we have much to learn from our "colleagues" the "native curers," the "sorcerers," and "healers." We have much to learn, not just about pharmacology, for example, the use of psychotropic plants and drugs, but also in an area that psychiatry is "discovering" in our times, for example, group dynamics, group psychotherapy, family therapy as well as the manipulation of social and communal problems. These are novelties for us, but native practitioners have always manipulated them with enviable ability. (Seguin, 1969: 159)

In the United States the ethnopsychiatrist E. Fuller Torrey (1972: 1) concludes from a cross-cultural survey of traditional therapists that "witchdoctors and psychiatrists perform essentially the same function in their respective cultures." He is a strong advocate of the integration of traditional and modern therapy, despite the resistance he perceives on the part of modern practitioners. As he puts it:

> Medicine can and will change. It can adapt itself to working with nonmedical therapists. Both these therapists and their techniques can be adopted and used to improve mental health services. The brew can be distilled, with the supernatant retained and the residue discarded. And this can be done despite the hoary traditions of medicine and psychiatry, feet firmly planted in the medieval guild system, voices echoing "You just can't do that!" with each footstep down the hall of innovation. (1972: 201)

Torrey (1972: 203) asks us to "put aside our ethnocentrism and look carefully at both witchdoctors and psychiatrists." He adds: "The world has become too small to accommodate arrogance."

In considering the feasibility of learning from the past, it might be well to recall that Eduardo himself, before being healed by a *curandera*, "didn't believe in these things." Of course, he had a cultural heritage that, once rediscovered, helped him to overcome his skepticism and eventually learn *curandero* therapy. But, as members of the family of man, we all share the same human heritage. This is a lesson that Eduardo, and men like him, can teach us—if we are willing to learn.

Appendixes

A: *MESA* ARTIFACTS

The following description of Eduardo's *mesa* is extracted from taped explanations given to me in the summer of 1970 and again in the fall of 1971, and updated in the winter of 1974. From other studies we know that images of saints, shells, archeological objects, jars of herbs, stones, crystals, staffs, swords, daggers, and rattles appear on all northern *mesas* (see Mac-Lain y Estenós, 1939, and 1942: 410, 412-13; Gillin, 1947: 123-25; Cruz Sánchez, 1948, 1951; Friedberg, 1959: 446-47, and 1963: 43-44, 101-11; Chiappe, 1968: 15-18; and Dobkin de Rios, 1968: 192-93, and 1968:69: 26). However, northern *curanderos* and *brujos* are very individualistic. Each sets up his *mesa* according to his own idiosyncratic needs and inspiration. Since no previous ethnographer has questioned shamans regarding the symbolic zoning of power objects, we do not know if the three fields of Eduardo's *mesa (Justiciero, Ganadero, Medio)* are his own creation or part of the tradition. His tutors made a vague distinction between benevolent right/malevolent left but did not have a middle zone. This is a question requiring research with other shamans.

Staffs

Campo Ganadero

I. *Bayoneta de Satanas* (Satan's Bayonet): Supposedly from the time of the French Revolution, when it was stained with human blood, this artifact symbolizes the malevolent powers of evil, such as Satan, his assistants, all the demons of Hell, and certain mountains where these powers are concentrated. Sorcerers conclude midnight pacts *(compactos negros)* with the Devil and petition his aid by applying *cañazo* (sugar-cane alcohol, water, and sugar) to this bayonet, followed by the appropriate ceremonies to invoke the thirteen and thirty thousand mystical accounts of Satan. For Eduardo, the bayonet is symbolically connected to Triton Shell (1), Snake Stone (2), and Deer Foot (3).

II. *Vara Lechuza* (Owl Staff): This is a rosewood staff with ambivalent referents. It is a symbol of wisdom and vision related to the owl's ability to see in the dark. However, it also symbolizes corpses, cemeteries, the spirits of the dead, and the spirits of the *huacas*, a term applied to pre-Columbian grave objects or ruins. *Brujos* use this staff for purposes of witchcraft, as opposed to *curanderos*, who use it for diagnosing and countering the effects of witchcraft. It is symbolically connected to Owl Stone (13), Vampire Bat Ceramic (14), Bound Corn Stone (28), and Bound Humans and Whirlpool Stones (29).

III. *Vara de la Señorita* (Staff of the Single Woman): This staff, made from black *chonta* wood, is symbolic of certain sacred highland lagoons and a shawl-wearing female guardian who protects these lagoons, along with the magical plants found near them and used in healing. *Brujos* use this staff to help a client (whether male or female) to perform *enredo*, entanglement of a mate or companion, a love spell; *curanderos* use it to bring about *desenredo*, disentanglement. In curing, it connects with sweet lime (77) in the *Campo Justiciero*.

Campo Medio

IV. *Vara Serpiente de Moisés y Solomón* (Serpent Staff of Moses and Solomon): This staff of *guayacán* wood is representative of the sun and the oceans, symbolizing the duality of light and water, as well as all mountains, lagoons, ancient shrines, streams, and magical herb gardens of northern Peru. Included in the realm of this staff are such personages as Moses, Solomon (the staff symbolizes his collarbone), and Saint Cyprian, who are all considered to have been masters of the magical and religious arts and therefore capable of harmonizing the two extremes of good and evil—which is the main function of the *Campo Medio* governed by this staff. Working in conjunction with the statue of Saint Cyprian, the Serpent Staff also symbolizes a red dragon and the three pyramids of Egypt. It is connected to Moses and the Red Sea Stone (57) in the *Campo Justiciero*.

Campo Justiciero

V. *Pico de Pez Espada* (Swordfish Beak): This is an authentic swordfish beak which symbolizes the seven seas, the powerful fish they contain, and the fish's speed of passage through the water. It is used to locate sailors or fishermen lost at sea, shipwrecks, drowned people, and sunken treasure, or to bring luck to fishermen and sailors. It is one of the artifacts associated with journeys to the underworld and is connected to the Sea and Winds Stone (33) in the *Campo Medio*.

VI. *Vara Águila* (Eagle Staff): The Eagle Staff is made of black *chonta* wood, with the dried head of an eagle and its claws affixed to the top. This staff is under the aegis of the Caesars of Rome and symbolizes great "vision" (related to the eagle's sharp sight), intelligence, power, ambition, triumph, good luck, and success in love, intellectual pursuits, and business. It is used to change bad luck, to bolster morale, or to guarantee good luck in present and future ventures. It is also a symbol of magical flight connected with sweet lime (77) and major mountain peaks such as Huascarán, Huandóy, Hualcán, Misti, Pelagato, Monte Aguja, and Machu Picchu.

VII. *Vara del Galgo* (Grayhound Staff): This is a black *chonta* wood staff with an ivory handle in the shape of a grayhound's head. Under the aegis of Saint Jerome, this artifact is used when the *curandero* is attempting to locate a lost person or object for his petitioner. The Grayhound Staff is also used to discover the whereabouts of people who have run away or stolen objects, because of its great tracking ability and sense of smell. It is another symbol for great speed and is often referred to as *alcosunca* (a spotted, short-haired dog) or *alcocala* (a hairless dog).

VIII. *Vara Chupaflor* (Hummingbird Staff): This is a rosewood staff used for removing sicknesses or pains by means of vomiting or sweating, because of its capacity to extract by sucking. In curing it connects symbolically with sweet lime (77) and "gardens" of magical herbs visited by the shaman in trances.

IX. *Vara de la Virgen de las Mercedes* (Staff of the Virgin of Mercy): This staff is made of black *chonta* wood capped with an expended military cartridge. It symbolizes the seven Churches of early Christianity and all the saints and prayers of the Roman Catholic Church, along with Moses and Solomon. It is used to promote good luck, especially in intellectual endeavors and marriage, for those who desire such luck for unselfish reasons. The Virgin of Mercy is the patron of the military forces of Peru. Thus the staff is a focal point of great force and power on the side of good and is connected to the Soldier Stone (54), sweet lime (77), Lord of Huamán (70), Saint Paul (61), and Saint Francis (41). The accounts of the Virgin, the Divine Judge, the saints, and Saint Joseph, patron of the home, are symbolically stored here.

X. *Espada de San Pablo* (Sword of Saint Paul): This sword, supposedly used by a Chilean soldier in the War of the Pacific in the late nineteenth century, symbolizes judges, lawyers (especially Saint Paul, the great lawyer of Christianity), soldiers, and justice in general. It is used to apply divine justice and to make rebellious spirits face reality in the same way as was done to Saul of Tarsus. It connects with the Soldier Stone (54).

XI. *Sable de San Miguel Arcángel* (Saber of Saint Michael the Archangel): This is a late-nineteenth-century cavalry officer's sword under the aegis of Saint Michael, chief of the celestial armies of Christianity. As a symbol of celestial justice, it is used to purge patients suffering from serious cases of *daño* and to ward off attacking evil spirits that might appear during a session. It is connected to the Soldier Stone (54) and Saint Michael's Dagger (47).

XII. *Espadín de Santiago el Mayor* (Sword of Saint James the Elder) (missing): This is a short hand-sword that symbolizes celestial courage, bravery, and vigilance. The sword is considered to be the defense of the *mesa* in connection with the Soldier Stone (54). It is also used to instill confidence and bolster the morale of patients undergoing treatment. The three swords of the *Campo Justiciero* (X, XI, XII) also imply the purging cross of Christian truth. In summer 1970 this sword was on loan from a friend who wanted it "charged" through placement at the head of Eduardo's *mesa*. By fall 1971 it had been reclaimed by its owner.

XIII. *Lata de San Pedro* (can of San Pedro brew): This five-gallon can holds the infusion made from the San Pedro cactus *(Trichocereus pachanoi)*, which is boiled for seven hours to extract the juice. The resulting brew is the catalyst or energy source for the activation of all the accounts of the *mesa*.

Ground Artifacts

Campo Ganadero

1. *Caracól Triton* (Triton Shell): This is a spirally formed shell found in an archeological ruin and connected with Satan's Bayonet (I). It is used for love magic and symbolizes the vulva as well as the spiral, one of the major symbols of the *mesa* associated with origins and with the "center." This symbol embodies the first subjective experiences related to San Pedro usage. Also called *remolino* (whirlpool), it is one of the first images seen by most people who take San Pedro.

2. *Piedra Culebra* (Snake Stone): This stone, found in an archeological ruin, is used to discover the cause of crop damage or to aid the growth of crops. Connected to Satan's Bayonet (I) and Wheat Stone (26), it is also called *colambo* and *macanche*, two alternate designations used in contemporary Moche folklore; *colambos* are trained snakes believed to protect small farms.

3. *Pata de Venado* (Deer Foot): This is the right front foot of a deer and is used to detect invading spirits as well as to exorcise spirits in cases of possession. It symbolizes the swiftness and elusiveness of spiritual flight and is connected to Satan's Bayonet (I).

4. *Botella de aguardiente* (bottle of cane alcohol) (missing): This is one of the ingredients used in the preparation of *tabaco* and as a libation to spirits that may be attracted to a séance. It is associated with the intoxicating powers of the Devil, which must be resisted in imbibing *tabaco* through the nostrils.

5. *Pedernales* (flints): These three colored flints (one black, one white, and one purple) are fire symbols for making sparks to chase off attacking spirits from the left. They balance the defensive functions of the three crystals (73) of the *Campo Justiciero*.

6. *Cerámica Mono* (Monkey Ceramic): This is a fragment of pre-Columbian pottery found at Chan-Chan, depicting a monkey and symbolizing its tricks. It is used to invoke jungle animals to play pranks and confuse a person with whom one may be annoyed, or to oppose such actions by another.

7. *Piedra Cuy Negro* (Black Guinea Pig Stone): Found in an archeological ruin, this stone is used in diagnostic practices along with a live guinea pig (when performing entrail divination) or in some cases alone. It symbolizes witchcraft.

8. *Piedra Loro Negro* (Black Parrot Stone): Found in an archeological ruin, this stone is used to discover whether damage to crops was caused by a *brujo*. It also symbolizes a black crow *(cuervo negro)*.

9. *Piedra Ojo* (Eye Stone): This meteoric eye-shaped stone from an archeological ruin is used to cure *daño* affecting human eyes. Once activated by the *curandero*, it manifests positively as an "eye of heaven."

10. *Piedra Corazón* (Heart Stone): Supposedly found in the mouth of a dead man in an ancient tomb near Moche, this heart-shaped stone is used to cure *daño* directed against the human heart.

11. *Piedra Riñon* (Kidney Stone): This stone from an archeological ruin is used to cure *daño* focused on the human kidneys.

12. *Piedra Pene* (Phallus Stone): This stone, found in an ancient tomb, is used to heal the male sex organ affected by *daño*.

13. *Piedra Lechuza* (Owl Stone): Shaped like an owl, this stone from the archeological ruins of Huaca Prieta is used to invoke the spirits of pre-Columbian peoples in order to break spells cast by users of black magic. It is connected to the Owl Staff (II).

14. *Cerámica Murciélago Vampiro* (Vampire Bat Ceramic): Found in the archeological ruins of Huaca del Sol, this fragment of pre-Columbian pottery depicts a vampire bat. It is used to enter the ancient *huacas*, or shrines, in order to invoke malicious spirits of the dead dwelling there and to detect the cause of witchcraft. This artifact is connected with the Owl Stone (13) and the Owl Staff (II).

15. *Piedra Laguna de Huaca Prieta* (Lagoon Stone from Huaca Prieta): Shaped like a highland lagoon, this stone was found in the ruins of Huaca Prieta, which are invoked by sorcerers. It is a water symbol used to invoke the powers and "charms" of the ancients, including a green toad *(sapo verde)* and ducks *(patos)*.

16. *Cerámica Zorro* (Fox Ceramic): This is a fragment of pre-Columbian pottery depicting a fox, which Eduardo associates with the moon. It was found in the ruins of Chan-Chan and is used to trick one's enemies. In addition to symbolizing ability to overcome setbacks and obstacles with the astuteness of a fox, it also symbolizes misfortune and danger caused by guile and deception.

17. *Piedra Rosa Candela* (Rose Fire-Stone): This red and black stone from Huaca Prieta is used to invoke the aid of the spirits of archeological ruins in undoing *daño* performed by fire.

18. *Piedra Ojos Dobles y Remolino* (Double-Eyed Whirlpool Stone): Associated with negative *ayatama* herbs, this stone from an archeological ruin is used to undo *daño* to the sight and to invoke the spirits of the ancients. It also symbolizes a spiral.

19. *Piedra Rodilla o Macana* (Knee or Club Stone): This knee-shaped stone is used to counter *daño*. It was found in an archeological ruin and is used to summon the spirits of this shrine. It also symbolizes a club *(macana)* or the blows *(golpes)* associated with *daño*.

20. *Pito para las huacas* (whistle for ancient shrines): This is an ancient ceramic ocarina from a tomb. It is used to invoke the spirits of the dead and of the pre-Columbian past. The spirit of the person with whom it was buried is believed to be captured inside it.

21. *Puros* (cigars): Cigar smoke is used to purify the *mesa* and overcome a sorcerer's spell effected with smoke. The *curandero* performs an operation called *fumada* (smoking), involving rapidly puffing on a cigar or cigarette until it is used up. Cigars are also placed in the mouth of the Maximón mask when it is used in a séance.

22. *Piedra de la Señorita* (Stone of the Single Woman): This stone, from the vicinity of the highland town of Santiago de Chuco, symbolizes a nearby lagoon and lagoons in general, as well as the shawl-wearing female guardian of these power loci. It is utilized with the Ancient Single Woman Ceramic (23) and the Staff of the Single Woman (III) in undoing love magic.

23. *Cerámica Señorita Gentila* (Ancient Single Woman Ceramic): This piece of pre-Columbian pottery was found at Chan-Chan. It is utilized with the Stone of the Single Woman (22) to overcome love magic. This ancient single woman is conceptualized as a shawl-wearing herbalist, guardian of the sacred lagoons and flora, who carries a bouquet of flowers in her hand symbolizing all the magical plants.

24. *Piedra Taco de Zapato de Mujer* (Stone of the Heel of a Woman's Shoe): This stone, shaped like its name, was found at Huaca Prieta. It is used to bring back women who are lost or who have run away.

25. *Piedra Paratón-Siete Suertes* (Elevated Seven Fortunes Stone): This stone, found on Cerro Paratón-Siete Suertes, a mountain located near the town of Pimentel, is used to aid the victims of *daño,* particularly when it affects business.

26. *Piedra Trigo* (Wheat Stone): This wheat-shaped stone, from an archeological ruin, is used to discover the cause of damage to crops or to promote their fertility. It connects with Snake Stone (2).

27. *Cerámica Pie Derecho de Hombre* (Right Foot of a Man Ceramic): This is a piece from a pre-Columbian pot found at Chan-Chan. Depicting a man's right foot, it is used to locate men who are lost or who have run away, as well as to discover theft. It is connected to Saint Cyprian (36) in the *Campo Medio.*

28. *Piedra Maíz Atado* (Bound Corn Stone): Shaped like two shocks of corn tied together, this stone is used for undoing love magic. It is from an archeological ruin and is connected to the Owl Staff (II).

29. *Piedras Humanos Atados y Remolino* (Bound Humans and Whirlpool Stones): These stones found at Huaca del Sol depict a bound male and female. They are used for undoing love magic. They also symbolize a spiral and are connected to the Owl Staff (II).

30. *Concha* (shell): Associated with the Bound Humans Stone (29) and love spells, this vulva-shaped shell is used for *rastreo* (tracing) of women patients to determine their character.

Campo Medio

31. *El Sol* (The Sun): This is a bronze sunburst symbolizing the sun as it climbs into the morning sky from 6:00 A.M. until noon. It is the fire symbol par excellence.

32. *Bola de bronce* (bronze disk): This disk represents a sun, complete with corona, and is identified with the light and the 24-hour day.

33. *Piedra del Mar y los Vientos* (Sea and Winds Stone): This stone, found in an ancient tomb near the ocean, is used to "see" drowned people, shipwrecks, and articles that have been lost at sea or on the beach. Like the Swordfish Beak (V) in the *Campo Justiciero*, with which it is connected, it symbolizes the seven seas.

34. *Seguro del curandero* (folk healer's glass herb jar): This is the place where the healer's power is most concentrated. It is his main talisman, his alter ego. He uses it for defense, divination, diagnosis, and treatment. In addition to certain standard ingredients (such as saints' medals, gold and silver coins, perfume, sugar candy, lime juice, and hair from the crown of the owner's head), it contains an assortment of magical herbs selected according to the healer's personal preferences. Seven accounts are stored here under the direction of Saint Jerome, tamer of wild animals. Saint Anthony, who helps to find lost objects, is also here along with the Peruvian mulatto Saint Martin, a miraculous healer, and the wise magician-king Solomon. The *seguro* (which literally means "protection") is also called *pomo* (glass jar) and *ajuste* (covenant).

35. *Piedra Laguna Shimbe* (Shimbe Lagoon Stone): Taken by Eduardo from the bottom of the Shimbe Lagoon during his first ritual bath in August 1970, this stone symbolizes the lagoon and don Florentino García, whose spirit is summoned to help out at Eduardo's séances. (See chapter 10 for further discussion.)

36. *San Cipriano* (Saint Cyprian): According to Christian folklore, this magician was converted to Christianity and became a martyr. He is the patron saint of many folk healers from northern Peru and the mediator between the *Campo Ganadero* and *Campo Justiciero*, since he is of these two realms himself. This statue is made of *sapote* wood and sits on a deck of Spanish divining cards with a red bag of divinatory runes at its feet, symbolizing the ambiguity of both fate and fortune. Cyprian is the saint in the best position to strike a bargain with Satan to cure witchcraft or to aid the *curandero* on a journey to the Underworld. Loomis (1948: 75) summarizes Saint Cyprian's story as follows:

> Cyprian was at one time a magician and teacher of sorcery. In his search for new kinds of magic, he came to the city of Antioch. While he was in that city, a young man who lusted for a young Christian virgin, Justina by name, came to him for help. When Cyprian had exhausted his arts to no avail in an attempt to win the maiden for the young man, he threatened the powers of evil that he would turn Christian if they could not overcome that girl. Having no power over the maiden, the satans substituted one of their number, disguised in her likeness. As soon as Cyprian mentioned Justina's name, this shadow vanished in smoke. Cyprian became a Christian and suffered martyrdom with Justina.

37. *Piedras Minerales y Caudales* (Mineral and Fortune Stones): These two stones from archeological ruins are used to bring wealth and good fortune. *Minerales* represents not only the mountains from which mineral wealth is extracted but also a sleeping lion, called a *carbunco* in local folklore, which protects the sec-

ond stone, a treasure chest representing the fortunes *(caudales)* obtained from the mountains.

38. *Espejo de cristál* (crystal "mirror"): This clear rock crystal from Río Seco is supposed to reflect events at a distance related to and explaining cases of *daño*. A cat fetish (described in chapter 5 and not included in figure 6-1) sits on it for defensive purposes; the sharp "vision," swiftness, and ferocity of the feline are used to discover and counter attacks by *brujos*. The twenty-five balanced accounts of the *Campo Medio* are stored in this mirror, which is also considered to be a pyramid.

39. *Paño de gentil* (cloth from an ancient tomb): This cotton cloth is used to wrap Saint Cyprian when *mesa* artifacts are stored. During a ceremony it is placed under the white linen cloth on top of which the artifacts are placed.

Campo Justiciero

40. *Seguro de paciente* (patient's herb jar): This is a glass bottle containing images of saints in plastic, gold and silver coins from the nineteenth century, three types of perfumes, white sugar, sweet lime juice, hair from the crown of the patient's head, and a large variety of magical herbs from the Andean highlands. The choice of saints and herbs depends on the individual. The *seguro* is used for protection, divination (like a gypsy's crystal ball), diagnosis, and treatment. Patient's may keep a *seguro* as an amulet for good luck. The one in figure 6-1 belongs to a patient who asked the *curandero* to place it at the head of his *mesa* during sessions in order to purify and "charge" it so as to bring good fortune in the petitioner's business.

41. *San Francisco de Asís* (Saint Francis of Assisi): The *curandero* modeled and fired his own ceramic statue of this, his favorite saint. Friend of wildlife, especially birds, Saint Francis is a symbol of divine strength and goodness and is especially powerful in exorcising evil spirits in connection with the Virgin of Mercy Staff (IX).

42. *Niño Jesus de Praga* (Child Jesus of Prague): This statue, carved in wood from the *sapote* tree, carries the world in its hand as if it were a toy. The world is also symbolized by the rattle (59), with which it is ritually connected. According to Jung, the Christ Child is a symbol of the self.

43. *Virgen del Carmen* (Virgin of Carmen): The statue of the Virgin Mary as she appeared at Carmen is carved in wood from the *sapote* tree. She is the overseer of Purgatory, and along with Saint Cyprian mediates journeys to the Underworld.

44. *Piedra Maria Magdalena* (Mary Magdalene Stone) (under rope): This stone from an archeological ruin is placed near the crucifix on the *mesa* at the feet of Christ. Mary Magdalene, converted from a life of sin as was Saint Cyprian, channels the power of evil constructively.

45. *Piedra Pecho de la Virgen* (Virgin's Breast Stone): Found in an archeological ruin, this stone is used for curing pains and burns and in petitions for mercy.

46. *Perla* ("Pearl" Shell): This is a flat, bivalve shell used in imbibing *tabaco*

through the nostrils. Since it is on the left, it is associated with the *Campo Ganadero* and is used by the *alzador* ("raiser" or assistant) to the *curandero's* left.

47. *Puñal de San Miguel Arcángel* (Dagger of Saint Michael the Archangel): This dagger is used for the defense of the *curandero*. He holds it in his left hand during the whole ceremony to protect himself against spirit attacks from the *Campo Ganadero*. In curing, it connects symbolically with the Saber of Saint Michael (XI).

48. *San Antonio* (Saint Anthony): Carved from *sapote* wood, this statue is used to discover lost or stolen objects.

49. *Virgen de la Purísima Concepción* (Virgin of the Immaculate Conception): This statue was carved by the *curandero* from a *palo de sangre* stick brought to him by a friend who had it baptized by a healer at Las Huaringas. It is used against *daño* involving hemorrhages, and it also symbolizes spiritual birth.

50. *Concha Fuente de la Virgen* (Fountain of the Virgin Shell): Found in an archeological ruin, this large oyster shell supposedly has a shape reminiscent of the Virgin Mary. Symbolizing a return from death (rebirth), it is used to hold a potent infusion of San Pedro and several purgative herbs in cases of *daño* induced by the mouth (i.e., poisoning).

51. *Cristo y el Calvário* (Crucified Christ): This crucifix of *pial* wood is the "center" of the *mesa*, from which the *curandero* draws his strength. It is placed on top of the prayer book of the Franciscan Tertiary Order (a lay order), which serves as an altar. The accounts relating to the seven miracles, or "justices," of Christ are stored here, as are the twelve thousand accounts of the *Campo Justiciero*. This is the axis of the entire *mesa*.

52. *Vasija para tabaco* (bowl for tobacco mixture): *Tabaco* contains the following ingredients: dried leaf tobacco (black, unprocessed, shown outside the lower right corner of the *mesa*); three perfumes—*agua cananga* (74), *agua florida* (75), and Tabu (76); sweet lime juice (77); cane alcohol (4); white sugar (66); and boiled San Pedro (XIII). *Tabaco* is "raised" (imbibed through the nostrils) by the *curandero*, his two assistants, and all patients and observers at certain intervals during the session. This is the auxiliary catalyst of a séance.

53. *Perla* ("Pearl" Shell): This is a flat, bivalve shell used for portions of *tabaco* served to patients undergoing therapy and to the *alzador* on the curer's right. It forms a set with a small shell used in measuring and serving ingredients for "raising."

54. *Piedra Militar* (Soldier Stone): This is a stone found in an archeological ruin near Cerro Paruque in the highlands. It works with the statue (61) and sword (X) of Saint Paul in applying divine justice and forms a power nexus with the last three staffs of the *Campo Justiciero:* Virgin of Mercy (IX), Saint Paul (X), and Saint Michael (XI).

55. *San Martín de Porres* (Saint Martin of Porres): Saint Martin was a Peruvian mulatto famous for his work among the poor and the sick. He is considered to

be a great "doctor." He carries a broom because during his lifetime he cheerfully performed menial chores. With this broom he is believed to sweep or cleanse the patient's soul.

56. *Concha San Juan Bautista* (Saint John the Baptist's Shell): This large oyster shell, brought from the ocean, is used for sprinkling holy water and for baptism. It symbolizes rebirth by means of a holy sacrament.

57. *Piedra Moisés y el Mar Rojo* (Moses and the Red Sea Stone): This stone from an archeological ruin is used to keep away evil spirits. It symbolizes miraculous passage, that is, rebirth, and is connected to the Serpent Staff of Moses (IV) governing the *Campo Medio* as well as the Staff of the Virgin of Mercy (IX) in the *Campo Justiciero.*

58. *Piedra Nacimiento de Jesus* (Birth of Jesus Stone): This stone is for protection against invading spirits. It is also a symbol of spiritual birth.

59. *Chungana* (gourd rattle): This wooden-handled gourd rattle containing dried *huarango* seeds activates all the *mesa* accounts. In conjunction with the *tarjos,* or songs, of the *curandero* and reinforced by sweet odors (perfumes), tastes (sugar), and the relaxed state caused by San Pedro, it is supposed to render all spirits (the patient's and those causing *daño)* susceptible to therapy. It symbolizes the world and its axis and the human skull, as well as being another manifestation of the spiral. It works in conjunction with the world carried in the hands of the Christ Child (42). Defensive functions are also attributed to it. It has the following incised on it: symbols for the three angels of light, the Star of David, the symbol of Christ and the Sacred Host, a spiral, the sun, and the moon.

60. *Soga de hábito de monje* (rope from a monk's habit): From a monastery in Lima, this gift from a grateful patient is worn around Eduardo's neck throughout the séance in support of the defensive functions of his dagger and rattle. By swinging it over his head, he can scourge and drive off evil spirits.

61. *San Pablo* (Saint Paul): This statue, carved from the wood of the *sapote* tree, is the symbol of divine justice, for Paul was a lawyer. It connects with the Virgin of Mercy Staff (IX) and the Sword of Saint Paul (X), which, together with the Saber of Saint Michael (XI), are instrumental in removing Judas from Satan's realm (the *Campo Ganadero)* during the raising of the twenty-five thousand accounts of the *Campo Medio.*

62. *Piedra de la cueva del Cerro Chalpón* (stone from the cave of Chalpón Mountain): This fire symbol, believed to have great curative powers, is from the cave of a Christian ascetic, Father Guatemala, who is believed to have ascended to Heaven. To this day people from all over Peru make pilgrimages to his holy shrine near the town of Motupe. Chalpón is volcanic; thus this stone symbolizes an erupting volcano, the account of which manifests at 3:00 A.M. during a séance. It is also symbolic of rebirth after an initiatory return to the earthwomb.

63. *Cristál Jacob* (Jacob's Crystal): This crystal, which is used as a defense against sorcerers' attacks, symbolizes rapid, clear "vision" resulting from regeneration.

64. *Cristál Ojo de Culebra* (Snake-Eye Crystal): This crystal depicts animate and inanimate defenses from nature as well as rapid, clear "vision" resulting from regeneration.

65. *Perla* ("Pearl" Shell): This is a flat, bivalve seashell used by the *curandero* for imbibing *tabaco* through the nostrils. Each of the five pearl-bearing shells (46, 50, 53, 56, 65) symbolizes the human hand, the moon, the sea (considered to be a great mirror), and spiritual rebirth.

66. *Azúcar blanco* (white sugar): This is a package of granulated white sugar used in *tabaco, seguros,* and purification ceremonies for the *mesa.* Like Tabu, it symbolizes sweetness and receptivity to therapy. Sometimes it is supplemented by hard sugar candy.

67. *Caracól en Rollo* (Roll "Snail" Shell): Found in the archeological ruins of Chan-Chan, this shell is used to undo love magic. It is another spiral symbol, this time with a phallic shape.

68. *Vasija para refresco* (bowl for "refreshment" or purification): This bowl is used to hold a mixture of holy water, white cornmeal, and lime, which "refresh" and purify both the *mesa* and the patients after the session is over.

69. *Agua bendita* (holy water) (missing): Holy water, a symbol of the purifying properties of water, is used with perfume in the petition to God during the ceremony. It is also used in the mixture with which the *mesa* and patients are purified after the session is over.

70. *El Señor de Huamán* (Lord of Huamán): This limestone statue of Christ on a throne in Heaven as Divine Judge after his ascension is a symbol of justice and humility. It is used in petitions, to win friends, and to lend general assistance when needed. It is connected to the Virgin of Mercy Staff (IX).

71. *Taza* (cup): This cup is used for serving San Pedro by itself at midnight. Normally it takes up the position occupied by white sugar (66) in figure 6-1, but it had to be moved to make room for the three perfumes (74, 75, 76), which were laid on their sides for better display in the photograph. (See photo insert.)

72. *Cristál Arca de Noé* (Noah's Ark Crystal): This crystal representing Noah's ark symbolizes a new beginning for human and animal life after emergence from the primal waters.

73. *Cristales Rayos Blancos* (White Ray Crystals): These three white quartz crystals are fire symbols used for defense. One is a bullet, another a car, and the third a single die. They were found near the ancient Huaca del Sol (Sun Temple) near Moche. Together they symbolize the speed and good fortune associated with magical flight.

74. *Agua cananga* (red perfume): This is a perfume used to prepare *tabaco,* found in *seguros,* used to purify the *mesa,* and occasionally used for a patient to imbibe through the nostrils. It symbolizes purifying fire.

75. *Agua florida* (scented water): This perfume is used like *agua cananga,* and in special cases a patient imbibes it through the nostrils without its being mixed with other ingredients. It symbolizes sacred herb "gardens" and flowers.

76. *Tabu* (Tabu cologne): For usage, see no. 75. This cologne is also used in the *curandero*'s petition to God during the mass. It symbolizes sweetness and receptivity to therapy.

77. *Lima dulce* (sweet lime): For usage, see no. 75. It is connected with Staffs III (Single Woman), VI (Eagle), VIII (Hummingbird), and IX (Virgin of Mercy).

78. *Mantél blanco de lino* (white linen cloth): This is the cloth on which the artifacts of the *mesa* are placed.

Tabaco negro (black tobacco). This is the principal ingredient in *tabaco,* a mixture of black tobacco, San Pedro juice, Tabu cologne, scented water, red *cananga* perfume, cane alcohol, sweet lime juice, and white granulated sugar. The mixture is imbibed during raising. Eduardo either calls the tobacco by the Quechua word for tobacco, *sayri,* or calls it *huaman tabaco* (falcon tobacco). The latter designation refers to the sharp sight of the falcon, since *tabaco* is believed to clear the mind and to stimulate great vision in divining and perceiving the attacks of sorcerers. Together with San Pedro, tobacco is supposed to activate a sixth sense in the individual.

B: *MESA* ACTS

The following description of Eduardo's ritual is based upon explanations he gave me of replays of sessions taped in the summer of 1970. Field notes of these explanations were compared with sessions and explanations taped in fall 1971 and again in winter 1974. From other studies we know that songs and whistling accompanied by a rattle, raising the San Pedro brew and other substances, orally spraying perfumes, and Catholic prayers are typical northern practices (see the synthesis of Gillin's 1947 report on Moche in chapter 7; Mac-Lain y Estenós, 1939, and 1942: 409-14; Cruz Sánchez, 1948: 256-57, and 1951: 163-64; Friedberg, 1960: 23-24, and 1963: 252, 359-60, 366-67, 378; Chiappe, 1968: 25-29; Dobkin de Rios, 1968: 193-94, and 1968-69: 27). However, since no other ethnographers have questioned northern shamans regarding the symbolism involved in their rituals, we do not know if the Apocalypse symbolism and power build-up implied in the magical numbers 7, 12, and 25 are traditional or a personal creation of Eduardo. Although he learned the numbers from his tutors, his application of this knowledge appears to be idiosyncratic. Research with other shamans is needed to clear up this matter.

Ceremonial Acts (Charging the Mesa)

1. *Apertura de la cuenta* (opening of the account). The *curandero* sets up the *mesa* in a special order: first, *Campo Justiciero* artifacts; second, *Campo Medio* artifacts; third, *Campo Ganadero* artifacts; last, staffs from right to left. Then, while invoking the forces of nature along with the four winds and four roads, he fills his mouth with sugar and Tabu. Next he sprays the mixture three times over the *mesa* to purify it. After another invocation, the same operation is repeated three times with sugar and *agua florida.* This is followed by another invocation and three more blasts of spray composed of sugar and *agua cananga.*

Finally sugar and sweet-lime juice are orally sprayed three times over the *mesa*. (Usually the total number of blasts is twelve.)

2. *Oraciones* (prayers) to the *Campo Justiciero* addressing God, the Virgin Mary, and the saints of the Roman Catholic faith. These prayers, mostly in Spanish, include the "Hail, Mary," "Our Father," a little Latin, and some Quechua.

3. *Llamada* (call) to sacred mountains and lagoons, ancient shrines, and *curanderos*, alive and dead, so that they will attend the session in spirit. The call is made by a *tarjo*. A *tarjo* starts with the *curandero* rhythmically shaking the *chungana*, or rattle. After a rhythm is established, the *curandero* whistles in time to the beat. Then he chants or breaks into a song, still shaking the *chungana*. Toward the end of the *tarjo* he resumes whistling, ending by once again shaking the *chugana* by itself.

4. The raising *(levantada)* of the *mesa* in general *con las siete mil cuentas* (with the seven thousand accounts). After another series of prayers, mainly within the realm of Roman Catholicism, the *curandero* imbibes *tabaco* through his nostrils. This is done seven times (for the seven "justices" of Christ—seven important events in the life of Christ); each time a whole shell is emptied and a short invocation is given. During the raising, the *curandero* holds the Dagger of Saint Michael, the crucifix, and the rattle above his head. When he is finished, his assistants imbibe one shell full of the same liquid. Not one drop of *tabaco* must be spilled. If it is, the person doing the raising must start over again. This operation activates the axis of the *mesa*—the crucifix.

5. Call to all the *encantos justicieros* (good charms). The *curandero* sings a *tarjo* addressed to personages of the Christian tradition—Jesus, the Virgin Mary, the apostles, saints, and angels—and to miraculous events in their lives.

6. Raising *con las doce mil cuentas* (with the twelve thousand accounts). The *curandero* invokes the twelve thousand accounts while either abstaining from or raising *tabaco*. Then he pours one shell of *tabaco* for each assistant to raise. This operation activates the forces of good from the *Campo Justiciero*.

7. *Tarjo* relating the birth, life, death, and resurrection of Jesus and the beginnings of the early Church. It is intended to invoke His presence in spirit.

8. Call and petition to God. The *curandero* imitates the consecration of the mass by raising a mixture of *agua bendita* and Tabu above his head and then drinking it. This act is followed by taking Tabu in his mouth and spraying the crucifix on the *mesa* three times. This ends the liturgical acts between the *curandero* and God.

9. The *mesa*'s raising *con las veinticinco y doscientos cincuenta mil cuentas justicieras y ganaderas* (with the twenty-five and two hundred fifty thousand accounts related to white and black magic). The number 25 in *curandero* symbology is composed of two 12s, each symbolizing the eleven faithful disciples and Paul, plus a 1 symbolizing Judas. Twenty-five is then multiplied by ten thousand to increase its power. In this way the *curandero* indirectly invokes the forces of evil associated with 13 to help his work (13 + 12 = 25), for these are the forces responsible for witchcraft, and therefore most capable of revealing its

causes. However, the forces of evil are carefully counterbalanced by the forces of good—the two 12s—in this operation: 12 + 12 + 1 = 25. A *brujo* would raise the *mesa con las treinta y trescientos mil cuentas* (symbolizing the thirty pieces of silver Judas received for betraying Christ), which would weigh the invocation toward the forces of evil. In this phase the two assistants each imbibe one shell of *tabaco* through the nose, but the *curandero* abstains. This operation activates the balanced forces of the *Campo Medio* and, in the process, the evil forces of the *Campo Ganadero*.

10. *Tarjo* addressed to all the forces of nature and of the ancients. In this *tarjo* the *curandero* invokes all the activated collective forces of both *campos*, *justiciero* and *ganadero*—the mountains, lagoons, ancient shrines, streams, gardens (of magical plants), herbs, and *curanderos*, alive and dead. At the end of this *tarjo* or in a separate one he sings all of his staffs to life, starting with the Saber of Saint Michael in the *Campo Justiciero* and ending with Satan's Bayonet in the *Campo Ganadero*.

11. Raising of the San Pedro remedy. The *curandero* pours *tabaco* into a shell, makes a cross with it over the *mesa*, and hands it to one of his assistants, who bends down beside the can of San Pedro, holding his shell at its base. Then the assistant raises his shell along the side of the can, makes a cross with it over the remedy, and imbibes the *tabaco* through his nose. This is repeated twice more, once with *agua cananga* by itself and once with Tabu by itself. The same procedure is performed by the second assistant—who is followed by everyone else present at the session (but once only with *tabaco)* except the *curandero*. If for some reason a patient cannot get the *tabaco* down his nostrils, he is allowed to swallow it.

12. Purification and presentation of the remedy and *curandero* to the *mesa*. One of the assistants brings a full cup of the remedy to the *curandero*, who places it on the *mesa* in front of him. Then the *curandero* picks up the *seguro* (herb jar), the dagger, and the cup of San Pedro and stands up. After serving themselves one shell each of *tabaco*, the assistants take positions on each side of the *curandero*. While the *curandero* performs a *tarjo* in his own name—holding the *seguro*, rattle, dagger, and cup of San Pedro all at the same time—both assistants simultaneously move their shells along his body from feet to waist, waist to neck, and neck to crown. Then they raise the *tabaco* mixture. When they have finished, the *curandero* performs *limpia*, or cleansing, of himself by rubbing the *seguro* all over his body from head to toes. Then he sits down, places everything back on the *mesa*, and orally sprays the *seguro* three times with *agua florida*, three times with Tabu, and three times with *agua cananga*.

13. The purification of self and San Pedro is followed by a raising performed by the *curandero* in the name of the remedy with one shell of *tabaco*. Then the *curandero* lifts the cup of San Pedro from the *mesa*, drinks it in one draft, massages his head with the empty cup, and ends by blowing into the cup three times. Patients and guests are not required to raise the San Pedro brew with *tabaco* as the *curandero* does, but at this point they go through the same ceremony of drinking the pure infusion as the *curandero*. To end this phase, the *curandero* serves pure San Pedro to his assistants, presenting their in-

dividual servings to the *mesa*, and making a special benediction in the name of each one. Both assistants follow the same procedure in drinking the remedy, as do the patients—drinking, rubbing the head, and blowing.

14. Cleansing of all present. The *curandero* stands beyond the staffs of the *mesa*, making sure that one of his assistants holds his seat at the *mesa* at all times, and has the patients and assistants come before him, one at a time. As each person comes forth, the *curandero* rubs him all around from head to foot with the *chungana*—ending by blowing on this instrument with a sharp expulsion of air *(sopla)*. When he has done this for everyone else, he performs the same procedure on himself. This ends the ceremonial division of the session at midnight.

Curing Acts (Discharging the *Mesa*)

1. Purificación (purification) of the *mesa*. The *curandero* orally sprays the table with the three perfumes and sugar as he did in the opening ceremony.

2. Rastreo (tracking, or tracing). The patient stands facing the *curandero* beyond the staffs and swords at the front of the *mesa*. The *curandero* sings a *tarjo* in the name of the patient. Then all present concentrate on the staffs to see which one vibrates. Once agreement is reached, this staff or sword is given to the patient to hold in his left hand over his chest. Now everyone concentrates on the patient and staff while the *curandero* chants a *tarjo* in the name of the staff. The *tarjo* includes all the accounts associated with the staff. It is intended to activate the patient's spirit, reveal his illness, and invoke the spirits that are antagonizing him, if any. The *tarjo* is followed by a silence that may last five or ten minutes.

3. Cuenta (account). As the persons and events of the patient's life begin to be "seen" by the *curandero*, he relates them—interspersing his narration with questions and comments. During this phase other patients or guests may share some of the *curandero*'s visions. It is during this phase of the curing session that the *curandero* "sees" the causes of *daño* (witchcraft), *enredo* (love magic), or *suerte* (bad luck), when these are the ailments bothering the patient. In serious cases this is a critical phase when many effects of the ailment may manifest themselves in the patient, requiring emergency measures by the *curandero*.

4. Desmarco or *descuenta* (removal or discount). The *curandero* sings a final song relating to the accounts of the staff.

5. Raising the patient. During the last song the *curandero*'s two assistants take positions on either side of the patient and raise him from feet to waist, waist to neck, and neck to the top of his head with one shell full of whatever substance is indicated by the *curandero*. This procedure is to help remove the cause of the patient's illness by "centering" him.

6. Raising the staff. The patient holds the staff over his head by its tip and imbibes whatever substance is specified by the *curandero*. In severe cases of *daño* the patient has great difficulty getting the substance down and often vomits (which is considered necessary in the treatment of *daño* induced by food or drink). This can be another critical period in the treatment of serious cases. If the patient cannot get the substance down, one of the assistants or the *curandero* himself may have to do so in his or her name, after which the *curandero* may still have to perform a sword battle and the seven somersaults *(siete mortales)* described in chapter 2.

7. Cleansing of the patient. Once the patient has raised the staff, an assistant takes it and rubs it all over the patient's body—even under the arms.

8. *Sopla* (blowing) and *chicotea* (violent shake) of the staff. One assistant or the *curandero* orally sprays the staff three times with whatever liquid is indicated by the account. Then he slices the air with the staff in whatever direction or directions of the compass are indicated by the account and returns it to its proper position at the front of the *mesa*.

9. *Salto sobre el fuego* (leap over the fire). After the curing acts are performed for all present, the victims of witchcraft must leap four times so that their movements form a cross over a small bonfire of straw, lit by the *curandero*'s assistants. After the jumps, each must stamp out the fire. Then, as the individual patient steps backwards, an assistant cuts the ground between his two feet with one of the *mesa* swords. This appears to be a symbolic act indicating "mastery over fire" or "magical heat," a shamanistic attribute (Eliade, 1964: 474–77) which is passed on to the patient in order to purge and purify him by exorcising evil spirits. In some cases *salto* may be performed before *rastreo* (step 2).

10. *Cierre de la cuenta* (closing of the account). This is the same as the opening ceremony. It is performed after the *curandero* has repeated steps 1 through 8 for all present except himself, as well as the fire ceremony (step 9) reserved for victims of witchcraft.

11. *Refresco* (purification, or "refreshment") of participants and locale. The two assistants orally spray a mixture of holy water, white cornmeal, white flowers, white sugar, sweet-lime juice, and powdered lime in the faces, on the necks (front and back), and over the hands (front and back) of everyone, including the *curandero* and each other. While they are "refreshing" the patients, the *curandero* gathers up his artifacts in the same order as he put them down at the beginning of the session—*Justiciero, Medio, Ganadero*, and staffs from right to left. Once he has packed them up, he uses the dagger to cut a cross three times in the earth where the *mesa* was laid. Then he sprinkles the same mixture used by his assistants three times along the cuts in the ground and once in each of the four corners of the *mesa* area, which must not be touched by anyone until noon of the day in progress. All of his artifacts have to be put away before sunrise to prevent sunlight from striking them. Any leftover San Pedro is buried for the same reason. All participants are required to abstain from condiments (especially salt, hot peppers, onions, and garlic), pork, beans, or any plant that grows on a vine or has twisting roots until noon of the day in progress.

C: ABORIGINAL *MESAS*

The *mesa*, an altarlike arrangement of power objects, occurs in a variety of forms—some more elaborate than others—in many parts of Latin America. What follows summarizes the ethnographic literature regarding the occurrence of this complex association of beliefs and practices.

Huastec

The Huastec Indians inhabit the eastern Mexican states of San Luis Potosí and Veracruz. Although geographically removed from the contemporary Maya, they are, nevertheless, linguistically related. In pre-Columbian times the Huastec extended Maya culture to its northernmost limit, and were then cut off from the Maya of southern Mexico, Yucatán, and Guatemala by the later migrations of Aztec-speaking peoples. Scholars who have worked among the Huastec do not know exactly how predominant native beliefs and customs are. At this time, however, little is known about Huastec shamanism, since few ethnographic studies have been conducted among these peoples and extreme secrecy is maintained by the shamans of the area.

Despite the lack of data, there are a few brief references to the *mesa* complex. Williams García (1972: 37, 56–57), in describing the native temple, or *lakachinchin*, in the town of Pisaflores, Veracruz, indicates that the altar has two *mesas*, or shelves. On the upper platform offerings are made to the sun and other deities. The lower platform, dedicated to the earth, holds closed boxes containing "seeds," anthropomorphic paper figures representing the major cultivated plants of the community. The shamans of the community, who make the figures, intercede with the supreme deity so that the figures will be animated by an "inner force."

After a severe storm or during a drought the shamans perform an all-night ritual in the temple to petition the ancestors not to interfere in the life of the community. At dawn paper figures representing the deities of wind, thunder, and plants are sprinkled with the blood of sacrificed chickens. Then a table is placed to one side of the altar. Male and female shamans gather around it to pray to the water god and offer forgiveness to each other as a symbol that they have performed their duties.

Another hint of the role of the *mesa* comes from Laughlin (1969: 308) in a discussion of curing in Aquismon, San Luis Potosí. One of the major curing ceremonies performed by shamans is the recovery of the patient's soul when it has been captured by supernatural beings. According to Laughlin, this is how the ceremony is concluded: "Returning to the patient's home, the curer and the patient dance around the table, the curer with *bolim* [a meat tamale prepared for festive occasions] in hand. At each corner of the table is piled an equal portion of the curer's fee, with a liter of cane alcohol in the center."

Mazatec

In a beautifully written essay on the use of hallucinogenic mushrooms among the Mazatec Indians of Huautla de Jimenéz, Oaxaca, Mexico, Munn (1973: 102–4) briefly mentions the role of the *mesa*. The shaman interviewed by Munn related how he came to his profession at about fifty years of age. After an apparently successful operation for appendicitis he developed a traumatic neurosis. Prior to the operation he had never been in a hospital in his life. Afterwards he became depressed and frightened. He lost his will to live and felt that his life was a failure. No matter how much the doctors treated him, he did not recuperate as he should have. Munn explains that "he remained apathetic and unresponsive, for he had been terrified by death and his spirit had flown away like a bird or a fleet-footed deer. He needed someone to go out and hunt it for him, to bring back his spirit and resuscitate him."

Eventually he sought the services of a famous shaman from a nearby village, who administered the mushrooms of vitality. The therapy worked, because the patient was convinced that the doctors' materialistic medicine could not really cure, divorced as it was from reliance on the supernatural and collaboration with the spirits.

During therapy the old shaman told the patient that he had to learn the shamanic art. When the patient protested that all he wanted was to be cured, the healer informed him that he was no longer in control of the situation. Then the old man told the patient that he was going to leave a table with ground tobacco on it and a cross underneath so that the reluctant apprentice could learn to cure. When told to choose the things he liked best, the patient resisted again. Once more he was informed that he really did not have a choice. At this point the patient heard the voice of his dead father urging him to accept his mission. Since the mushrooms had cured him, the patient, recognizing his obligation to cure others, told the old shaman that he wanted to learn everything.

Munn explains that the table, tobacco, and cross are "signs of the shaman's work." Mazatec mushroom sessions are referred to as masses, with the shaman assuming a sacerdotal role in directing the rituals. According to Munn, "the table is an altar at which to officiate. . . . The tobacco, San Pedro, is believed to have powerful magical and remedial values. The cross indicates a crossing of the ways, an intersection of existential paths, a change, as well as being the religious symbol of crucifixion and resurrection."

Mayan Tzotzil

In the south Mexican Tzotzil Indian town of Zinacantán, Vogt (1969: 406-76; 1970: 26-29, 90-99) found that rectangular tables play an important role in ritual meals performed during semiannual ceremonies dedicated to the crosses of the community as well as to the Ancestral Gods and the Earth Owner, and in private curing rites. These tables are placed with the long axis running east-west, the eastern end, or "head," of the table being the most important. In community rituals involving several shamans (h'iloletik, from h'ilol, seer), these ritual specialists are seated in order of rank; those who have been shamans longest are seated at the eastern end of the table, and the newest shamans are at the western end.

The Zinacantán shaman is one who has dreamed three times that his "inner soul" (as opposed to the "companion animal spirit") has been called before the Ancestral Gods inside Senior Large Mountain, the home of the chief ancestor (Gran Alcalde). In the first dream, which usually occurs at the age of ten or twelve, a supernatural guide brings the inner soul of the novice before a long table at the east end of which Gran Alcalde is seated, flanked by all the shamans of Zinacantán, seated in order of their rank. After bowing to all present, the novice kneels at the west end of the table. Gran Alcalde asks him if he is ready to become a shaman. Zinacantecos believe that if he does not say yes he will die. He is given candles and flowers, the requisite paraphernalia for curing, and instructed in the proper rituals and prayers. Then he is given a ceremonial robe and must kneel again while Gran Alcalde swears him in by making the sign of the cross on his forehead. As a final test, a patient is brought in and the novice must cure his or her ailment.

In the second and third dreams, which occur within the next two years, the novice must cure other patients. After that he becomes ill, which indicates to him that he must respond to his "call" by a public debut. Thus he goes to the highest-ranking shaman in his hamlet, recounts his dreams, and asks for permission to reveal his shamanic calling. The veteran shaman prays to the Ancestral Gods in the sacred mountains and then grants permission. All that remains for the new shaman to do is to travel to the lowlands to cut a bamboo staff. Carried in his left hand, this staff becomes a symbol of his office.

There are two kinds of shamans in Zinacantán: "good" shamans, who know only how to cure, and "bad" shamans, who not only know how to cure, but also know how to make others sick. A bad shaman is called *h'ak'chamel h'ilol* (thrower-of-illness shaman). Similarly, there are two kinds of curing ceremonies. "Good" ceremonies, called "asking for pardon," are performed to treat the loss of part of the inner soul or to obtain release of the patient's animal-spirit companion from its corral in Senior Large Mountain—both being punishments by the ancestors for bad behavior. "Bad" ceremonies are called "on account of witchcraft" and performed to retrieve part of the patient's inner soul from the Earth Owner, to whom it has been "sold" in cave rituals practiced by throwers of illness.

A major curing ceremony is called a Great Vision. It consists of nineteen steps, the highlights of which include prayers and a ritual meal at a table oriented east-west in the patient's house; bathing the patient in a boiled mixture of plants and water from seven sacred water-holes; a pilgrimage to mountain crosses (usually four are visited) and Catholic churches, where the shaman offers incense, candles, rum, and prayers to the ancestors (a chicken is sacrificed and left at the last mountain cross, and a ritual meal is eaten); and a final ritual meal at the table in the patient's house (on entering the house, the first greeting is addressed to the table).

Besides curing and community cross ceremonies, shamans in Zinacantán also perform maize-field and new-house ceremonies (emphasizing the four corners and the center), rain-making ceremonies, and year-renewal ceremonies.

Mayan Mam

Maud Oakes (1951) found *mesas* used by the *chimanes* (shamans) of the Mam village Todos Santos Cuchumatán in the Cuchumatán Mountains of northwest Guatemala. She informs us that "each *chimán* owns a table, considered holy, which serves for casting the sacred beans of divination and as an altar." (1951: 24n.) *Chimanes* are divided into (1) practitioners of "white" magic, those "who know"; (2) practitioners of "black" magic, or *brujos;* and (3) novice shamans, or *zajorines*. All three can perform magic, soothsaying, or healing, individually or all at once. Their ritual activity is referred to as *costumbre*. According to Oakes (1951: 90–91):

> When a man becomes a *chimán,* he is given his table of *costumbre* (the teacher of a *zajorín* designates when he is ready to receive it). The night he "graduates" he conducts his first mass at the table and summons the Spirit, or *dueño de cerro* [a guardian or mountaintop master, a supernatural being supposed to dwell in a mountain or other natural formation]. On his table is a wooden cross, never a crucifix. (A Catholic crucifix is considered *ladino* [of Indian-Spanish cultural background]). A *chimán* always has a wooden cross on his table of

costumbre though it is usually hidden. . . . Later he goes to the *cerros* [hills or mountains] many times with his teacher and establishes contact with the *dueño*. Then he is given his chain of office. . . . of metal, similar to a dog chain, with links and a metal ring at the end.

In Todos Santos the *mesa* is an actual table made of white cypress without a nail in it. A novice shaman's *mesa* is often referred to as the daughter of his teacher's *Santa Mesa* (Holy Table) during prayers addressed to *Santa Mesa*, Christ, *Santa Justicia* (Holy Justice), and the four *Alcaldes del Mundo* (Mayors or Governors of the World) (1951: 116–17).

The beginning shaman is initiated into the use of the *mesa* in a night ceremony during which the legs of his *mesa* are sprinkled with the blood of a rooster sacrificed at the house of the initiating shaman-teacher. The initiate must also say his first mass behind a curtain in a darkened room and then offer money to the *mesa* of his teacher. Then the tutor ceremonially carries the new table, which is tied around his neck with his sash, to the house of the novice, where it is placed in a four-posted divinatory stall, or *corral*, used for communing with the Spirit and is again sprinkled with sacrificed rooster blood. This is followed by drinking and celebration until 5:00 A.M., at which time guests and spectators depart (1951: 145–49).

After further preparation under his tutor, the novice eventually learns how to cure with the aid of his *mesa* and invocations to *Santa Vara* (Holy Staff) and *Santa Letra* (Holy Knowledge) (1951: 152). Another interesting detail is that masks worn in ritual community dances and at public festivals are considered to be sons of the *chimán's mesa* who look for a ritual prayer ceremony from his table (1951: 223).

Mayan Tzutuhíl

The *mesa* concept is also found in the Tzutuhíl town of Santiago Atitlán, located on Lake Atitlán in the midwestern highlands of Guatemala. The best material on the activities of the *atiteco ajkún* (shaman) comes from Mendelson (1957: 280–81), whose comments on the *mesa* deserve extensive quotation. Mendelson asked his shaman-informant, Baltazár, how an *ajkún* began:

> He said that a young man who wished to be an *ajkún* tried to learn the prayers, bit by bit, from another *ajkún* but that there were no direct courses of lessons given by an old man to a pupil and that there could not be since these things came from God. For this reason each *ajkún* had a different way of praying.

At this point Baltazár began talking about himself:

> "When I was twenty years old I did not yet have a wife and was a mere boy *(puro patojo)*. I had some dreams in which Don Pedro (i.e., Maximón, Don Pedro Alvarado, or perhaps, San Pedro Apostol) appeared to me and told me that I should be his *mozo* [servant] and recite such and such prayers. But I was very young and afraid and did not want to accept my table *(mesa)*. I went mad for three days and three nights: it was like a cloud descending upon me and I walked about undressed and said very bad words and was in a terrible temper until I realized that I would have to accept the *mesa*, for I had heard that if one did not accept it, one died."

Mendelson later (1957: 282) provides more insights regarding the *mesa* in Atitlán that show some similarity to Mam and Tzotzil concepts and practices:

> With regard to the *mesa*, I believe it refers also to the table which Baltazár had in his house and which formed his house altar. Upon this he kept a few saints to whom candles were burned and who were incensed three times a day on rising, at midday, and at six P.M. The dedication of candles and other cult objects is always made before a *costumbre* on this table and there are similar tables in front of the altars of all *cofradías*. The "holy table" *(Santa Mesa)* is always referred to in prayers.

Warao

The Warao are fishermen and gatherers who inhabit the swamps and waterways of the Orinoco River delta of Venezuela. Wilbert (1972: 55–83) provides extensive information on Warao shamanism.

There are three religious practitioners among the Warao: (1) the priest-shaman *(wishiratu)*, who visits the Supreme Spirits *(Kanobos)* in dreams or tobacco-induced trance to intercede on behalf of the community in addition to presiding over an annual festival; (2) the "light" shaman *(bahanarotu,* owner or master of the arrow), who presides over an ancient fertility cult and travels in his dreams or tobacco-induced trance state to the eastern part of the cosmic vault, maintaining a celestial bridge of tobacco smoke connecting his people with the eastern House of Tobacco Smoke *(Bahana),* which guarantees abundant life on earth; (3) the "dark" shaman *(hoarotu),* who maintains the connection between the Warao in the center of the universe and the spirits of the west, whose requirements of human flesh and blood are acquired by killing with magic projectiles sent by means of tobacco smoke. All three specialists can be either benevolent or malevolent in their actions.

Our major concern here is with the second practitioner, the light shaman, or *bahanarotu,* for it is in the mythology that provides the rationale for his initiation as a shaman and in his magical practices that we find the *mesa* concept once again (1972: 65–72). According to *bahanarotu* lore, the Creator-Bird of the Dawn created the House of Tobacco Smoke halfway between the junction of sky and earth and the zenith of the cosmic vault. This was done at the beginning of time, when the bird spirit arose in the east. His body, bow, two arrows (carried with his left wing), and rattle (carried with his right wing) were all made of solidified tobacco smoke. The house created by his thoughts was round and white and also made of solidified tobacco smoke.

Next the Creator-Bird desired four companions, so he called up Black Bee, Red Wasp, Yellow Termite, and Blue Honey Bee to share his solitude. They all were transformed into tobacco smoke. The four companions chanted and smoked cigars, thus becoming *bahanarao,* those who blow smoke—the prototypes of the Warao shaman of light.

Wilbert (1971) points out that the four companions are all social, productive insects that fly, metamorphose, sting, produce honey from nectar, and build nests similar in shape to the House of Smoke. Flight and metamorphosis are apt symbols for spiritual procreation out of an undivided, bisexual unity as represented by the Creator-Bird. The stinger is a symbol for the male sex organ, and honey symbolizes semen. Here we have the idea of the first human act of creation being rooted in the secret of cosmic procreation—a rationale for human existence and social life. It is interesting to note that the Creator-Bird, as the unifying principle relating the four insect companions, is the fifth member of the prototypical group. Thus, although four is the sacred number of the Warao, it implies five as a unifying catalyst or center.

To continue with the creation myth: The thoughts of the Bird of the Dawn now turned to the middle of the House of Smoke, where there was a table draped in white holding four dishes, all made of smoke and corresponding to his four companions. He laid his bow with two arrows in the upper righthand section of the table, bringing the total of artifacts on the table up to five (the bow and arrows are counted as one item). Wilbert points out that the placing of the weapon on the table represents an act of decision, of sheer potency or stored energy ready for action, with the implied threat that he who created can destroy.

Then the Creator-Bird proceeded to finish what Wilbert referred to as the Game of *Bahana*. On Black Bee's dish there appeared a sparkling rock crystal, on Wasp's a ball of white hair, on Termite's white rocks, and on Honey Bee's tobacco smoke—the four-fold set of the Game of *Bahana*. Wilbert compares this table to a battery capable of generating considerable power. Like an altar, it is a place of action where Heaven and earth meet. The four plates on the table function together as a set. Together they are power. Thus the House of Smoke of the Creator-Bird of the Dawn became the birthplace of *Bahana*, the shamanistic therapy involving smoke blowing and sucking out of sickness.

To this day, when a young novice is initiated by a teacher, he begins by smoking four wads of black tobacco containing the four insect-companions of *Bahana*, who come to open his chest. They reside around the heart and cleanse the novice. Four days of fasting follow. When this purification period is completed, there are four additional days of abstinence and constant cigar-smoking until the initiate goes into a trance that takes him on a spirit journey to an encounter with the Supreme *Bahana* in the House of Tobacco Smoke.

When the new shaman awakens from his ecstatic trance his chest contains the gift of *Bahana:* White Smoke and White Rocks. But these guardian spirits are still feeble and require much care. The young man eats little, smokes a great deal, and observes celibacy for over a month. A brown spot appears in the palm of each hand and grows in proportion to the growing *Bahanas* in his chest. At the end of the training period the initiate must swallow two pairs of sticks and make them travel past the spirits in his chest and through his arms to be "born" in the palms of his hands. The second pair of sticks, which are white, are born as white crystal beads. By passing this final test the student proves that he can direct his spirit sons through the holes in his hands to assist him in trances or curing sessions. He can now play the supernatural Game of *Bahana* with its four pieces, which he carries in a basket.

Ecuadorian Indians

The chief source for information on curing in the town of Peguche in the Imbabura Valley of northern Ecuador is Parsons (1945). Here the Rainbow is considered to be a malevolent disease- or death-causing spirit that must be smoked out of the victim. Some sicknesses may be sent by the wind *(aire)* or witch-sent "worms." Curing is performed by professional *curanderos* who may also be sorcerers *(brujos)* in night healing sessions focused on the *mesa,* or altarlike arrangement spread on a cloth placed on the ground. The types and quantity of artifacts placed on the *mesa* vary from practitioner to practitioner, but seem to include as a bare minimum: a cross, shells, stones (which, according to Parsons's informant, are given to *brujos* by the spirits or *duendes* who accompany them), quartz crystals, and remedies used in healing.

During the session in Peguche (which may be conducted to cure, divine, or learn about a marriage or robbery) the healer sucks the diseased area, sprays the patient with rum, and blows tobacco smoke over him. It is interesting to note that healers have many Caucasian patients. Parsons noticed *ayahuasca (Banisteriopsis caapi)* for sale in the nearby Otavalo market, which suggests that potent hallucinogens may also be used by practitioners. Two species of *Datura (arborea* and *stramonium)* are also recorded as growing near the town. Parsons does not, however, report the use of these hallucinogens.

Recent work by Mena (1969) in the Imbabura Valley (town of La Calera) involved extensive interviewing of a shaman who was willing to share some of his curing lore. In this region the shaman, referred to as *Yachag Taita,* is a wise man who "talks" with the mountains, divines, and knows how to cure all kinds of sickness. Commanding greater respect than the political and religious authorities, he is a person "predestined" to exercise the "profession" of shaman, which in the majority of cases is passed on from father to son.

One of the major duties of the *Yachag Taita* is to train a successor, usually his most promising son or—if he has no male descendant—a member of a nearby family or other candidate who demonstrates intelligence, respect, and shamanic capacity. The novice begins service as the shaman's major assistant *(Mapa Shitador),* attending all curing sessions, seated to the right of the healer. His major task is to carry away the pathogens (such as lizards, worms, and frogs) that the *Yachag Taita,* through sleight of hand, pretends to have sucked out of patients during the night. The assistant carries a whip in his left hand and smokes three cigarettes in order to protect himself from evil spirits. During a session, the *Yachag Taita* also protects his assistant by invoking the mountains on his behalf.

When the *Mapa Shitador* is believed to have learned enough, he is given an "exam" to test his knowledge. If he passes, he enters the second stage of training, during which he is allowed to treat certain ailments under the direction of his tutor. This period lasts about a year or a year and a half. During this time the apprentice is approached by many neighbors to test his emerging abilities to divine and diagnose. Once the novice terminates his training, after his twenty-sixth birthday, a date is set for his "coronation." It must be on a Friday at midnight, sometime after the full moon. Only the oldest men of the community are present, and women are excluded. In the middle of the "curing room" a table is laid with a banquet consisting of twenty-four kinds of food. At the appointed time the candidate kneels before the *Yachag Taita,* who invokes his "companions," the mountains. Then the shaman orally sprays cane alcohol three times on the top of the apprentice's head and blows three puffs of cigarette smoke at him. Next, after dipping his forefinger in the alcohol, he makes the sign of the cross on the initiate's forehead while whispering "secret words." After this the shaman proceeds to "clean" the patient by rubbing his body from head to toe with a flask of purple dye. Finally he exhales into the flask to transmit "powers" and delivers it to the novice while whispering to him the secret words. The investment ceremony terminates at about 4:00 A.M. with the apprentice taking a solemn oath to use his wisdom and knowledge solely in the service of good and never to cause evil. The banquet foods from the table are gathered up and taken to the volcanoes Imbabura and Cotacachi, where they are left as offerings.

Mena also describes the use of a table in a ritual to cure extreme cases of witchcraft when the patient is close to death. Two dolls representing the victim and his enemy are made from rags and cotton. The patient is placed naked on a table and covered with a white sheet. Four assistants holding candles stand at the four corners of the table while the *Mapa Shitador* covers the patient's face with his hands. The *Yachag Taita* sprays the doll representing the victim with cane alcohol and blows cigarette smoke over it. After ordering the patient to rise and take his own seat, the shaman cuts the sheet that covered the victim in two. Next he places the victim's doll on top of the one representing the enemy and spears the two through the heart. His palmwood lance is then held up so that the two dolls can be burned. When this is over, the *Mapa Shitador* takes the lance in his right hand, a whip in his left, and departs to throw the burned dolls in the river. The four assistants act as a rear guard, carrying candles in their right hands and whips in their left.

Atacameño

In the 1930s, while excavating pre-Columbian ruins near Chiu-Chiu in the interior regions of northern Chile, Latcham (1938: 61–63) noted group burials in cylindrical caverns. Accompanied by burial offerings, the dead were wrapped in ponchos or blankets and placed in either an elevated gallery or an extended niche excavated around the circumference of the cave floor. Mummies included adults of both sexes as well as children, which led Latcham to conclude that these were family mausoleums.

Through local natives, Latcham discovered that people still buried their dead in family mausoleums like those he had excavated. The elevated gallery was replaced, however, by a great round table made of planks, which occupied the entire floor of the cavern. According to Latcham's informants, when a family member was close to death, he was carried to the mausoleum, seated on the table, and propped up against the wall with blankets and ponchos behind his back. Food, drink, clothing, jewels, and personal belongings were placed on the table in front of the dying person. His relatives gathered, and with weeping, dancing, and singing they helped him "to die well."

Once he was dead they arranged the corpse with the chin on the knees and the arms around the shins. Then they wrapped the corpse in blankets tied with wool cords, or they left it seated on the table surrounded by the offerings. The entrance to the mausoleum was closed with branches, earth, and stones. A year after the funeral—to the accompaniment of weeping, dances, and songs—the sepulcher was opened to renew the offerings. As other members of the family died, these rites were repeated until the table became full.

In San Pedro de Atacama, Latcham discovered similar funeral customs. Here, however, the dead person was first buried according to the rites of the Catholic Church. But the next day the corpse was disinterred and carried to its home, where it was placed on a round table in the midst of offerings. The food and drink was consumed by the mourners in the midst of weeping, dancing, and singing. In one to three days, the rituals were concluded and the corpse was buried again.

Other Examples

There are two other minor examples of the *mesa* complex which, like the Warao example, involve a concept as opposed to an actual artifact or grouping of artifacts. The first example comes from central Mexico, where the word *mesa* is used by a traveling dance group, the *Danzantes de la Conquista,* who perform at Catholic festivals in Mexico City and throughout the states of Mexico, Hidalgo, and Querétaro. The term *mesa* denotes the membership principle by which the dancers organize themselves. They are very secretive, maintaining a body of esoteric lore and a hierarchical structure in which the leaders are known as captains and captains-general (Joyce Bishop, personal communication).

Toor (1947: 323) has the following to say regarding the *Danzantes de la Conquista* (popularly known as *concheros):*

> [E]ach group of anywhere from fifty to a hundred *concheros* is called a *mesa* or table, referring to the altar around which it is organized. Sometimes the *mesa* stands in a little separate oratory, but mostly it is part of the furnishings where the family eats and sleeps. It is covered with a beautifully embroidered cloth, and on it are the saints of their devotion, an image of a soul in purgatory, glasses with artificial and fresh flowers, censers, and other adornments.

The second example, from the Mapuche Indians of southern Chile, is found in the autobiography of an elderly Mapuche chief transcribed in Mapuche and translated into Spanish by Father Moesbach (1973). Two chapters deal with the initiation and curing practices of a shamaness *(machi).* (Among these people most shamanic practitioners are female.) Several songs addressed to the bisexual creator-god of the Mapuche are included. In these songs the Creator is described as located in the sky, seated at a "beautiful table of silver." (1973: 334, 343, 346, 352, 361.) One of the songs is performed by old *machis* when initiating a novice; two are sung by the novice herself once her sacred ladder or symbolic tree *(rehue)* has been planted; and two more songs are used in a curing ceremony. The *rehue* is the pivot of curing rituals. It is interesting to note that during the initiatory ritual the *rehue* is planted over a cache of silver coins (1973: 342). In addressing the Creator, the novice says that once invested she will direct her future petitions to the Creator on behalf of her people "in the midst of silver" and that she will "dance on top of silver," possibly indicating that the *rehue* is seen as a table of silver similar to that of the Creator.

D: ABORIGINAL COSMOLOGIES

Furst's outline of the cosmology of the American Indian shaman (1973–74: 40) reveals the remarkable similarity of concepts found throughout the New World:

> The universe is multi-layered or stratified, with an Underworld below and an Upperworld above as principal divisions. Underworld and Upperworld are usually further divided into several levels, each with its respective spirit rulers and other supernatural denizens. There are also gods of the principal world directions or quarters, and supreme beings that rule respectively over the celestial and chthonic spheres (for example, sky gods, lords of the dead, etc.). . . .
> [T]he multi-layered universe might be represented in the shaman's material culture or art by notched staffs.. . . . The several levels of the universe are in-

terconnected by a central axis (*axis mundi*) which merges conceptually with the shaman's "sky ladder" and world tree, and which . . . might be symbolized . . . in the shaman's art again by the notched or unnotched staff, or even the handle of the sacred rattle as symbolic vertical path to the gods at the top of the sky vault.

What follows is a summary of aboriginal cosmological notions recorded in the ethnohistorical and ethnographic literature:

Aztec

Nicholson (1971: 403–408) provides a description of the cosmology of the prehispanic peoples of Central Mexico based on a review of all the written sources from the early colonial period. The Aztecs thought of the earth as a mass of land surrounded by water. The ocean was believed to merge vertically with the sky, forming a continuous support for the lowest heaven. In a more metaphoric sense, the earth was visualized as a monstrous spiny crocodile or as a huge toad with gaping teeth and snapping mouths at the elbows and knees that swallowed the sun in the evening, disgorged it at dawn, and ate the blood and hearts of sacrificial victims and the souls of the dead. Both monsters floated on the primeval universal sea.

From the center, or "navel," of the earth four regions extended out to the four cardinal points: East, "Place of Dawn"; North, "Region of the Underworld"; West, "Region of Women"; South, "Region of Thorns." Each region had a sacred tree with a sacred bird perched upon it, along with a color association. The ethnohistorical sources reflect considerable regional variation regarding these trees, birds, and colors but the most common scheme seems to have been: East, mesquite-quetzal-yellow; North, ceiba-eagle-red; West, cypress-hummingbird-blue/green; South, willow-parrot-white (black may have been the color of the Center). Occasionally the jaguar, serpent, and rabbit are also assigned to the directions.

Four deities supporting the lowest heaven at each cardinal point have been identified as: East, Venus-like goddess; North, a fire deity; West, Quetzalcoatl as rain god; South, god of death and the Underworld. Four "temple deities" were also associated with the different directions, and all the deities had four aspects — each assigned to a particular direction — as well as, in many cases, a fifth aspect assigned to the Center. Since time and space were intimately linked in the Aztec world view, the four year-signs, the twenty day-signs, and the twenty "divinatory week" signs were associated with the propensities of each directional deity — for example East: good, fertile; North: bad, barren; West: unfavorable, too humid; South, indifferent.

Supplementing this horizontal dimension of the universe, the vertical dimension consisted of a series of levels under and above the earth's surface. For example, at the time of the Conquest the celestial sphere was conceived of as a varicolored, thirteen-tiered system with certain phenomena assigned to each layer; it was intimately associated with the thirteen deities governing successive days in the special Aztec divinatory calendar. It is possible that a more ancient scheme included only nine tiers. At the time of the Conquest, the Underworld was believed to be stratified in nine tiers, which were conceived of as hazard stations that had to be passed by each dead soul on its journey to the ninth and lowest stratum of eternal rest.

Mayan

Thompson (1970: 194–96) summarizes our present knowledge of Mayan cosmology. The Maya conceived the world to be a flat square block with the heavens above and the lower worlds below. The heavens were supported at the four cardinal points and also at intercardinal points by the four Bacabs, the Opossum Actors, and the gods of bees and the apiary. Reflecting the Aztec interrelationship of space and time, these world bearers also supported time by carrying the year bearers on their backs during new-year calendrical ceremonies. As in Aztec cosmology, there were thirteen celestial layers in the skies and nine in the Underworld. However, the Mayan system, unlike that of the Aztecs, was not a strictly vertical arrangement: The thirteen celestial layers were viewed as six steps ascending from the eastern horizon to the seventh step, the zenith, and as six more steps that led down from the zenith to the western horizon. In the Underworld four steps led down from the west to a fifth step, the nadir, and four steps led up to the east. Thus in actuality there were seven heavenly layers and five lower-world layers. It is possible that a creator deity lived in the seventh heaven and a death god occupied the fifth level of the Underworld. The model for this stepped, pyramidal structure was provided by the sun (*kin*), which "followed this sort of stepped rhomboid on his daily journey across the sky and his nightly traverse of the underworld to return to the point of departure each dawn." (1970: 195)

At the center of the earth stood the sacred green ceiba tree, with its roots deep in the Underworld and its trunk and branches piercing the layers of the sky. In addition, ceiba trees—possibly with *chacs* (Yucatec rain gods) and birds perched in them—were associated with each of the four directions and their respective colors: for example, East, red ceiba; North, white ceiba; West, black ceiba; South, yellow ceiba. East was always the most important direction. A fifth direction, either at the zenith in celestial matters or below the ground in terrestrial affairs, was also recognized.

Hopi

Waters (1963: 231–35) explains the Hopis' cosmology as summed up in their concept of man's Road of Life, which is synonymous with the path of the sun—that is, "both describe the perfect rounded whole with the same clockwise circuit about the dual division of space and time."

Each day the sun travels in a circular path above the earth from its sun-house in the east at sunrise to its sun-house in the west at sunset. At night it completes its circular journey by traveling through the Underworld from west to east. Thus day and night are reversed in the two worlds (upper and lower); the sun rises in the Lower World as it sets in the Upper World and vice versa.

The "diurnal reversal" is replicated in the annual passage of the seasons. Every year at the winter solstice (December 21) the sun leaves its winter house on a journey to its summer house, which is reached at the summer solstice (June 21). In the six-month interval—regarded as summer by the Hopis—increasingly longer days that are used for planting are experienced in the Upper World. During the six-month period from the summer solstice to the winter solstice (June 21 to December 21)—regarded as winter in the Upper World—the sun returns to its winter house. During the biannual journeys of the sun conditions are reversed in the two worlds; it is winter in the Lower World when summer prevails in the Upper World and vice versa.

The basic premise underlying the idea of the "year's duality" is that life in the Upper World is duplicated by life in the Lower World. The sun marks the "dual phases of time" (day-night, summer-winter) along its daily and yearly path through the "dual divisions of space" (Upper World, Underworld), describing "the circular form of the perfect rounded whole of life."

The "pattern of creation" also regulates man's life, which is lived in two stages of one overall cycle: that is, one stage from birth to death in the Upper World and a second stage from death to birth in the Underworld. So the Hopis maintain that the solar cycle coincides with the human cycle, or the Road of Life. Waters (1963: 233–34) describes this parallel as follows:

> Like the sun emerging from his sun-house in the east, which serves as a *sipápuni* leading from the underworld, the newly born also emerge to this earth from the underworld through the *sipápuni* (navel, path from). Their birth too is associated with the east and the sun. . . .
>
> Also like the sun, man travels west at death to re-enter the *sipápuni* and return to the world below. Here he is reborn, like a baby, to live another stage of existence in the same great cycle.

The Hopis' *kiva* (altar) reflects their cosmology, for it is

> set facing east and west. Novices are always seated on the raise to the east, as they are being reborn by ritual initiation; the lower altar level lies to the west, as it holds the *sipápuni*, fire-pit, and altar which function in the ritualism of death and rebirth. (1963: 234)

Although we can no longer observe the dramatization of Inca cosmology as we can the Hopi ceremonials, the sketchy details we have indicate that Inca cosmology, too, may have included such concepts as the dual nature of time and space.

Mayan Tzotzil: Zinacantán

Vogt (1970: 3–4), in a section entitled, "The Quadrilateral Cosmos," discusses the cosmology of the contemporary *zinacantecos*. The visible world is considered to have the shape of a huge cube, the center or "navel" of which is an earth mound in Zinacantán's ceremonial center. This cubical world is supported by Four Corner Gods (*Vashakmen*).

The Lower World (*Olon Balamil*), which is separated from the surface world by an open space, also has a quadrilateral form. However, it is shaped more like a layer of an ancient Mayan Pyramid. It is inhabited by dwarfs, who, along with monkeys, were created in the mythical past when the gods tried to make men.

The Sky (*Vinahel*) above the top of the cubical world is the realm of the Sun, Moon, and Stars. Father Sun, associated with God, circles the cubical world each day, preceded by the Sweeper of the Path (the Morning Star). Each day the Sun appears in the morning, pauses at noon to survey his people, and disappears at evening, making the ocean boil as he sets. At night his path passes between the world of the earth's surface and the Lower World, where he makes it so hot for the dwarfs that they have to wear mud hats as protection.

The Sun's path marks the basic directions recognized by the *zinacantecos*. East is called the "place where the Sun rises." West is referred to as the "place where the Sun sets." South and North, "the sides of the path of the Sun," are distinguished by facing east and differentiating the right hand from the left. East is the primary direction in Zinacantán, and most rituals are oriented in this direction.

The Moon, referred to as Our Holy Mother and associated with the Virgin Mary, circles the world on a path similar to that of the Sun. But she appears here at night while the Sun is traversing the Lower World. The Stars occupy a layer of the Sky below the paths of the Sun and Moon but above the clouds. At night they provide light above and below their layer.

In addition to the Ancestral Gods, who occupy the mountains around Zinacantán, there is an ambivalent deity known as the Earth Owner who governs all the products of the land and can be communicated with in caves, limestone sinks, and water holes.

Mayan Tzotzil: Larráinzar

Larráinzar, a town near Zinacantán, is more isolated from civilization. Holland (1964) gives the following information regarding the cosmology of this Tzotzil community. Here the earth

> is conceived of as the center of the universe, the flat and rectangular surface of which is sustained on the shoulders of a bearer at each of the four corners. The heavens, formed by thirteen levels, are conceived as a cupola or cup over the earth: six layers in the east, six in the west, and the thirteenth one in the zenith, heart of the heavens.
>
> Seen from a distance, this sphere looks like a huge mountain or pyramid. The concept of "the mountain of the earth" is often symbolized in the prehispanic codices. . . .
>
> Some of the Tzotzil Indians still keep the Ancient Maya belief . . . in the ceiba . . . , which ascending from the center of the earth, penetrates and connects the thirteen levels of the heavens. This central point is, for that reason, of a green color. Beneath the earth there exist nine, thirteen, or even an undetermined number of layers that form the underworld of *Olontik*. (1964: 14)

Regarding the sun's movements, the people of Larráinzar believe that

> at dawn the sun rises in the east preceded by Venus, the morning star, a large plumed serpent called *Mukta Ch'on* by the Tzotzil. As it was conceived in prehispanic times, Venus is the precursor and the herald of the sun, and the Tzotzil still identify it with the serpent deity, as it was among all Middle-American Indians. . . .
>
> The sun ascends the thirteen layers of the heavens, which form a path ornamented with flowers as if it were carried in a two-wheel cart. Ascending a layer every hour, it reaches at noon the thirteenth one; this is the heart of the heavens, where the sun remains one hour, this being the time when it watches the happenings on earth. In the afternoon, it descends the western layers, and disappearing into the sea, gives way to the evening. During the night it passes by under the layers of the *Olontik*. When it is night on the surface of the earth, the

home of the living, it is day in the domain of the dead, and vice-versa. At the next dawn the sun appears in the east, and gives birth to the new day. (1964: 14–15)

In Larráinzar there are

five classes of gods: (1) gods of the three levels of the sky of which the most important are Jesus Christ (the sun), the Virgin (the moon), and the Catholic saints; (2) gods of the earth that control the rain, the fertility of the soil, and wild life, all with names of Catholic saints; (3) *Vashak Men* formed by the bearers in the four corners of the world as well as the four gods in the four cardinal points—the god of the rain in the east is white, the god of corn in the north is also white, the god of the wind in the south is red, while the god of death in the west is black . . . ; (4) gods of death in the underworld; (5) ancestral and lineage gods. (1964: 15–16)

Mayan Tzotzil: Chamula

Gossen (1974: 18–36) describes the cosmology of the community of Chamula. Here the earth is believed to be an island and one of three horizontal layers: sky, earth, Underworld. The sky in turn is composed of three concentric domes: The first level is unoccupied; the second is traversed by the stars, moon, and minor constellations; and the third is occupied by the sun, Saint Jerome (guardian of animal souls), and the major constellations. The Underworld, habitat of the dead, experiences day while it is night on earth since the sun passes through this region each day on its circular path around the earth. It is the point at which the world is supported, whether by a single earth-bearer or by four located at the intercardinal points.

The Chamulas maintain the ancient Mayan solar calendar of 365 days divided into eighteen months of twenty days and one month of five days. They perceive it to be a natural cycle created by the oscillation of the sun from sunrise and sunset in the extreme south on December 26 to sunrise and sunset in the extreme north and back again. Gossen maintains that the native calendar "is more closely tuned to the solstices" than the Gregorian (1974: 27). Also, for the modern Chamulas "time and space form a single structural primordial reality. . . . For them, as for their Ancient Maya forbears, time and space are a unitary concept whose primary referent is the sun deity." (1974: 30)

Gossen (1974: 32–33) explains how this solar cosmology structures ritual activities:

Chamula cosmological symbolism has as its primary orientation the point of view of the sun as it emerges on the eastern horizon each day, facing "his" universe, with north on his right hand and south on his left hand. . . . Thus, there is an overwhelming tendency of almost all Chamula ritual motion to follow a counterclockwise pattern. This direction is the horizontal equivalent of the sun's daily vertical path across the heavens from east to west.

This transformation of the sun's path according to Chamula premises could be derived by imagining oneself facing the universe from the eastern horizon, as the sun does each morning, and "turning" the vertical solar orbit to the right so that it lay flat on the earth. . . . This horizontal transformation allows

[political-religious] officials to "move as the sun moves," thereby restating symbolically both the temporal and spatial cycles for which the sun is responsible.

Mayan Tzutuhíl

O'Brien (1975: 42-47, 136-51, 242-53) delineates the cosmology of the Tzutuhíl
Maya of Santiago Atitlán, Guatemala. In their system the shape of the Holy World or
Face of the Earth—conceptualized as the cosmic body of San Martín—is that of a flat
rectangle, with the corners at the four solstice points placed within the spherical vault
described by the path of the sun, in the center of which is Santiago Atitlán. Spirits
called *Martín* (aspects of San Martín), the ancestors-become-gods (*nawals*), and the
Catholic saints live on mountains and in the sky at the intercardinal points at the ends
of the earth. They control the forces of nature and the destinies of men on the earth
and in the Underworld. Their realms are connected with the center (the central plaza
of Santiago Atitlán) by roads running from sacred mountains at the intercardinal or
solstice points. The Saint Andrew's cross formed by these roads shares its plaza-center
with another cross: the vertical axis from the zenith of the sky to the nadir of the
Underworld, crossed horizontally by the east-west path of the equinoctial sun. The
equinox line also divides the sky into two sectors: the northern half of the vault,
through which the sun travels between March 21 and September 21, and which is the
light, warm side associated with the color white; and the colder southern side,
associated with the color yellow. These vertical and horizontal crossroads represent the
physical cosmos as well as the communication channels to the cosmic powers at the
"four corners," which permit the interaction between men and the gods.

O'Brien (1975: 249-50) relates this "geography of power" to religious practices and
the cult of Maximón (or Mam) as follows:

> At the central meeting point of these roads, particularly in the Church and the
> *cofradías* of Santiago Atitlán, the power and presence of the gods are focused
> and concretized in the holy images, so that the transcendental macrocosm of the
> Martins is made immanent in the microcosm of the Church and the *cofradías* of
> Atitlán. At this focal point, in the *cofradía* "Holy Cross" (*Santa Cruz*), stands
> the image of Old Mam. He is "the Man" *par excellence,* the shaman whose
> power enables him to cross on the roads to the four corners, to ascend to "the
> ancient chairs, the ancient tables" of the gods on the mountaintops. He can fly
> to the sky to draw down the blessings of the spirits of nature, especially the sun,
> upon men. He is the pre-eminent Lord over all aspects of fertility that are ac-
> tivated by the agency of man: the bearing and implanting of seeds. . . . He is
> lord of the realms above and below the earth, and their inhabitants, of light and
> darkness, of the good and evil that are in men, of life, death, and the renewal of
> life.

The cult of San Martín is performed in the *cofradía* San Juan. Here the spirits of
nature (the Company of the World)—headed by San Martín, whose power is focused
in a sacred bundle kept in a box—are embodied in images arranged on the altar in two
groups. On the left side, near the bundle of San Martín, are the spirits governing such
affairs of men as crops, rain, good weather, tools, and trade. On the right side are the
spirits in charge of the affairs of women: weaving, birth, child-rearing, and so forth. A

wooden box ("the cradle"), containing sacred objects used in rituals for women, hangs by ropes from the rafters on the far right. This box is referred to as "the umbilicus of the world, the heart of the world, the source of the life of men." Thus the *cofradía* San Juan focuses the powers of the spirits of the generation of life and the cycles of nature.

In discussing the Tzutuhíl concept of time embodied in the myth of Mam, O'Brien (1975: 251) pinpoints the capacity of Mayan thought to revitalize itself:

> In this concept of time, the history of the world is a repeating cycle of events and deeds that have occurred before and which are expected to recur. In each new cycle, however, certain elements are transformed, renamed or reclothed, according to the influences which converge upon the culture in each era. But the basic symbols of the economy of the cosmos, the exchanges between the gods and men, remain unchanged, in the fundamental structural features of the myth.

Mayan Chorti

The Chorti of eastern Guatemala and western Honduras, as studied by Girard (1966), are another example of a contemporary Mayan people among whom many of the cosmological notions of their pre-Columbian ancestors are still very much alive. This is particularly apparent in the beliefs and practices surrounding their conception of the sacred *mesa,* a quadrilateral construction oriented to the east that is laid out on the ground and on tables and altars within the native temples and during fertility rituals, performed at critical periods during the agricultural cycle. The parameters of the *mesa* are provided by the movement of the sun.

At the beginning of the native year, Indian priests make a pilgrimage to the sacred water holes of the community located to the west of the temple. In making the pilgrimage the priests consider themselves to be following the route of the sun from sunrise in the east to sunset in the west. At the springs in the west, considered to be the entrance to the Underworld, the first *mesa* of the year is established by extending a ceremonial cloth on the ground oriented along the east-west axis. Then four fiber rings (each is called *kin,* meaning sun, day, time) are laid on the cloth to suggest a rectangular shape: two in the east and two in the west. A fifth ring is placed in the center. The cloth symbolizes the horizontal "cosmic plane" and each ring symbolizes a sun and a cosmic deity. Girard points out that the four gods of the "corners of the world" are oriented not toward the four cardinal points, but toward the solstices. This first *mesa* is the scene of a banquet offered to the gods and the spirits of the dead, who are petitioned to provide rain, abundance, and good health for the community. After the banquet the pilgrims select five smooth, round river stones from the vicinity of the water holes, and return to their temple.

That night in the temple, a rectangular but five-pointed cosmic ideogram is constructed on the ground below the main altar and on the altar itself. The construction under the altar, which symbolizes the Underworld, is formed as follows. First two clay jars filled with "virgin" water from a sacred water hole near Esquipulas are placed in the east. This water in the east, the direction of rain and clouds, is meant to attract the precious liquid during the forthcoming rainy season. Then two more jars, which are ritually filled with "captured" air, are stopped up and placed in the west. In this way the winds, considered to be the escape valve of malevolent forces, are imprisoned in the Underworld so that they cannot damage crops and bring sickness to the community. Finally, a miniature canoe filled with water is placed in the center. During the rituals to initiate the rainy season, the canoe will be filled with frogs and fish brought on a pilgrimage from the "center of the world" at the headwaters of a major river.

On the altar itself, in a ceremony symbolizing the re-creation of the world and of time, another cosmic ideogram is formed with the five stones brought back from the sacred water holes to the west. This structure defines the cosmic plane, or surface, of the earth. The seat of the major saint of the temple is placed over the second ideogram, since this divinity is believed to hold sway over the earth and its fertility. The marriage of the temple saint with the Virgin Mary is believed to give birth to the young corn god and produce the regeneration of vegetation during the rainy season, as symbolized by the decoration of the temple with fresh green leaves and the branches of young trees. Often a foliated cross, symbolizing the Tree of Life or Cosmic Axis uniting Heaven and earth, is associated with the altar during the planting season. During rites held at specific times in the rainy season, other *mesas* are laid out on the ground at the foot of the altar and on sacred tables, the latter symbolizing either the earth (low tables) or the heavens (high tables). Girard also discusses thirteen rain gods of the heavens and nine "lords of the night" associated with the Underworld and the growth of corn seeds.

The arrangement of the artifacts forming the cosmic ideogram follows a special order and has certain color associations. For example, the two corners on the north side of the *mesa*, which are laid down first, are associated with the colors red and black, corresponding to the dark skies of the rainy season that prevail during half of the year, when rituals are esoteric and performed at night. The two corners on the south side, which are laid down next, are associated with white and yellow, corresponding to the clear skies of the dry season that prevail during the other half of the year, when rituals are held publicly in daylight. The center, which is laid down last, is colored green, corresponding to the Tree of Life at the center of the world that unites the three planes of the cosmos. Regarding this five-point cosmic symbol, Girard makes a statement which it is well to remember when dealing with native cosmologies: "It does not represent the world, it is the world itself." (1966: 29)

Kogi

Reichel-Dolmatoff (1951: 239-59) provides an excellent summary of the cosmology of the Kogi,* who inhabit the Sierra Nevada de Santa Marta in northeastern Colombia.

The Kogi describe the universe as a large egg balanced point-upright on two beams which are held on the shoulders of four men, two in the east and two in the west. Under the egg there is water. Floating on the water is a large flat stone supporting the Universal Mother, who, in addition to rubbing the men's arms, shoulders, and backs, gives them food and water. The egg itself is composed of nine round, flat worlds shaped like plates. Each world has its own Mother, sun, moon, stars, and people. Our earth is the middle "plate"; there are four "bad" worlds of night below it and four "good" worlds of the sun above. The nine worlds personify the nine daughters of the

---

*Like the Chorti, the Kogi depict their cosmology through *mesa*-like configurations laid out on the ground (Gerardo Reichel-Dolmatoff, personal communication).

Universal Mother; our world (the Black Earth) is the ninth and best daughter. Reichel-Dolmatoff sees the myth of creation relating the formation of the nine worlds as being patterned after the development of a child in its mother's uterus from conception to birth, the moment of "dawning." He points out that the uterine fantasy of the creation and structure of the universe is evident in the symbol of the "great egg," which is none other than the primigenial uterus in which we all live. The myth also expresses the dichotomy of nature in making the distinction between the good worlds of the sun and the bad worlds of night. The positioning of these two sets of worlds "up" and "down" represents two poles between which our world is situated, exposed to the influence of both.

The Kogi also have specific associations for the four cardinal points. For example, the "owners" of the East are the jaguar and his wife the wild boar. White is associated with this direction, which is "good" because it is where the sun (an important son of the Universal Mother and brother to the solar hero *Sintana*, the first man of creation) is "born." The owners of the West are the owl and the snake. Black is associated with this direction, which is considered "bad" because it is the place where the sun "dies." The owners of the North are the fox and the armadillo. Blue is associated with this direction, which is considered bad because it is the area of sickness and cold weather. The owners of the South are the puma and the deer. Red is associated with this direction, considered to be good or bad because it gives rise to warm weather, which the Kogi associate with sexuality (said to have its good and its bad aspects). The Zenith and the Nadir do not have owners, but the point "in the middle," the center of the universe where the Kogi live, is under the sign of the Red Jaguar, accompanied by a mythical personage.

Supplementing the concepts of good and bad applied to the major divisions of the world and the universe is the idea that a close relationship exists between South and East as opposed to a similar relationship between North and West. This idea underscores a basic dichotomy between the earth and day, on the one hand, and water and night, on the other. The theme of dualism is also associated with the human body; that is, the right side and right hand are considered good, while the left side and hand are considered bad. The Kogi view nature as a confusing testing ground on which the individual walks between day and night, right and left, good and evil. But they find consolation in the fact that the Mother is present in the world and never abandons her children. All the depressions of the earth, such as caves, gorges, and gullies, are orifices in her body and are designated as her uterus. Even the Kogi's circular houses with their conical roofs represent the Mother's uterus, and the apex of the ceremonial house is her vagina. All the prominent hills are sons and daughters of the Mother inhabited by the Ancients and the ancestors (the latter also inhabit large rocks and boulders). The ancient Kogi priests (*mamas*) knew the entrances to the hills and how to get into them.

Three animals receive a great deal of attention in the world of the Kogi: the jaguar, the frog, and the snake. The jaguar, especially, is a central figure throughout Kogi mythology. It is a symbol of vital force or energy, which finds expression in sex and eating. It is said that all of the ancestors had the ability to convert themselves into jaguars at night. The frog symbolizes the feminine sex organ in its aggressive and insatiable aspects. The third animal, the snake, represents the male sex organ and is a symbol of death. Under the dominion of these three signs the Kogi live out their lives: in the East is the jaguar, an expression of positive energy; in the West is the snake, which symbolizes the death of this energy; on the earth among men is the frog, prolific and terrible.

As far as their immediate geography is concerned, the Kogi consider the coastal regions to the north, at the foot of the Sierra Nevada, to be bad, dangerous country. That is where the Ancients (the *Tairona*) lived, the land of sickness. The land at an altitude of a thousand to two thousand meters, where the Kogi live, is considered good for agriculture. From two thousand to four thousand five hundred meters, below the snow line, the country is considered to be sacred, land of the Mother, where the sick are taken to be cured. This is where the sacred lagoons, ceremonial centers, and sites for offerings and divination are located. From four thousand five hundred meters on up (snow country) is the habitation of the dead, where no mortal can go.

For the Kogi, the concrete, tangible world—the world of the animals, plants, and stones—diverges from the world of the sun, moon, winds, and clouds. Faced with this opposition of forces, the Kogi are constantly preoccupied with "putting them in agreement." The basic formula of Kogi religion says: "One must be in agreement, then all is well." This agreement is the object of the public religious ceremonies and dances, which also "sustain the earth." Resignation to the "law of the Mother," which was established when order was brought to the universe as related in numerous myths, is the key to Kogi society.

Warao

Our information on Warao cosmology comes from Wilbert (1975b: 164–68). According to the Warao, mankind lives in the center of a flat, saucer-shaped earth surrounded by water. In the ocean and surrounding the earth is the Snake of Being in an *uroborus* position—his head and tail approach each other in the east. Below the earth and ocean is a solid, boxlike realm of darkness inhabited by the Goddess of the Nadir and the Earth Monster, a four-headed serpent. This realm serves as the bottom to the ocean, supports the earth, and supports the world mountains at the cardinal and intercardinal points. These mountains in turn support the bell-shaped cosmic vault, the center of which is held up by the World Axis.

The world mountains at the cardinal points on the horizon are occupied by deities, three of whom have companions inhabiting lesser mountains toward the center of the world. The different directions and their respective deities are: South, two Toad Gods, the most powerful of the Warao pantheon; North, the Butterfly God and his companion, Father of the Waves; East, the God of Origin and his companion, the Creator-Bird of the Dawn, who governs the House of Tobacco Smoke and sponsors light shamanism; West, body of the Macaw God (his soul occupies the Zenith), who rules the Underworld as the lord of dark shamanism and death.

The mountains of the intercardinal points seem to correspond to the observable points of sunrise and sunset during the solstices. These directions and their respective deities are: Southeast, soul of the Mother of the Forest, one of the deities of the world of light; Southwest, body of the Mother of the Forest, patron of male artisans; Northeast, Mother of Moriche Flour; Northwest, God of the Dance. The deities of the Northeast and Northwest are associated with sustenance and fertility as provided by the moriche palm, the "tree of life" of the Warao. The patronesses of this tree—the Grandmothers, who sponsor female weavers—are also identified with the winter solstice.

There are three gods inhabiting the Zenith: the First Shaman, God of the Center of the World, who lives in a house of light with his son; a psychopomp who guides traveling spirits and souls across a white bridge of tobacco smoke lined with flowers to the House of Tobacco Smoke in the east; and the soul of the Macaw God, living with his son in a house of darkness.

There are five stratified cosmic levels in the Warao universe. From top to bottom these are: (1) the zone at the Zenith, occupied by the Gods of the Center of the World; (2) the Celestial Equator, inhabited by the lesser companions to the gods of the cardinal and intercardinal points and the House of Tobacco Smoke; (3) the horizontal mountaintops at the cardinal and intercardinal points, occupied by their respective gods; (4) the flat surface of the earth; and (5) the dark Underworld, the abode of the Goddess of the Nadir and the Earth Monster.

Desana

The Desana, a subgroup of the Tukano Indians who inhabit the jungles of the Vaupés territory of the Colombian northwest Amazon, have an interesting cosmology as described by Reichel-Dolmatoff (1971: 41–47). The following is Reichel-Dolmatoff's summary:

> [F]irst . . . the creative principle is masculine (Sun, yellow) and acts upon the biosphere (red) that, although composed of a masculine element and a feminine one, is imagined essentially as a feminine element. . . . [S]econd . . . the Universe consists of three superimposed planes. The upper zone is divided into a solar sphere (orange-yellow-white) and a blue sphere of communication, this last being constituted by the Milky Way. While the solar sphere is exclusively beneficent, the stellar sphere is ambivalent because it contains an ambiguous seminal concept (semen = sickness); both spheres are eventually subject to the manipulations of human beings who are endowed with the capacity of trance and, therefore, with communication. The intermediate zone of the biosphere is not divided except in its western part, associated with sickness. The lower zone [Ahpikon-dia] has a paradisical-uterine character (coca, green) and is, at the same time, the dwelling place of the Creator Sun, once again combining a masculine principle with a feminine one. (1971: 47)

Reichel-Dolmatoff's discussion of the Desana conception of the relationship between the Creator Sun and the present sun explains the presence of the Creator in the lower zone:

> The Creator Sun . . . , after the Creation, remained in Ahpikon-dia together with the Moon. . . . [T]he sun which today shines on our earth is only a representative of the true divine Creator. When the sun goes down every day in the west and arrives in Ahpikon-dia, it loses its light before the resplendence of in Creator Sun and passes without light under the earth. The same happens with the moon, which is also a representative of the first Moon which accompanied the Sun in the Creation. (1971: 45)

Siona

Langdon (1974: 126-55) presents a comprehensive and insightful description of the cosmology of the Siona, who are located along the upper Putumayo River of southern Colombia. The Siona universe is composed of five horizontal levels, all of which are conceptualized as flat disks modeled after the disk-like griddles used to cook cassava (tapioca). The first three levels are equal in size, the fourth and fifth levels are con-siderably smaller—the fifth level being about two feet in diameter (the size of the cassava grill). The first and lowest level, the Underworld ("inside the earth"), rests on a tripod of three clay cylinders like those used by the Siona to support cooking pots over the fire. It is the level of least importance, since its inhabitants, the Earth People, have little influence on the Siona.

The second level, the First Heaven, includes the earth's surface and the sky as far up as the eye can see. It has three major subdivisions: the home site, which is the cultural or domestic realm over which humanity has control; the jungle; and the river—the lat-ter two representing what is beyond humanity's control and therefore major sources of potential danger. Each of these realms contains two realities: that which is normally seen and an unseen supernatural reality which is a replica of the known world. (In a similar fashion, the other levels of the Siona universe reflect life on earth.) Thus the jungle—governed by father or mother spirits—contains the various "home sites" of numerous animistic spirits and the underground houses of animals (such as the Jaguar People, who—along with the *Yagé* People of the Second Heaven—set the pattern of life for the Siona); while the river is occupied by the Father of the Fish (the anaconda), the River Jaguar People, and other supernatural beings. Although the Siona recognize the natural dangers of the jungle and river, the dangers from the supernatural alter-reality are the ones that concern them the most.

The third level, the Second Heaven, begins beyond the point where the human eye can see up into the sky. It is separated from the First Heaven by a large river system that flows in the opposite direction of the rivers on earth. The sun sails in this "sky river" every day in his huge motor canoe. The Second Heaven is inhabited by a large number of spirits: sickness spirits of many kinds, souls of dead shamans, Wind People, Thunder People, Lightning Man, Moon People, a malevolent father of the spirits possibly derived from Christian and Inca religions, and—most important of all—the *Yagé* People, who introduce the Siona to the other spirits and teach them how to deal with the supernatural.

The fourth level, the Third Heaven, is perceived as being only six feet in diameter. It is inhabited by God, his angels, and doves that write on paper. God keeps a book of all his remedies. At the end of this Third Heaven there is a door that leads to nothingness.

The fifth and top level (Little Metal Heaven), like the fourth level is reduced in size, being only two feet in diameter—the size of the cassava grill itself. It contains a tree branch with a spirit hanging from it. Both these upper levels are often described by the Siona as being just pure clouds.

The region around the circumference of the first three disks is referred to as the Ending Place, beyond which there is nothing, or—according to some informants—an infinite expanse of water. The Ending Place serves as an intermediate area between the first three levels, from which it is possible either to ascend to the Second Heaven or descend into the Underworld at the point where the sun sets. The most important section of the Ending Place is in the southeast, where the rivers end to form a deep lake. According to the Siona, this is the part of the world where God left everything fresh and new. Here God left his footprint, along with implements used to bless the lake, which are also used by shamans for healing and for blessing the *yagé* used in Siona ceremonies: a metal bench, a curing "broom," and a metal plate full of a milky sap.

In the Ending Place there is a long shiny hollow tube, the "water tube," which revolves around the disks every twenty-four hours. Described as a "large mirror," this tube extends into the Second Heaven and the Underworld. To ascend into the Second Heaven it is necessary to enter the tube, but only after purging oneself in the lake. After the sun's daily journey on the "sky river," as he sets at the Ending Place, he enters the water tube in order to descend to the Underworld. There he travels along a river that crosses the Underworld, passing below the disk of the earthly First Heaven to rise again the next day.

Finally, Langdon (letter of 8 October, 1974) provides some information on a table used in *yagé* rituals, as compared with Eduardo's *mesa:*

> With regard to the Siona, the table is actually considerably different and missing most of the Christian elements, although I suspect that the present form was influenced by the early Catholic missionaries when they performed mass for the Siona two centuries ago. The table consists mainly of a "chalise" for holding the *yagé* and a drinking cup placed on top of it. There is a "broom" of leaves for chasing away evil spirits and a feather staff used when the shaman sings. The staff contains some of the power of the shaman. I know very little about the symbolism of their placement, for it was a topic that I was unable to research due to the deaths of the shamans of the tribe.

References

Agurell, Stig
    1969a   "Identification of Alkaloid Intermediaries by Gas Chromatography-Mass Spectometry: Potential Mescaline Precursors in *Trichocereus* Species." *Lloydia* 32:40-45.
    1969b   "Cactaceae Alkaloids." *Lloydia* 32:206-216.

Aranguren Paz, Angélica
    1975   "Las Creencias y Ritos Mágicos Religiosos de los Pastores Puneños." *Allpanchis Phuturinqa* 8:103-132.

Arriaga, Pablo Joseph de
    1968   *The Extirpation of Idolatry in Peru.* Lexington, Ky.: University of Kentucky Press.

Backeberg, Curt
    1959   *Die Cactaceae.* Handbuch der Kakteenkunde, vol. 2. Jena: Gustav Fischer Verlag.

Bandelier, Adolph
    1910   *The Islands of Titicaca and Koati.* New York: The Hispanic Society of America.

Barth, Fredrik
    1967   "On the Study of Social Change." *American Anthropologist* 69:661-669.

Bastien, Joseph W.
    1973   "Qollahuaya Rituals: An Ethnographic Account of the Symbolic Relations of Man and Land in an Andean Village." Latin American Studies Program, Dissertation Series no. 56, Cornell University.

Bolton, Ralph
    1973   "Kallawaya Sorcery: Description of a Session." *Fortieth International Congress of Americanists, Proceedings,* vol. 2, pp. 541-551. Rome-Genoa.
    1974   "To Kill a Thief: A Kallawaya Sorcery Session in the Lake Titicaca Region of Peru." *Anthropos* 69:191-215.

Bolton, Ralph, and Bolton, Charlene
    1976   "Rites of Retribution and Restoration in Canchis." *Journal of Latin American Lore* 2, no. 1:97-114.

Britton, N. L., and Rose, N. J.
  1920   *The Cactaceae: Descriptions and Illustrations of Plants of the Cactus
            Family.* Publication no. 248, vol. 2. Washington, D.C.: Carnegie In-
            stitute.

Brundage, Burr C.
  1963   *Empire of the Inca.* Norman, Ok.: Oklahoma University Press.

Buechler, Hans C., and Buechler, Judith-Maria
  1971   *The Bolivian Aymara.* New York: Holt, Rinehart, and Winston.

Cabieses, Fernando
  1972   "Neuro-Farmacología en el Antiguo Perú." *Revista Médica Peruana*
            35, no. 340:167–171.

  1974   *Gods and Disease: Medicine in Ancient Peru.* Lima: Artegraf.

Calancha, Antonio de la
  1638   *Crónica Moralizada del Orden de San Agustín en el Perú, con Sucesos
            Ejemplares de Esta Monarquía.* Barcelona: Pedro Lacavalleria.

Camino Calderón, Carlos
  1942   *El Daño.* Lima: Gil.

Campbell, Joseph
  1959   *The Masks of God: Primitive Mythology.* New York: Viking Press.

Carnero Checa, Luis
  1971   "Las Huaringas: Reducto de Brujos." *Siete Días del Perú y del Mundo.*
            Año 20, no. 655:49–58.

Casaverde Rojas, Juvenal
  1970   "El Mundo Sobrenatural en una Comunidad." *Allpanchis Phuturinqa*
            2:121–243.

Castaneda, Carlos
  1968   *The Teachings of Don Juan: A Yaqui Way of Knowledge.* New York:
            Ballantine Books.

  1971   *A Separate Reality: Further Conversations with Don Juan.* New York:
            Pocket Books.

  1972   *Journey to Ixtlán: The Lessons of Don Juan.* New York: Simon and
            Schuster.

  1974   *Tales of Power.* New York: Simon and Schuster.

  1977   *The Second Ring of Power.* New York: Simon and Schuster.

Chiappe, Mario
  1967   "Alucinógenas Nativas." *Revista del Viernes Médico* 18:3:293–299.

  1968   *Psiquiatría Folklórica Peruana: El Curanderismo en la Costa Norte del
            Perú.* Anales del Servicio de Psiquiatría, vol. 11, nos. 1–2. Lima:
            Hospital del Obrero, Sección de Psiquiatría.

  1969a   "El Curanderismo con Alucinógenas de la Costa y la Selva del Perú."
            In *Psiquiatría Peruana* (Primer Congreso Nacional de Psiquiatría).
            Edited by Oscar Valdivia P. and Alberto Péndola, pp. 318–325. Lima:
            Editorial Imprenta "Amauta."

  1969b   "El Síndrome Cultural de 'Daño' y su Tratamiento Curanderíl." In *Psi-
            quiatría Peruana* (Primer Congreso Nacional de Psiquiatría). Edited

by Oscar Valdivia P. and Alberto Péndola, pp. 330-337. Lima: Editorial Imprenta "Amauta."

Cobo, Bernabe
1956   *Historia del Nuevo Mundo.* Obras del P. Bernabe Cobo, vols. 1, 2. Edited by P. Francisco Mateo. Biblioteca de Autores Españoles, vols. 91, 92. Madrid: Ediciones Atlas.

Cruz Sánchez, Guillermo
1948   "Informe sobre las Aplicaciones Populares de la Címora en el Norte Perú." *Revista de Farmacología y Medicina Experimental* 1, no. 2:253-258.
1951   "Estudio Folklórico de Algunas Plantas Medicamentosas y Tóxicas de la Región Norte del Perú." *Revista de Medicina Experimental* 8, no. 1:159-166.

Custred, Harry Glynn, Jr.
1973   "Symbols and Control in a High Altitude Andean Community." Dissertation, Indiana University, Bloomington.

Dalle, Luis
1969   "El Despacho." *Allpanchis Phuturinqa* 1:139-154.
1971   "Mosoq Wata, Año Nuevo." *Alpanchis Phuturinqa* 3:34-44.

Dammert Bellido, José
1974   "Procesos por Supersticiones en la Provincia de Cajamarca en la Segunda Mitad del Siglo XVIII." *Allpanchis Phuturinqa* 9:179-200.

Danielou, Jean
1961   *Primitive Christian Symbols.* Baltimore, Md.: Helicon Press.

Delgado Aragón, Julio G.
1971   "El Señalakuy." *Allpanchis Phuturinqa* 3:185-197.

De Mille, Richard
1976   *Castaneda's Journey: The Power and the Allegory.* Santa Barbara, Calif.: Capra Press.

Dobkin de Rios, Marlene
1968   "*Trichocereus Pachanoi*—A Mescaline Cactus Used in Folk Healing in Peru." *Economic Botany* 22, no. 2:191-194.
1968-69 "Folk Curing with a Psychedelic Cactus in the North Coast of Peru." *International Journal of Social Psychiatry* 15, no. 1:23-32.
1969a   "Curanderismo Psicodélico en el Perú: Continuidad y Cambio." *Mesa Redonda de Ciencias Prehistóricas y Antropológicas,* vol. 1, pp. 139-149. Lima: Publicacciones del Instituto Riva-Aguero, no. 53A.
1969b   "Fortune's Malice: Divination, Psychotherapy, and Folk Medicine in Peru." *Journal of American Folklore* 82, no. 324:132-141.

Dragunsky, Luis
1968   "El Curanderismo en la Costa Norte Peruana." Unpublished manuscript.

Drysdale, Robert S., and Myers, Robert G.
1975   "Continuity and Change: Peruvian Education." In *The Peruvian Experiment: Continuity and Change under Military Rule.* Edited by Abraham F. Lowenthal, pp. 254-301. Princeton, N.J.: Princeton University Press.

Earls, John, and Silverblatt, Irene
1976   "La Realidad Física y Social en la Cosmología Andina." *Forty-second International Congress of Americanists, Proceedings.* Paris: in press.

Eliade, Mircea
1958   *Patterns in Comparative Religion.* New York: Meridian Books.
1960   *Myths, Dreams, and Mysteries.* New York: Harper Torchbooks.
1964   *Shamanism: Archaic Techniques of Ecstasy.* Princeton, N.J.: Princeton University Press (Bollingen Books).
1965   *The Two and the One.* New York: Harper Torchbooks.

Favre, Henri
1968   "Tayta Wamani: Le Culte des Montagnes dans le Centre Sud des Andes Péruviennes." *Etudes Latino-Américaines* 3:121-140. Université d'Aix-Marseille: Faculté des Lettres et Sciences Humaines d'Aix-en-Provence.

Flores Ochoa, Jorge
1976   "*Enqa, Enqaychu, Illa, y Khuya Rumi:* Aspectos Mágico-Religiosos entre Pastores." *Journal of Latin American Lore* 2, no. 1:115-134.

Friedberg, Claudine
1959   "Rapport Sommaire sur une Mission au Pérou." *Journal d'Agriculture Tropicale et de Botanique Appliquée* 6, nos. 8-9:439-450.
1960   "Utilisation d'un Cactus à Mescaline au Nord du Pérou *(Trichocereus pachanoi)."* *Sixth International Congress of Anthropological and Ethnological Sciences,* vol. 2, pt. 2, pp. 21-26.
1963   "Mission au Pérou—Mai 1961-Mars 1962." *Journal d'Agriculture Tropicale et de Botanique Appliquée* 10, nos. 1-9:33-52, 245-258, 344-386.

Frisancho Pineda, David
1973   *Medicina Indígena y Popular.* Lima: Libreria-Editorial Juan Mejía Baca.

Fung Pineda, Rosa
1969   "Las Aldas: Su Ubicación Dentro del Proceso Histórico del Perú Antiguo." *Dédalo* 5, nos. 9-10:5-207.

Furst, Peter T.
1965   "West Mexican Tomb Sculpture as Evidence for Shamanism in Prehispanic Mesoamerica." *Antropológica* 15:29-80.
1967   "Huichol Conceptions of the Soul." *Folklore Americas* 27, no. 2:39-106.
1968a   "A Possible Symbolic Manifestation of Funerary Endo-Cannibalism in Mexico." *Thirty-eighth International Congress of Americanists, Proceedings,* vol. 2, pp. 385-399, Stuttgart-Munich.
1968b   "The Parching of the Maize: An Essay on the Survival of Huichol Ritual." *Acta Ethnologica et Linguistica,* no. 14, pp. ii-42. Vienna: E. Stiglmayr.
1968c   "The Olmec Were-Jaguar Motif in the Light of Ethnographic Reality." In *Dumbarton Oaks Conference on the Olmec.* Edited by Elizabeth P. Benson, pp. 143-174. Washington, D.C.: Dumbarton Oaks Research Library and Collection, Trustees for Harvard University.

1968-69   "Myth in Art: A Huichol Depicts His Reality." *Los Angeles County Museum of Natural History Quarterly* 7, no. 3:16-25.

1972   "To Find Our Life: Peyote among the Huichol Indians of Mexico." In *Flesh of the Gods: The Ritual Use of Hallucinogens.* Edited by Peter T. Furst, pp. 136-184. New York: Praeger.

1973   "An Indian Journey to Life's Sources." *Natural History* 82, no. 4:34-43.

1973-74   "The Roots and Continuities of Shamanism." *Artscanada,* December 1973/January 1974, nos. 184-187, pp. 33-60.

1974   "Psychotropic Flora and Fauna in Pre-Columbian Art." In *Art and Environment in Native America.* Lubbock, Tex.: Special Publications of the Museum of the Texas Technological University.

Furst, Peter T., and Myerhoff, Barbara G.

1966   "Myth as History: The Jimson Weed Cycle of the Huichols of Mexico." *Antropológica* 17:3-39.

Furst, Peter T., and Reed, Karen B.

1970   *Stranger in Our Midst: Guided Culture Change in Highland Guatemala.* Los Angeles: Latin American Center, University of California.

Garr, Thomas M.

1972   *Cristianismo y Religión Quechua.* Cuzco: Instituto de Pastoral Andina.

Geertz, Clifford

1965   "Religion as a Cultural System." In *Anthropological Approaches to the Study of Religion.* Edited by M. Banton, pp. 1-46. New York: Praeger.

Gillin, John

1947   *Moche: A Peruvian Coastal Community.* Smithsonian Institution, Institute of Social Anthropology, Publication no. 3. Washington, D.C.: U.S. Government Printing Office.

Girard, Rafael

1966   *Los Mayas.* Mexico City: Libro Mex.

González Huerta, Inez

1960   "Identificación de la Mescalina Contenida en el *Trichocereus pachanoi* (San Pedro)." *Revista del Viernes Médico* 11, no. 1:133-137.

Goodenough, Ward H.

1957   "Cultural Anthropology and Linguistics." In *Report on the Seventh Annual Round Table Meetings on Linguistics and Language Study.* Edited by P. Garvin, pp. iii-219. Washington, D.C.: Georgetown University Monograph Series on Language and Linguistics, no. 9.

1961   "Comment on Cultural Evolution." *Daedalus* 90:521-528.

Gossen, Gary H.

1974   *Chamulas in the World of the Sun: Time and Space in a Maya Oral Tradition.* Cambridge, Mass.: Harvard University Press.

Gow, David D.

1976   "The Gods and Social Change in the High Andes." Dissertation, University of Wisconsin, Madison.

Gow, David D., and Gow, Rosalinda
1975   "La Alpaca en el Mito y el Ritual." *Allpanchis Phuturinqa* 8:141-174.

Gow, Rosalind, and Condori, Bernabe
1976   *Kay Pacha.* Cuzco: Editorial de Cultura Andina.

Graves, Ted, and Woods, Clyde M.
1973   *The Process of Medical Change in a Highland Guatemalan Town.* Los Angeles: Latin American Center, University of California.

Griaule, Marcel
1965   *Conversations with Ogotemmêli: An Introduction to Dogon Religious Ideas.* London: Oxford University Press.

Gushiken, José
1977   *Tuno: El Curandero.* Lima: Universidad Nacional Mayor de San Marcos.

Gutiérrez-Noriega, Carlos
1950   "Area de Mescalinismo en el Perú." *America Indígena* 10, no. 3:215-220.

Haley, Harold B., and Grollig, Francis X.
1976   "Amulets in the Lake Titicaca Region." *Forty-first International Congress of Americanists, Proceedings,* vol. 3, pp. 172-182, Mexico City.

Hissink, Karin, and Hahn, Albert
1961   *Die Tacana: Ergebnisse der Frobenius-Expedition nach Bolivien, 1952 bis 1954.* Vol. 1: *Erzahlungsgut.* Stuttgart: W. Kohlhammer.

Holland, William R.
1964   "Conceptos Cosmológicos Tzotziles como una Base para Interpretar la Civilización Maya Prehispánica." *America Indígena* 24, no. 1:11-28.

Isbell, Billie Jean
1976   "La Otra Mitad Esencial: Un Estudio de Complementariedad Sexual Andina." *Estudios Andinos 12, La Mujer en los Andes,* año 5, no. 1:37-56.

Jaffé, Aniela
1964   "Symbolism in the Visual Arts." In *Man and His Symbols.* Edited by Carl G. Jung, pp. 255-322. New York: Dell.

John the Divine
1611   The Revelation of Saint John the Divine. Holy Bible, King James ed.

Jung, Carl G.
1958   *Psyche and Symbol.* Edited by Violet S. de Laszlo. New York: Doubleday.

1971   *The Portable Jung.* Edited by Joseph Campbell. New York: Viking Press.

1972   *Mandala Symbolism.* Princeton, N.J.: Princeton University Press.

Kauffmann-Doig, Federico
1969   *Arqueología Peruana: Vision Integral.* Lima: Iberia.

Kubler, George
1946   "The Quechua in the Colonial World." In *Handbook of South American Indians.* Edited by Julian Steward. Smithsonian Institution, Bureau of American Ethnology, Bulletin no. 143, vol. 2, pp. 331-410. Washington, D.C.: U.S. Government Printing Office.

La Barre, Weston
- 1948   *The Aymara Indians of the Lake Titacaca Plateau.* Memoir Series of the American Anthropological Association, no. 68. Menasha, Wisc.
- 1972   "Hallucinogens and the Shamanic Origins of Religion." In *Flesh of the Gods: The Ritual Use of Hallucinogens.* Edited by Peter T. Furst, pp. 261–278. New York: Praeger.

Lama, Abraham
- 1965   "Amanecer Milenario." *Caretas* 15, no. 305:26–27.

Langdon, E. Jean
- 1974   "The Siona Medical System: Beliefs and Behavior." Dissertation, Tulane University, New Orleans.

Larco Hoyle, Rafael
- 1941   *Los Cupisniques.* Lima: Editorial "La Crónica" y "Variedades."
- 1944   *Cultura Salinar.* Buenos Aires: Sociedad Geográfica Americana.

Latcham, Ricardo E.
- 1938   *Arqueología de la Región Atacameña.* Santiago: Prensas de la Universidad de Chile.

Laughlin, Robert M.
- 1969   "The Huastec." In *Handbook of Middle American Indians.* Edited by Evon Z. Vogt, vol. 7, pt. 1, pp. 298–311. Austin, Tex.: University of Texas Press.

Leach, Edmund
- 1976   *Culture and Communication: The Logic by Which Symbols Are Connected.* Cambridge, England: Cambridge University Press.

Lehmann-Nitsche, R.
- 1928   "Coricancha: El Templo del Sol en el Cuzco y las Imagenes de Su Altar Mayor." *Revista del Museo de la Plata* 31, no. 3a: 1–260.

Lévi-Strauss, Claude
- 1950   Introduction to *Sociologie et Anthropologie* by Marcel Mauss. Paris: Presses Universitaires de France.

Lira, Jorge
- 1969   "El Cambio de la Suerte." *Alpanchis Phuturinqua* 1:29–41.

Llosa Porras, Fernando
- 1974   "Chavin: An Ancient Temple Ruin in Peru." *Graphis* 30, no. 172: 146–151.

Lommel, Andreas
- 1967   *The World of the Early Hunters.* London: Evelyn, Adams, and Mackay.

Loomis, C. Grant
- 1948   *White Magic.* Cambridge, Mass.: Medieval Academy of America.

Mac-Lain y Estenós, Roberto
- 1939   "La Brujería en el Perú." *Twenty-seventh International Congress of Americanists, Proceedings,* vol. 2, pp. 295–306. Lima.
- 1942   *Sociología Peruana.* Lima: Gil.

Marzal, Manuel
- 1971a   *El Mundo Religioso de Urcos.* Cuzco: Instituto de Pastoral Andina.

1971b   "¿Puede un Campesino Cristiano Ofrecer un 'Pago a la Tierra'?" *Allpanchis Phuturinqa* 3:116-128.

Mayorga, Silvia; Palacios Rios, Felix; and Samaniego Díaz, Ramiro
1975   "El 'Despacho.' " Paper presented at the Seventy-fourth Annual Meeting of the American Anthropological Association, symposium on Sorcery, Divination, and Magical Curing in Andean Societies, San Francisco.

Meighan, Clement W.
1973   "California Indian Shamanism," January 26 lecture in Anthropology 106-A, "Native Peoples of California," University of California, Los Angeles.

Mena, Vicente
1969   "Algunos Aspectos de Medicina Popular en La Calera, Provincia de Imbabura." *Revista de Folklore Ecuatoriano* 3:3-39.

Mendelson, E. Michael
1957   "Religion and World-View in Santiago Atitlán." Microfilm Collection of Manuscripts on Middle American Cultural Anthropology, no. 52, University of Chicago.
1965   *Los Escándalos de Maximón.* Guatemala City: Seminario de Integración Social Guatemalteca, no. 19.

Métraux, Alfred
1944   "Le Shamanisme chez les Indiens de l'Amérique du Sud Tropicale" (2 parts). *Acta Americana* 2, no. 3:197-219; 2, no. 4:320-341.

Mishkin, Bernard
1940   "Cosmological Ideas among the Indians of the Southern Andes." *Journal of American Folklore* 53, no. 210:225-241.
1946   "The Contemporary Quechua." In *Handbook of South American Indians.* Edited by Julian Steward, Smithsonian Institution, Bureau of American Ethnology, Bulletin no. 143, vol. 2, pp. 411-470. Washington, D.C.: U.S. Government Printing Office.

Moesbach, Ernesto Wilhelm de
1973   *Vida y Costumbres de los Indígenas Araucanos en la Segunda Mitad del Siglo XIX.* Santiago: Instituto de Capacitación e Investigación en Reforma Agraria.

Molina of Cuzco, Cristóbal de
1959   *Ritos y Fábulas de los Incas.* Buenos Aires: Editorial Futuro.

Monast, J. E.
1972   *Los Indios Aimaraes.* Buenos Aires: Ediciones Carlos Lohlé.

Munn, Henry
1973   "The Mushrooms of Language." In *Hallucinogens and Shamanism.* Edited by Michael Harner, pp. 86-122. New York: Oxford University Press.

Murúa, Martin de
1946   *Historia del Origen y Genealogía Real de los Reyes Incas del Perú.* Madrid: C. Bermejo.

Myerhoff, Barbara
    1968   "The Deer-Maize-Peyote Complex among the Huichol Indians of Mexico." Dissertation, University of California, Los Angeles.
    1970   "The Deer-Maize-Peyote Symbol Complex among the Huichol Indians of Mexico." *Anthropological Quarterly* 43:64-78.
    1974   *Peyote Hunt: The Sacred Journey of the Huichol Indians.* Ithaca, N.Y.: Cornell University Press.

Nachtigall, Horst
    1975   "Ofrendas de Llamas en la Vida Ceremonial de los Pastores." *Allpanchis Phuturinqa* 8:133-140.

Naranjo, Claudio
    1973   "Psychological Aspects of the Yagé Experience in an Experimental Setting." In *Hallucinogens and Shamanism.* Edited by Michael Harner, pp. 176-190. New York: Oxford University Press.

Nicholson, Henry B.
    1971   "Religion in Pre-Hispanic Central Mexico." In *Handbook of Middle American Indians.* Edited by Robert Wauchope, vol. 10, pp. 395-446. Austin, Tex.: University of Texas Press.

Nuñez del Prado, Juan Victor
    1970   "El Mundo Sobrenatural de los Quechuas del Sur del Perú a través de la Comunidad de Qotobamba." *Allpanchis Phuturinqa* 2:57-119.

Oakes, Maud
    1951   *The Two Crosses of Todos Santos.* Princeton, N.J.: Princeton University Press (Bollingen Books).

Oblitas Poblete, Enrique
    1963   *Cultura Callawaya.* La Paz: Editorial Talleres Gráficos Bolivianos.
    1971   *Magia, Hechicería, y Medicina Popular Boliviana.* La Paz: Ediciones ISLA.

O'Brien, Linda
    1975   "Songs of the Face of the Earth: Ancestor Songs of the Tzutuhíl-Maya of Santiago Atitlán, Guatemala." Dissertation, University of California, Los Angeles.

Oliva, Anello
    1895   *Historia del Reino y Provincias del Perú.* Lima: Imprenta y Librería de San Pedro.

Otero, Gustavo Adolfo
    1951   *La Piedra Mágica: Vida y Costumbres de los Indios Callahuayas de Bolivia.* Mexico City: Instituto Indigenista Interamericano.

Pachacuti-Yamqui Salcamaygua, Juan de Santa Cruz
    1950   "Relación de Antigüedades deste Reyno del Pirú." In *Tres Relaciones de Antigüedades Peruanas.* Edited by Marcos Jiménez de la Espada, pp. 204-281. Asunción: Editorial Guarania.

Paredes, Manuel Rigoberto
    1963   *Mitos, Supersticiones, y Supervivencias Populares de Bolivia.* La Paz: Ediciones ISLA.

Parsons, Elsie C.
1940 "Cosmography of the Indians of Imbabura Province, Ecuador." *Journal of American Folklore* 53, no. 210:219–224.
1945 *Peguche, Canton of Otavalo, Province of Imbabura, Ecuador: A Study of Andean Indians.* Chicago: University of Chicago Press.

Poisson, J.
1960 "The Presence of Mescaline in a Peruvian Cactus." *Annales Pharmaceutiques Françaises* 18:764–765.

Polo de Ondegardo, Juan
1916 "Los Errores y Supersticiones de los Indios, Sacados del Tratado y Averiguación que Hizo el Licenciado Polo." *Colección de Libros y Documentos Referentes a la Historia del Perú.* Edited by Horacio H. Urteaga and Carlos A. Romero, 1st series, vol. 3, pp. 3–43. Lima: Sanmarti y Ca.

Poma de Ayala, Felipe Guaman
1966 *La Primera Nueva Crónica y Buen Gobierno, Tercera Parte.* Lima: Imprenta Gráfica Industrial.

Quispe M., Ulpiano
1969 *La Herranza en Choque Huarcaya y Huancasancos, Ayacucho.* Lima: Instituto Indigenista Peruano.

Ramirez, Miguel Justino
1966 *Huancabamba: Su Historia, su Geografía, su Folklore.* Lima: Imprenta del Ministerio de Hacienda y Comercio.

Redfield, Robert
1941 *The Folk Culture of Yucatán.* Chicago: University of Chicago Press.

Reiche, Maria
1969 "Giant Ground-Drawings on the Peruvian Desert." *Thirty-eighth International Congress of Americanists, Proceedings,* vol. 1, pp. 379–384. Stuttgart-Munich.

Reichel-Dolmatoff, Gerardo
1951 "Los Kogi" (pt. 1). *Revista del Instituto Etnológico Nacional* 4:1–314.
1971 *Amazonian Cosmos: The Sexual and Religious Symbolism of the Tukano Indians.* Chicago: University of Chicago Press.
1972 "The Cultural Context of an Aboriginal Hallucinogen." In *Flesh of the Gods: The Ritual Use of Hallucinogens.* Edited by Peter T. Furst, pp. 84–113. New York: Praeger.
1975 *The Shaman and the Jaguar.* Philadelphia: Temple University Press.

Rodríguez Suy Suy, Victor Antonio
1973 "La Medicina Tradicional en la Costa Norte del Perú Actual." *Boletín Chiquitayap* 1, no. 1.

Rowe, John Howland
1946 "Inca Culture at the Time of the Spanish Conquest." In *Handbook of South American Indians.* Edited by Julian Steward, Smithsonian Institution, Bureau of American Ethnology, Bulletin no. 143, vol. 2, pp. 183–330. Washington, D.C.: U.S. Government Printing Office.
1948 "The Kingdom of Chimor." *Acta Americana* 6:26–59.

1957   "The Incas under Spanish Colonial Institutions." *Hispanic Historical Review* 37:155–199.

Sawyer, Alan
1968   *Mastercraftsmen of Ancient Peru.* New York: Solomon R. Guggenheim Foundation.

Schultes, Richard E., and Hofmann, Albert
1973   *The Botany and Chemistry of Hallucinogens.* Springfield, Ill.: Charles C. Thomas.

Seguin, Carlos Alberto
1969   "Psiquiatría Folklórica." In *Psiquiatría Peruana* (Primer Congreso Nacional de Psiquiatría). Edited by Oscar Valdivia P. and Alberto Péndola, pp. 154–159. Lima: Editorial Imprenta "Amauta."
1970   "Folk Psychiatry." In *World Biennial of Psychiatry and Psychotherapy.* Edited by Silvano Arieti, vol. 1, pp. 165–177. New York: Basic Books.

Sharon, Douglas
1972a   "The San Pedro Cactus in Peruvian Folk Healing." In *Flesh of the Gods: The Ritual Use of Hallucinogens.* Edited by Peter T. Furst, pp. 114–135. New York: Praeger.
1972b   "Eduardo the Healer." *Natural History* 81, no. 9:32–47.
1976a   "A Peruvian *Curandero*'s Séance: Power and Balance." In *The Realm of the Extra-Human: Agents and Audiences* (Ninth International Congress of Anthropological and Ethnological Sciences, Chicago). Edited by Agehananda Bharati, pp. 371–381. The Hague: Mouton Publishers.
1976b   "Becoming a *Curandero* in Peru." In *Enculturation in Latin America: An Anthology.* Edited by Johannes Wilbert, pp. 359–375. Los Angeles: UCLA Latin American Center Publications.
1976c   "Distribution of the *Mesa* in Latin America." *Journal of Latin American Lore* 2, no. 1:71–95.

Sharon, Douglas, and Donnan, Christopher B.
1977   "The Magic Cactus: Ethnoarchaeological Continuity in Peru." *Archaeology* 30, no. 6:374–381.

Sidel, Victor W., and Sidel, Ruth
1974   *Serve the People: Observations on Medicine in the People's Republic of China.* New York: Josiah Macy, Jr., Foundation.

Siegel, Ronald K.
1973   "Visual Imagery Constants: Drug-Induced Changes in Trained and Untrained Observers." *Eighty-first Annual Convention, American Psychological Association, Proceedings,* pp. 1033–1034.

Spiro, Melford E.
1951   "Culture and Personality: The Natural History of a False Dichotomy." *Psychiatry* 14:19–46.

Steward, Julian H., and Faron, Louis C.
1959   *Native Peoples of South America.* New York: McGraw-Hill.

Tamayo Herrera, José
    1970   "Algunos Conceptos Filosóficos de la Cosmovisión del Indígena Quechua." *Allpanchis Phuturinqa* 2:245-254.

Tello, Julio C.
    1923   "Wira Kocha." *Inca, Revista Trimestral de Estudios Antropológicos* 1:93-320; 3:582-606.
    1959   *Paracas, Primera Parte.* Lima: Empresa Gráfica T. Scheuch.

Thompson, J. Eric S.
    1970   *Maya History and Religion.* Norman, Ok.: University of Oklahoma Press.

Toor, Frances
    1947   *A Treasury of Mexican Folkways.* New York: Crown Publishers.

Torrey, E. Fuller
    1972   *The Mind Game: Witchdoctors and Psychiatrists.* New York: Bantam Books.

Tschopik, Harry
    1946   "The Aymara." In *Handbook of South American Indians.* Edited by Julian Steward, Smithsonian Institution, Bureau of American Ethnology, Bulletin no. 143, vol. 2, pp. 501-573. Washington, D.C.: U.S. Government Printing Office.
    1951   *The Aymara of Chucuito, Peru.* 1: *Magic.* Anthropological Papers of the American Museum of Natural History, vol. 44, pt. 2.

Valcárcel, Luis E.
    1959   *Etnohistória del Perú Antiguo.* Lima: Universidad Nacional Mayor de San Marcos.

Vogt, Evon Z.
    1969   *Zinacantán: A Maya Community in the Highlands of Chiapas.* Cambridge, Mass.: Belknap Press of Harvard University Press.
    1970   *The Zinacantecos of Mexico: A Modern Maya Way of Life.* New York: Holt, Rinehart, and Winston.

von Franz, M. L.
    1964   "The Process of Individuation." In *Man and His Symbols.* Edited by Carl G. Jung, pp. 157-254. New York: Dell.

von Hagen, Victor W.
    1964   *The Desert Kingdoms of Peru.* New York: Mentor Books.

Wassén, Henry S.
    1967   "Anthropological Survey of the Use of South American Snuffs." In *Ethnopharmacological Search for Psychoactive Drugs.* Edited by Daniel H. Efron, pp. 233-289. Washington, D.C.: U.S. Public Health Service Publication no. 1645.

Waters, Frank
    1963   *Book of the Hopi.* New York: Ballantine Books.

Wilbert, Johannes
    1971   "The Warao *Bahanarotu* Tradition." May 18 lecture in Anthropology 257, "Indians of South America: Vision and Ecstasy in Shamanism," University of California, Los Angeles.

1972a   "Cultural Relevance and Specificity of Amerindian Education."
         January 26 Latin American Study Center Chalk Talk, University of
         California, Los Angeles.
1972b   "Tobacco and Shamanistic Ecstasy among the Warao Indians of
         Venezuela." In *Flesh of the Gods: The Ritual Use of Hallucinogens.*
         Edited by Peter T. Furst, pp. 55–83. New York: Praeger.
1975a   "Magico-Religious Use of Tobacco in South America." In *Cannabis
         and Culture* (Ninth International Congress of Anthropological and
         Ethnological Sciences, Chicago). Edited by Vera Rubin, pp. 439–461.
         The Hague: Mouton Publishers.
1975b   "Eschatology in a Participatory Universe: Destinies of the Soul among
         the Warao Indians of Venezuela." In *Dumbarton Oaks Conference on
         Death and the Afterlife in Pre-Columbian America.* Edited by
         Elizabeth P. Benson, pp. 163–189. Washington, D.C.: Dumbarton
         Oaks Research Library and Collection, Trustees for Harvard Univer-
         sity.

Williams García, Roberto
   1972   *Mitos Tepehuas.* Mexico: SepSetentas.

Wolf, Eric R.
   1955   "Types of Latin American Peasantry." *American Anthropologist*
           57:452–471.

Zuidema, R. T.
   1969   "El Cuzco." Unpublished manuscript.
   1971   "Meaning in Nasca Art: Iconographic Relationships between Inca,
           Huari, and Nasca cultures in Southern Peru." *Göteborg Etnografiska
           Museet, Abstracts,* pp. 35–44.

Zuidema, R. T., and Quispe, U.
   1968   "A Visit to God: The Account and Interpretation of a Religious Ex-
           perience in the Peruvian Community of Choque-Huarcaya." *Bijdragen
           Tot de Taal-Land-en-Volkenkunde* 124:22–39.

Index